UNCITRAL MODEL LAWS ON DIGITAL TRADE

This book provides a detailed analysis of two UNCITRAL texts: the Model Law on Electronic Transferable Records (MLETR) and the Model Law on the Use and Cross-border Recognition of Identity Management and Trust Services (MLIT).

The MLETR is the legal tool that enables the use of trade documents such as bills of lading and promissory notes in electronic form. The book discusses core MLETR provisions and illustrates national variations in enactment techniques and substantive content, including in France, Singapore, and the United Kingdom.

The MLIT provides the legal framework to manage identity management and trust services, including electronic signatures. The book explains the different approaches to giving legal recognition and effect to identity management and trust services, both domestically and across borders. It discusses the legal framework to accommodate functions and needs of identity management, describes trust services against the background of pre-existing UNCITRAL texts, and takes into account the revised EU eIDAS Regulation.

Providing an article-by-article commentary as well as an overview of implementation trends, the book is a fundamental resource for commercial, maritime and banking lawyers, digital economy policymakers, legislative drafters, supply chain management and paperless trade specialists, and for anyone interested in understanding the legal aspects of the transition from documents to data in trade.

Hart Studies in Commercial and Financial Law: Volume 19

Hart Studies in Commercial and Financial Law

Series Editors: John Linarelli and Teresa Rodríguez de las Heras Ballell

This series offers a venue for publishing works on commercial law as well as on the regulation of banking and finance, and the law on insolvency and bankruptcy. It publishes works on the law on secured credit, the regulatory and transactional aspects of banking and finance, the transactional and regulatory institutions for financial markets, legal and policy aspects associated with access to commercial and consumer credit, new generation subjects having to do with the institutional architecture associated with innovation and the digital economy including works on blockchain technology, works on the relationship of law to economic growth, the harmonisation or unification of commercial law, transnational commercial law, and the global financial order. The series promotes interdisciplinary work. It publishes research on the law using the methods of empirical legal studies, behavioural economics, political economy, normative welfare economics, law and society inquiry, socio-legal studies, political theory, and historical methods. Its coverage includes international and comparative investigations of areas of law within its remit.

Volume 1: The Financialisation of the Citizen: Social and Financial Inclusion through European Private Law
Guido Comparato

Volume 2: MiFID II and Private Law: Enforcing EU Conduct of Business Rules
Federico Della Negra

Volume 3: Reforming Corporate Retail Investor Protection: Regulating to Avert Mis-Selling
Diane Bugeja

Volume 4: The Future of Commercial Law: Ways Forward for Change and Reform
Edited by Orkun Akseli and John Linarelli

Volume 5: The Cape Town Convention: A Documentary History
Anton Didenko

Volume 6: Regulating the Crypto Economy: Business Transformations and Financialisation
Iris H-Y Chiu

Volume 7: The Future of High-Cost Credit: Rethinking Payday Lending
Jodi Gardner

Volume 8: The Enforcement of EU Financial Law
Edited by Jan Crijns, Matthias Haentjens and Rijnhard Haentjens

Volume 9: International Bank Crisis Management: A Transatlantic Perspective
Marco Bodellini

Volume 10: Creditor Priority in European Bank Insolvency Law: Financial Stability and the Hierarchy of Claims
Sjur Swensen Ellingsæter

Volume 11: Chinese and Global Financial Integration through Stock Connect: A Legal Analysis
Flora Huang

Volume 12: The Governance of Macroprudential Policy: How to Build Regulatory Legitimacy Through a Social Justice Approach
Tracy C Maguze

Volume 13: A Socio-Legal Theory of Money for the Digital Commercial Society: A New Analytical Framework to Understand Cryptoassets
Israel Cedillo Lazcano

Volume 14: Venture Capital Investment and Government Incentives: Law, Regulation and Policy Design
Tamara Wilkinson

Volume 15: Regulating Primary Markets in the Capital Markets Union: Between Uniformity and Differentiation
Konstantinos Serdaris

Volume 16: Regulating Innovation in the Digital Age: A Demand-Centred Toolbox for the Data-Driven Economy
Nikita Divissenko

Volume 17: Digital Assets in Enforcement and Insolvency: Securing Creditor Access and Protecting Customer Interests in the Crypto World
Edited by Christian Koller and Matthias Lehmann

Volume 18: Transnational Mortgage Law: Reconstructing the Global Framework for Housing Finance
Guido Comparato and Irina Domurath

Volume 19: UNCITRAL Model Laws on Digital Trade: Electronic Transferable Records, Digital Identity and Trust Services
Luca G Castellani

UNCITRAL Model Laws on Digital Trade

Electronic Transferable Records, Digital Identity and Trust Services

Luca G Castellani

•HART•
OXFORD • LONDON • NEW YORK • NEW DELHI • SYDNEY

HART PUBLISHING

Bloomsbury Publishing Plc

Kemp House, Chawley Park, Cumnor Hill, Oxford, OX2 9PH, UK

1385 Broadway, New York, NY 10018, USA

Bloomsbury Publishing Ireland Limited, 29 Earlsfort Terrace, Dublin 2, D02 AY28, Ireland

HART PUBLISHING, the Hart/Stag logo, BLOOMSBURY and the Diana logo are trademarks of Bloomsbury Publishing Plc

First published in Great Britain 2025

A catalogue record for this book is available from the British Library.

A catalogue record for this book is available from the Library of Congress.

Library of Congress Control Number: 2025942728

ISBN: HB: 978-1-50993-741-7
ePDF: 978-1-50993-742-4
ePub: 978-1-50993-743-1

Typeset by Compuscript Ltd, Shannon

For product safety related questions contact productsafety@bloomsbury.com

To find out more about our authors and books visit www.hartpublishing.co.uk. Here you will find extracts, author information, details of forthcoming events and the option to sign up for our newsletters.

FOREWORD

The United Nations Commission on International Trade Law was established almost 60 years ago by the United Nations General Assembly to harmonise and modernise international trade law. Over the years, it has built bridges between the principal legal systems of the world, developing harmonised instruments to facilitate cross-border trade in areas such as trade finance, transport, e-commerce, payments and dispute resolution. It has also developed substantive business law on insolvency, adapted trade law to address the needs of micro-small and medium-sized enterprises and adopted frameworks for States entering into business relations with private parties, enterprises and investors.

In recent years, UNCITRAL has devoted much of its legislative activities to modernising international trade law and adapting it to the profound changes in business practice resulting from advances in digital technologies, including most recently the increased deployment of artificial intelligence.

Moving beyond traditional concerns about effective enforcement and legal certainty in a peculiarly cross-border setting that engages different legal frameworks and jurisdictions, UNCITRAL's work in the digital space is increasingly focused on new forms of trading. In particular, it is concerned with the rise of new actors providing services to support digital trade, including trading and supply chain and dispute resolution platforms, new assets and commodities, and new ways of transacting, all of which have one feature in common: less human intervention and more trade carried out by machines programmed to operate autonomously. Far from science fiction, the COVID-19 pandemic has given digital trade a boost that has accelerated a transition already in the making through technological developments.

When opening this book, prepare yourself for an interesting journey and let yourself be guided through two cornerstones of UNCITRAL's legislative framework supporting the digital transformation: the UNCITRAL Model Law on Electronic Transferable Records and the UNCITRAL Model Law on the Use and Cross-border Recognition of Identity Management and Trust Services. The author has first-hand experience of the conceptualisation, drafting, development and adoption of these texts, as well as their promotion and dissemination in different legal systems and by jurisdictions at varying stages of economic development. By following him through the chapters of this book, the reader will gain a clear understanding of the core principles underpinning this framework, such as non-discrimination and technology neutrality, and the functional equivalence approach that has allowed established legal requirements formulated in the era of paper-based in-person trade to be applied to new forms of trading. They will see how the pursuit of these principles and approaches has evolved over time and how they are finding new expression in legislative efforts to address emerging challenges presented by the cross-border recognition of digital identities and the shift from documents to data.

The book is timely as the digital transformation is accelerating. It is important for lawyers, lawmakers and policymakers to recognise how these principles and approaches have responded to the progressive waves of electronic commerce, and how the enabling mechanisms and legislative techniques developed in these two texts provide the tools to confront future challenges. The author follows a chronological approach of the two recent texts but cleverly compares their main features and origins. He analyses how they relate to the widely used UNCITRAL framework. He examines their uptake and the opportunities that they offer for future developments in technology and in international trade.

I can only recommend to read and re-read this seminal piece on the international legislative response to the digital transformation of trade and the enduring principles and approaches that UNCITRAL has honed over the decades. I commend the author for his project and for his contribution to the legal embrace and facilitation of digital trade.

Anna Joubin-Bret
Secretary of UNCITRAL
Vienna, 27 May 2025

ACKNOWLEDGEMENTS

The views expressed herein are those of the author and do not necessarily reflect the views of the United Nations or of UNCITRAL. The texts of the UNCITRAL Model Law on Electronic Transferable Records and of the UNCITRAL Model Law on the Use and Cross-border Recognition of Identity Management and Trust Services are reproduced by permission of the UNCITRAL Secretariat. The author would like to thank Vivienne Bath, Tom Smedinghoff and Meixian Song for their comments.

TABLE OF CONTENTS

ABBREVIATIONS

ADB	Asian Development Bank
AGC	Attorney General's Chambers
AML	Anti-Money Laundering
APEC	Asia-Pacific Economic Cooperation
ASEAN	Association of Southeast Asian Nations
BIMCO	Baltic and International Maritime Council
CISG	United Nations Convention on Contracts for the International Sale of Goods
CLOUT	Case Law on UNCITRAL Texts
CMI	Comité Maritime International
CMNI	Budapest Convention on the Contract for the Carriage of Goods by Inland Waterway
CMR	Convention on the Contract for the International Carriage of Goods by Road
CNUDCI	See UNCITRAL
CNUDMI	See UNCITRAL
CPTA	Framework Agreement on Facilitation of Cross-border Paperless Trade in Asia and the Pacific
CRVS	Civil Records and Vital Statistics
DAPL	Principles on Digital Assets and Private Law
DCSA	Digital Container Standard Association
DEPA	Digital Economy Partnership Agreement
DIFC	Dubai International Financial Centre
DLT	Distributed Ledger Technology
DOI	Digital Object Identifier

EBRD	European Bank for Reconstruction and Development
ECC	United Nations Convention on the Use of Electronic Communications in International Contracts
eCMR	Additional Protocol to the Convention on the Contract for the International Carriage of Goods by Road concerning the Electronic Consignment Note
EDI	Electronic Data Interchange
eFBL	Negotiable FIATA Multimodal Transport Bill of Lading
eFTI	Regulation (EU) 2020/1056 of the European Parliament and of the Council of 15 July 2020 on Electronic Freight Transport Information
eIDAS	Regulation (EU) No 910/2014 of the European Parliament and of the Council of 23 July 2014 on electronic identification and trust services for electronic transactions in the internal market and repealing Directive 1999/93/EC
eIDAS 2	Regulation (EU) 2024/1183 of the European Parliament and of the Council of 11 April 2024 amending Regulation (EU) No 910/2014 as regards establishing the European Digital Identity Framework
EMCRI	Electronic Monetary Claim Recording Institutions
ENISA	European Union Agency for Cybersecurity
ERMC	Electronically Recorded Monetary Claims
ERMCA	Electronically Recorded Monetary Claims Act
ESIGN	Electronic Signatures in Global and National Commerce Act
ETDA 2023	Electronic Trade Documents Act 2023
ETSI	European Telecommunications Standards Institute
EU	European Union
FIATA	International Federation of Freight Forwarders Associations
FIT Alliance	Future International Trade Alliance
G7	Group of 7
GSBN	Global Shipping Business Network
HGB	Handelsgesetzbuch

ICC	International Chamber of Commerce
ICC DSI	International Chamber of Commerce Digital Standards Initiative
ICT	Information and Communications Technology
IG P&I Clubs	International Group of the Protection and Indemnity Clubs
ILNAS	Institut luxembourgeois de la normalisation, de l'accréditation, de la sécurité et qualité des produits et services
IMDA	INFOCOMM Media Development Authority
IMF	International Monetary Fund
ISO	International Organization for Standardization
ITU	International Telecommunication Union
KFTC	Korea Financial Telecommunications and Clearings Institute
KYC	Know Your Customer
LNTS	League of Nations Treaty Series
MLAC	UNCITRAL Model Law on Automated Contracting
MLEC	UNCITRAL Model Law on Electronic Commerce
MLES	UNCITRAL Model Law on Electronic Signatures
MLETR	UNCITRAL Model Law on Electronic Transferable Records
MLIT	UNCITRAL Model Law on the Use and Cross-border Recognition of Identity Management and Trust Services
MLWR	UNCITRAL – Unidroit Model Law on Warehouse Receipts
NFT	Non-Fungible Token
NIST	National Institute of Standards and Technology
OECD	Organisation for Economic Co-operation and Development
PKI	Public Key Infrastructure
RADIAN	Registro de factura electrónica de venta considerada título valor
TAPED	Trade Agreement Provisions on Electronic-commerce and Data
UCC	Uniform Commercial Code
UCP	Uniform Customs and Practice for Documentary Credits

UETA	Uniform Electronic Transactions Act
UK	United Kingdom
UN	United Nations
UN/CEFACT	United Nations Centre for Trade Facilitation and Electronic Business
UNCITRAL	United Nations Commission on International Trade Law
UNCTAD	United Nations Trade and Development (formerly, United Nations Conference on Trade and Development)
UN/ESCAP	United Nations Economic and Social Commission for Asia and the Pacific
UNGA	United Nations General Assembly
UNIDROIT	International Institute for the Unification of Private Law
UNTS	United Nations Treaty Series
URC	Uniform Rules for Collections
URDTT	Uniform Rules for Digital Trade Transactions
US	United States of America
WTO	World Trade Organization

1

Introduction

1.1. From Paper to Electronic Documents and Beyond

Producing, sharing, and storing information is a basic need of human societies: knowledge is necessary to conduct daily activities and to promote innovation. Information must be understandable and accessible to serve as reference in case of need. For this reason, the ability to record information and the form in which the information is recorded are particularly important.[1] Among the different media suitable for information storage, paper emerged over time, thanks to innovations in its production process, as the technology offering the best compromise between usability, trustworthiness, security, durability and cost. The use of particular methods and procedures, such as signatures and seals, and the intervention of third parties such as public notaries, may give additional assurance of certain qualities of a paper-based document. Yet, paper-based documents have also significant limitations, such as the need for physical transmission and storage, and the impossibility of reusing and analysing automatically the information contained therein.

Against this background, it is possible to appreciate why the pervasive and ubiquitous use of electronic communications has become a defining feature of our age. Electronic means, though not a recent technology, only became available to the wider public after the 1980s.[2] The developments in their use may be described in three phases.

At the onset, users of electronic transactions focused on the ability to share information instantaneously at long distance by converting information available on paper to the electronic medium (so-called 'digitisation'). For instance, documents on paper may be scanned and sent by fax, or as an email attachment. A human being may thus immediately read the information contained in the attachment.

However, it soon became clear that analysing, reusing, and sharing information across entities and applications could make business processes more efficient.

[1] C Herrenschmidt, *Les trois écritures : langue, nombre, code* (Paris, Gallimard, 2007).

[2] J Coopersmith, *Faxed: The Rise and Fall of the Fax Machine* (Baltimore, Md, Johns Hopkins University Press, 2015).

To do so, information needs to be structured so that its content may be processed correctly by different applications. For instance, the information relating to a passenger boarding a flight may be shared with border control authorities for law enforcement purposes provided the person is sufficiently identified. Applications are tasked with processing information with varying degrees of automation and human beings may access information selectively. This second phase may be referred to as 'digitalisation' and is increasingly common.[3]

The third phase is digital transformation, where the use of electronic means allows a complete overhaul and re-engineering of business processes. This approach, also called 'end-to-end trade digitalisation' is still at an early stage and assumes the management of documents and data exclusively in electronic form. Data flows seamlessly in dedicated ecosystems, thus overcoming fragmentation of information in multiple paper documents. To achieve this goal, it is necessary to have rules on how to use all types of documents in electronic form as well as rules on how to assure the quality of the data contained in those documents. This book discusses those rules.

There may be significantly different understandings of what 'digital trade' means today as terminology evolves with technology. In this book, in line with prevailing practice it is assumed that 'electronic commerce' refers to the purchase of goods and services online, and to the delivery of services online; and that 'digital trade' refers to the use of commercial, financial and trade-related documents in electronic form. However, defining digital trade may not always be necessary: nowadays, virtually all trade is digital, because no trader may carry out commercial operations without using any electronic means. It is important to appreciate the shift in the essence of digital trade: ie from the reproduction of paper documents in electronic form; to the creation of electronic documents but still based on paper-based requirements; to the generation of native electronic documents as output of the re-engineered trade dataflow. In short the transition from documents to data.

1.2. The Path Towards Digital Transformation

Success in promoting the effective use of electronic means – be it nationally or across borders – relies on several elements, which include: sound policy decisions; a robust technical infrastructure; a modern and balanced legal and regulatory framework supported by proactive trade policies; and the buy-in of the private sector. Each element alone is necessary but not sufficient.[4]

[3] On the difference between digitisation and digitalisation, see, eg P Hyatt, 'Unpacking the Digital Transformation of Trade' (29 November 2023) www.tradeready.ca.

[4] See, generally, International Monetary Fund (IMF); Organisation for Economic Co-operation and Development (OECD); United Nations Conference on Trade and Development (UNCTAD); World Bank, and World Trade Organization (WTO); *Digital Trade for Development* (Geneva, 2023);

With regard to policy decisions, governments must embrace a coherent and comprehensive approach to the use of electronic means. Documents which outline national information and communication technology policies, or national digital strategies (and similar) provide guidelines for the effective use of electronic means in commercial and non-commercial settings, including exchanges with public entities.[5] However, these policy documents focus on telecommunications infrastructure development and issues such as e-government. They may discuss regulatory matters such as data privacy and protection, cybersecurity, and consumer protection, but seldom consider commercial and trade facilitation aspects.[6]

Moreover, the effective implementation of digital policies relies significantly on the effectiveness of the coordinating authority. Public entities with significant digital transformation needs and sufficient resources may decide to develop solutions that satisfy specific needs, but which do not comply with general legal requirements and technical standards. This may result in the creation of data silos that may hinder dataflows. In the trade field, single windows for customs operations may be an example of such stand-alone applications.[7]

A robust technical infrastructure, including not only hardware and software for exchange of electronic information, but also factors of general relevance such as reliable access to electricity and adequate human resources, is another key requirement of digital transformation. An insufficient technical infrastructure is a recurring issue, especially in developing countries. For instance, geographical remoteness and insufficient market demand may impede connectivity through high-speed fibre cables.

A comprehensive, modern, efficient, and effective legal framework is also needed for digital transformation. Legal rules relevant for the use of electronic means may be of a regulatory or enabling nature and may have application across different fields and business sectors, or in specific areas only. Regulatory rules set forth conditions to carry out certain activities, while enabling rules remove legal obstacles arising from existing laws and provide guidance on the application of those laws in an electronic setting. Core elements of the regulatory framework include data privacy and data protection, consumer protection and cybercrime laws. These matters require monitoring and enforcement, which are often carried out by one, or several, dedicated agencies. Core elements of the enabling

Commonwealth Telecommunications Organisation, *Digital Transformation: Critical Success Factors and Challenges in the Commonwealth* (London, Commonwealth Telecommunications Organisation, 2024).

[5] D Gierten and M Lesher, 'Assessing National Digital Strategies and their Governance' (2022) OECD Digital Economy Papers No 324.

[6] See, eg, Malawi National Information and Communications Technology (ICT) Policy 2013; Somalia National ICT Policy & Strategy 2019–2024; Zimbabwe National ICT Policy 2022–2027.

[7] WTO and World Economic Forum, *The Promise of TradeTech: Policy Approaches to Harness Trade Digitalization* (Geneva, WTO, 2022) ch 4; H Shah and A Srivastava, 'Authentication and Recognition Issues in Cross-Border Single Window' (2013) 47 *Journal of World Trade* 1225.

framework include the law relating to electronic transactions and electronic signatures, which are matters regarding the form of the communication and, more generally, contract law.

Public sector engagement alone may not be sufficient to achieve digital transformation. Historically, private sector investments have driven technological developments, promoted the build-up of technical infrastructures and of human capacity, and helped to establish confidence in digital solutions.

Developing and developed countries are not in the same position vis-à-vis digital transformation. Developing countries and smaller economies may be more agile in decision-making and thus able to adopt laws quickly. However, legislative agility does not always translate in the effective implementation of laws, as these countries often suffer from lack of technical infrastructure, including connectivity at a reasonable cost, and skilled human resources.[8] The measures to mitigate the digital divides aim to address these challenges at an international level.[9]

Finally, it is imperative to develop, test and disseminate modern business processes and practices. The human factor is critical in digital transformation and the need for capacity-building applies to private and public sector alike. This is particularly important in those economies whose market size may not justify developing locally those processes and practices. For instance, some Pacific jurisdictions have adopted modern legislation enabling the use of electronic transferable records. However, the limited size of their banking and financial sector does not permit the actual use of those records in business practice. It is expected that such use will increase once major business partners – for example, Australian banks – utilise those records in their daily operations.

1.3. The Case for Electronic Transferable Records

As noted above, the use of electronic means in trade has become ubiquitous and pervasive. Communications are exchanged continuously, and increasingly in an automated manner. While special form requirements remain, both with regard to specific documents and business types (for example, transfer of certain rights in real estate; family and succession law matters), the trend towards digital uptake is clear.

Many arguments are put forward in favour of digitalising trade. Electronic communications may be exchanged much more quickly than paper-based ones,

[8] UNCTAD, *E-commerce and Digital Economy Programme Year in Review 2022 – Looking Beyond Current Crises: Boosting Digital Readiness in Developing Countries* (Geneva, UNCTAD, 2023).

[9] See, eg the measures for achieving Sustainable Development Goal 9, aimed at the need to 'Build resilient infrastructure, promote inclusive and sustainable industrialization and foster innovation', and the World Summit on the Information Society, 'Plan of Action' (12 December 2003) UN Doc WSIS-03/GENEVA/DOC/5-E, Action Line C7, para 16.

with a higher number of partners, and at reduced cost: hence, gains in both speed and efficiency are possible. Electronic data may be analysed and reused in a much more complex and effective manner than paper-based data. The availability of additional information provided by data sharing and its more effective and focused analysis leads to increased governance and transparency of business processes. This results in a higher level of compliance at reduced cost and simplified procedures (for instance, thanks to the use of persistent digital identifiers). Savings may be especially beneficial for small- and medium-sized enterprises and may translate into lower costs for final users. Moreover, the electronic management of a supply chain may make it more resilient to external disruptions, such as changes in transport conditions, or in the availability of goods, thanks, in part, to data redundancy and real-time monitoring. Electronic means may also enable new applications that result in innovative services, reduced prices, and increased user-friendliness.

These and other strong and valid arguments explain the seemingly unstoppable race to digital trade. However, there is an exception: the digitalisation of documents incorporating the right to delivery of goods or payment of a sum of money has proven to be particularly challenging. These documents, referred to as 'transferable documents or instruments', or as 'documents of title', are of great relevance for logistics and paperless trade, and for trade financing and access to credit, as they allow trading in goods during transportation (typically, by ships) and facilitate payments. Moreover, these documents contain data of great importance for compliance purposes due to completeness, timeliness, accuracy and authenticity.

In the last few decades, several attempts have been made to provide an adequate legal framework for electronic transferable records.[10] In line with the general trends in the evolution of the use of electronic means in trade, the first attempts were aimed at improving the speed of transmission of documents. For instance, in short sea voyages the ship may reach the port of destination before the courier delivers the original paper-based bill of lading necessary to unload the goods: the use of electronic bills of lading would avoid this situation.

Awareness of the importance of enabling the use of electronic transferable documents and instruments has progressively increased, namely regarding their integration in single windows for customs operations and in the framework of efficient supply chain management. At the same time, technology has made significant advances, placing analysis and reuse of data at the centre of innovation through notions such as the Internet of Things, which generates big data, and artificial intelligence, which processes big data to provide analysis and forecasts.

However, security concerns, among other factors, may discourage commercial operators from fully transitioning to the electronic environment. This is

[10] See ch 2.

particularly true for conservative business such as banking and finance, which may feel comfortable with the well-established risk assessment of the use of paper-based documents and instruments, and fear venturing into uncharted digital territory. In particular, the concern for 'double spending', ie the risk that electronic transferable records will be replicated, thus exposing the debtor to multiple claims for the same obligation, has been a major reason limiting the uptake of electronic transferable records. However, documentary fraud also takes place regularly, and involves significant amounts of money, when paper documents are used. The use of electronic records provides more information on the transaction and in real time. If the information is managed correctly, governance of the transaction improves, and compliance costs are reduced.[11] In short, the reluctance to using electronic transferable records seems to be due to parties being comfortable with known risk patterns rather than an actual higher risk in the digital space.

When the COVID-19 pandemic highlighted the fragility of cross-border supply chains, the need for increased digital uptake of transferable documents and instruments became apparent, and related efforts multiplied. This, in turn, triggered considerations that went beyond streamlining and increasing the resilience of supply chains. Digital technologies are engines of growth that may increase productivity by reducing production costs, support economies of scale and more efficient financing, promote innovation by fostering exchange of ideas and expand and diversify export by reducing cross-border trade costs. Digitalisation can promote resilience to shocks, a wider services-led growth model and more inclusive growth.[12] Specifically, digitalisation of transferable documents and instruments may reduce transport costs and their environmental impact by replacing paper-based with paperless documents.[13] It may also improve governance of trade processes, including traceability of goods and certification of their compliance with environmental, social, and governance (ESG) and similar standards.

While discussions on the digitalisation of transport documents have been taking place for some time, awareness of the need to promote new trade finance solutions has also increased. Financial services have traditionally been offered by regulated operators on the basis of legacy business practices that limit information-sharing and innovation. The emergence of innovative solutions and

[11] Deutsche Bank, 'Fighting trade-related fraud' *Flow* (19 April 2023) flow.db.com. See also generally C Hare and D Neo (eds) *Trade Finance: Technology, Innovation and Documentary Credits* (Oxford, Oxford University Press, 2021) pts II and III; H Alavi, 'Mitigating the Risk of Fraud in Documentary Letters of Credit' (2016) 6 *Baltic Journal of European Studies* 1, 139.

[12] IMF, *Digital Trade for Development*, 3. See also UNCTAD 'Maritime Transport in Times of Polycrisis' (14 August 2024) UN Doc TD/B/C.I/MEM.7/32, para 56 and passim. According to the Digital Container Shipping Association 'State of the Industry Report, 2024', 41% of interviewed shippers consider supply chain visibility and access to real-time data as top operational priorities.

[13] For an estimate of the environmental benefits arising from the wide adoption of electronic bills of lading, see Global Shipping Business Network – SIA Partners, 'Impact of Digitalization in Driving Decarbonization in the Shipping Industry' (2024) www.gsbn.trade/publications.

new players has forced the rethinking of the traditional approach and the placing of data at the centre of trade financing operations.[14] Fully enabling digital trade finance is a first step in that direction.

To sum up, digitalisation of transport and finance documents may lead to their integration, with less trade financing costs, easier access to credit, and an increase in financing profitability. These benefits contribute to achieving strategic economic goals such as reinforcing or establishing a strong financial sector and providing additional credit to export operations, especially for small- and medium-sized enterprises. Importantly, digitalisation of transport and finance documents completes the process of digitalisation of trade documents and enables end-to-end digital trade.

1.4. The Role of UNCITRAL

The transition from paper-based to electronic documents requires a favourable enabling legal environment. Such an environment is often based on the texts prepared by the United Nations Commission on International Trade Law (UNCITRAL). UNCITRAL is the core body in the United Nations system for the harmonisation and modernisation of commercial law. It has prepared several legal texts on commercial contracts, company law and alternative dispute resolution. Over the last three decades, UNCITRAL has drafted uniform legislative texts on the law of electronic transactions that have been adopted in more than 100 states.[15]

UNCITRAL texts on electronic commerce (as they are traditionally referred to) have an enabling nature: they provide legal certainty by introducing rules that adapt contract law to the online environment and remove legal obstacles to the use of electronic means arising from form requirements of contract law. The comprehensive and harmonious suite of UNCITRAL legislative texts thus enables and facilitates the use of electronic transactions, including in relation to contracts and commercial documents. UNCITRAL provisions have been incorporated in electronic transactions laws across the world to give legal effect to the use of data messages, to ensure that all technologies are treated equally, and to adjust well-settled contract law rules tailored for the use of paper to the needs of the online world, for example, by referring to physical locations.

UNCITRAL has for decades aimed to legally enable the use of transferable documents and instruments in electronic form, especially bills of lading. It first

[14] On the use of data in financing, see GG Castellano, ĒK Selga and DW Arner, 'The Emergence of Financial Data Governance and the Challenge of Financial Data Sovereignty' in A Chander and H Sun (eds), *Data Sovereignty* (Oxford, Oxford University Press, 2023) 178.

[15] Texts, status, and other information on UNCITRAL texts is available on the UNCITRAL website at uncitral.un.org in the six official languages of the United Nations.

discussed the matter in 1994[16] and regularly thereafter, formulating different solutions.[17] Other entities – both public and private – have also made several attempts in the last decades to legally enable electronic transferable records and to promote their business use. However, all those efforts have been met with limited success due to several reasons.

First, early legal solutions assumed a business model based on the use of centralised registries, often managed by licensed operators. This model may work for documents exchanged only on domestic markets among a limited number of participants, such as promissory notes. It is not viable when the documents circulate among a very large number of participants dispersed across different jurisdictions, as is the case with bills of lading. Moreover, licensed service providers may not have an incentive to establish open interoperable ecosystems, but prefer pursuing proprietary lock-in, which may eventually create data silos that hinder interoperability.

A similar issue may arise with solutions that rely for legal recognition solely on a contractual network, which presumes the exclusive use of a service provider and is reflected in a rulebook. Clients may be wary of excessive reliance on a single service provider, which may lead to proprietary lock-in. Moreover, contract-based electronic documents do not replicate all functions of a document of title, but only a few of them, as their effect is limited to contractual network participants.

The creation of open trade ecosystems, in which service providers may compete freely provided they assure data exchange interoperability, may overcome these challenges. Those ecosystems rely on a law that enables the use of transferable documents and instruments in electronic form, as opposed to a rulebook or other contractual mechanisms. The proposed law is the UNCITRAL Model Law on Electronic Transferable Records (MLETR).[18]

The legislation on electronic equivalents of transferable documents and instruments enacted before the adoption of the MLETR followed a piecemeal approach, applying only to a specific type of document or instrument.[19] The MLETR offers a comprehensive legal regime for the use of electronic transferable records, which are defined as transferable documents and instruments in electronic form. It does not modify existing law but permits its application to online environments, thus enabling the joint management of all types of transferable documents and instruments in electronic form: this paradigm shift may dramatically increase efficiency in business practice.

[16] UNGA, 'Report of the United Nations Commission on International Trade Law. Twenty-seventh Session' (1994) UN Doc A/49/17, para 201.

[17] See ch 2, sections 2.1 and 2.2.

[18] UNCITRAL, *Model Law on Electronic Transferable Records* (New York, United Nations, 2018). This publication contains an Explanatory Note to the MLETR (the 'Explanatory Note').

[19] See ch 2, section 2.4.

The MLETR represents a legal turning point in trade digitalisation. To complete the transition from documents to data, the MLETR and other laws on electronic documents and electronic transactions need to rely on an equally robust legal mechanism for data quality assurance, including cross-border. It is necessary to build trust in the origin, integrity and other relevant features of the electronic document or message exchanged. UNCITRAL has addressed that need by preparing the UNCITRAL Model Law on the Use and Cross-border Recognition of Identity Management and Trust Services (MLIT),[20] which is based on pre-existing UNCITRAL texts, especially on electronic signatures, as well as on regional experience. In a nutshell, the MLETR completes the enabling legal framework to allow end-to-end trade digitalisation, and the MLIT provides the legal tools to establish trust in trade digitalisation with regard to data quality assurance, including identity.

1.5. What is in this Book?

This book provides a detailed legal analysis of MLETR and MLIT complemented by information on related texts.

Chapter two discusses texts predating the MLETR and the MLIT. It contains an overview of UNCITRAL texts on electronic commerce and discusses their underlying fundamental principles, which are shared with the MLETR and the MLIT, as well as those provisions that have been used in drafting the MLETR and the MLIT, or that have been amended or repealed by MLETR and MLIT. It also discusses UNCITRAL texts on the carriage of goods by sea which contain provisions on the use of electronic bills of lading, and other uniform texts. Finally, it illustrates those national laws dealing with electronic transferable records that have been used as references during MLETR preparation as well as contract-based solutions.

Chapter three offers an article-by-article commentary on the MLETR preceded by a description of its drafting history. Following the structure of the MLETR, it first illustrates its general principles and scope of application. It then discusses functional equivalence rules, including the assessment of the reliability of the methods used to achieve functional equivalents, and the use of electronic transferable records, including cross-border. Finally, it provides an overview of certain matters relevant for the interpretation and application of the MLETR that are not directly reflected in the MLETR provisions.

Chapter four contains a description of the national enactments of the MLETR, including variations and additions to the uniform text. It also discusses some

[20] UNCITRAL, *Model Law on the Use and Cross-border Recognition of Identity Management and Trust Services* (Vienna, United Nations, 2023). This publication contains a Guide to Enactment of the MLIT (the 'Guide to Enactment').

aspects of other national legislation on electronic transferable records. Finally, it provides an overview of uniform texts influenced by the MLETR.

Chapter five contains an introduction to the notions of identity management and trust services, a summary of the drafting history of the MLIT and an article-by-article discussion of the MLIT general provisions.

Chapter six illustrates the notion of identity management, which is defined as the identification of physical and legal persons with the use of electronic means, including the evolution of the notion of identification in time. It then discusses the provisions of the MLIT relating to identity management, which include functional equivalence provisions to achieve identification as well as a list of obligations of the identity management service provider, and a liability regime for their violation. It also elaborates on the options for assessing the reliability of the methods used in delivering identity management services.

Chapter seven deals with MLIT provisions on trust services, which are services for the assurance of data quality. Besides discussing obligations and liability of trust service providers, it illustrates the legal features of each trust service named in the MLIT. Particular attention is given to the discussion of electronic signatures, which are one type of named trust service.

Chapter eight illustrates the provisions of the MLIT on cross-border use and recognition of identity management and trust services.

Chapter nine discusses matters related to the adoption and implementation of the MLETR and the MLIT, including technical cooperation and other promotional activities, policy issues, and the relationship with trade agreements. It also deals with the use of these model laws in specific business sectors.

2

Legislation on Electronic Transferable Records Predating the UNCITRAL Model Law on Electronic Transferable Records

The mandate of the United Nations Commission on International Trade Law (UNCITRAL) refers to the 'promotion of the progressive harmonization and unification of the law of international trade'.[1] This goal is pursued by preparing treaties and model laws for consideration and adoption by states. This work traditionally required the application of the comparative law method to identify common elements in national laws and formulate a universally acceptable legislative text. A thorough analysis must go beyond statutes and include case law, jurisprudence, business practice and any other element that contributes to defining the law in the broad sense.[2]

Over time, the focus of UNCITRAL's work has shifted slowly from the unification of commercial law to its harmonisation, which may bring a lower level of uniformity but possibly in a higher number of jurisdictions due to the increased ability to reconcile diverse legal traditions. The outcome is not limited to defining the minimum legal common denominator but may also include legislative developments and innovations that are deemed broadly acceptable. For instance, Part III of the United Nations Convention on Contracts for the International Sale of Goods[3] is considered as innovating on the prior existing remedies for non-performance of obligations arising from a contract for the international sale of goods.

The traditional comparative approach needs to be adapted when it is used to address new business needs. In such a case, which includes the desire to legally enable and facilitate the use of electronic transactions, national laws do not exist or are not well established, and national legislators seek uniform guidance to fill the

[1] UNGA Res 2205 (XXI) (17 December 1966), I.

[2] See the classic formulation of the 'theory of formants' in R Sacco, 'Legal Formants: A Dynamic Approach to Comparative Law' (1991) 39 *American Journal of Comparative Law* 1 (Instalment I), 343 (Instalment II).

[3] United Nations Convention on Contracts for the International Sale of Goods (adopted 11 April 1980, entered into force 1 January 1988) (CISG) 1489 UNTS 3.

legislative gap. Uniformity is thus achieved by basing the legislation on a common model from the origin, rather than by reconciling existing laws.[4] In this case, the focus of the legislative exercise shifts again from legislative harmonisation to modernisation based on uniform models.

This legislative gap-filling function is evident in the field of electronic commerce law,[5] where UNCITRAL's pioneering work has been remarkably successful. As noted above, taken together, UNCITRAL texts on electronic commerce have been adopted in more than 100 states. Given their relevance and importance to cross-border trade, they are increasingly referenced in trade agreements between states.[6]

2.1. UNCITRAL Legislative Texts on Electronic Commerce

UNCITRAL began its work on electronic commerce in 1985 with the adoption of Recommendations to Governments and International Organizations concerning the Legal Value of Computer Records.[7] It then dealt with the use of electronic means in payments, with the adoption in 1987 of the UNCITRAL Legal Guide on Electronic Funds Transfer,[8] and in 1992 of the UNCITRAL Model Law on International Credit Transfers,[9] which applies the notion of 'authentication' to online payments.

The UNCITRAL legislative texts on electronic commerce are:

- the UNCITRAL Model Law on Electronic Commerce (1996);
- the UNCITRAL Model Law on Electronic Signatures (2001);
- the United Nations Convention on the Use of Electronic Communications in International Contracts (2005);

[4] L Castellani, 'Uniform Law and the Production and Circulation of Legal Models' in G Low (ed), *Convergence and Divergence of Private Law in Asia* (Cambridge, Cambridge University Press, 2022) 7, 30–31.

[5] This area of work of UNCITRAL is traditionally referred to as 'electronic commerce'. However, it covers mostly electronic transactions and electronic signatures law, which is considered part of 'digital trade' law. Nowadays, the notion of 'electronic commerce' is often associated with consumer protection law, which is a topic outside the mandate of UNCITRAL. For consistency of terminology, UNCITRAL texts on electronic commerce will be referred to with their traditional name. For an introduction to these texts, L Castellani, 'UNCITRAL texts on electronic commerce' in R Gulati, T John, and B Köhler (eds), *The Elgar Companion to UNCITRAL* (Cheltenham, UK, Edward Elgar Publishing, 2023) 512; on the early legal issues addressed by those texts, T Smedinghoff, 'The Legal Requirements for Creating Secure and Enforceable Electronic Transactions', in International Monetary Fund, *Monetary and Financial Law*, vol 3 (Washington, DC, International Monetary Fund, 2005) 757.

[6] See ch 9, section 9.5.

[7] UNGA, 'Report of the United Nations Commission on International Trade Law. Eighteenth session' (1985) UN Doc A/40/17, para 360.

[8] UNCITRAL, *Legal Guide on Electronic Funds Transfer* (New York, United Nations, 1987).

[9] UNCITRAL, *Model Law on International Credit Transfers* (Vienna, United Nations, 1994).

- the UNCITRAL Model Law on Electronic Transferable Records (2017);
- the UNCITRAL Model Law on the Use and Cross-border Recognition of Identity Management and Trust Services (2022); and
- the UNCITRAL Model Law on Automated Contracting (2024).

2.1.1. The UNCITRAL Model Law on Electronic Commerce

The UNCITRAL Model Law on Electronic Commerce (MLEC)[10] was the first legislative text of UNCITRAL in this field and, as such, contains the first formulations of the principles of non-discrimination against (or legal recognition of) the use of electronic means, technology neutrality and functional equivalence, which are the foundations of modern electronic commerce law.[11]

The principle of legal recognition of the use of electronic means requires that an electronic record is not denied legal effect, validity or enforceability solely on the grounds that it is in electronic form. This principle is also known as the principle of non-discrimination against the use of electronic means because it is formulated in negative form to stress that other factors – for instance, the use of an unreliable method – may prevent legal recognition.

The principle of technology neutrality ensures that the law does not mandate or favour the use of any specific technology, method, or product. This makes the law future-proof, promotes innovation and prevents proprietary lock-in. In most UNCITRAL texts on electronic commerce it is not formulated in specific provisions but is reflected throughout the legislative texts.

The principle of functional equivalence sets out the criteria by which electronic communications are deemed to satisfy form requirements applicable to paper-based documents.[12] Functional equivalence is not established between paper-based and electronic form, but between the functions pursued with the use of paper and those fulfilled with the use of electronic means. Therefore, this principle presupposes the existence of a law that applies to paper-based documents.

[10] UNCITRAL, *Model Law on Electronic Commerce with Guide to Enactment, 1996, with additional article 5 bis as adopted in 1998* (New York, United Nations, 1999). For an introduction to the MLEC, see H Burman, 'United Nations: UNCITRAL Model Law on Electronic Commerce' (1997) 36 *International Legal Materials* 197; for the MLEC drafting process, see: H Gabriel, 'The New United States Uniform Electronic Transactions Act: Substantive Provisions, Drafting History, and Comparison to the UNCITRAL Model Law on Electronic Commerce' (2000) 5 *Uniform Law Review* 651.

[11] For an application of these principles, see ch 3, commentary on the UNCITRAL Model Law on Electronic Transferable Records (MLETR), art 3, para 2.

[12] For an in-depth discussion of this principle, see: M Demoulin, *Droit du commerce électronique et équivalents fonctionnels. Théorie critique* (Bruxelles, Larcier, 2014). See also: E Caprioli, 'La Loi-type de la CNUDCI sur les documents transférables électroniques : analyse et perspectives' (2023) *Journal du droit international 'Clunet'* 465, 484, for the historical development of the notion of functional equivalence.

Moreover, the MLEC establishes rules for the formation and validity of contracts concluded by electronic means and on various aspects of data message exchanges such as attribution of data messages, acknowledgement of receipt, and determination of time and place of dispatch and receipt of data messages. The MLEC is the foundational and most adopted UNCITRAL text in this field, having been enacted in some 90 states, and is regularly referenced in trade agreements.

MLEC provisions establishing the requirements for functional equivalence between the paper-based notions of 'writing' and 'signature' and their electronic counterparts are directly relevant for MLETR enactment and implementation.[13]

MLEC, arts 16 and 17 establish functional equivalence between documents used in conjunction with the carriage of goods and electronic records based on the use of a method providing reliable assurance of uniqueness of the electronic record.[14] Articles 16 and 17 of the MLEC may apply to all documents related to the transport of goods, transferable or not, and to any means of transport, and presuppose the existence of a paper-based transport document. They therefore also apply to electronic bills of lading.

MLEC, art 17, paras 3 and 4 are the core provisions for establishing functional equivalence between transferable documents and electronic records. They set up a mechanism providing not only guarantee of uniqueness (or, in MLETR terminology, singularity) of the record but also assurance that multiple claims shall be prevented.[15] The preparatory study for those provisions recognised identifying with certainty the person in control of the electronic record who could request delivery of the goods and ensuring the uniqueness of the electronic record incorporating the title to the goods as conditions to achieve those goals.[16] A subsequent study stressed the desirability of drafting rules that permit establishing control over the electronic transferable record in a manner functionally equivalent to physical possession of transferable documents and instruments to fully enable the digitalisation of those documents and instruments.[17]

The MLEC has been enacted in a very large number of jurisdictions, but not arts 16 and 17. Moreover, in those few jurisdictions where these articles have been enacted their use in business practice has not been reported.[18]

[13] See ch 3, commentary on the MLETR, arts 8 and 9.

[14] For an early commentary on these articles focusing on their implementation through electronic data interchange (EDI), see: J Livermore and K Euarjai, 'Electronic Bills of Lading and Functional Equivalence' (1998) 2 *The Journal of Information, Law and Technology* available at: elj.warwick.ac.uk.

[15] MLEC Guide to Enactment, para 115.

[16] UNCITRAL, 'Electronic Data Interchange' (31 January 1996) UN Doc A/CN.9/WG.IV/WP.69.

[17] UNCITRAL, 'Possible future work on electronic commerce. Transfer of rights in tangible goods and other rights' (20 December 2000) UN Doc A/CN.9/WG.IV/WP.90.

[18] See arts 26 and 27 of Law 527 of 1999 of Columbia; arts 31 and 32 of Decree No 47 of 2008 of Guatemala; ss 25 and 26 of the Electronic Commerce Act, Republic Act No 8792 of the Philippines. Canada has incorporated the MLEC, arts 16 and 17 in uniform model legislation: see ss 24 and 25 of the Uniform Electronic Commerce Act prepared by the Uniform Law Conference of Canada. These

The reluctance to adopting and using these provisions may be explained with the then prevalence of a business model based on contractual agreements and siloed applications and the lack of adequate supporting technology.

UNCITRAL did not take an explicit position on whether the MLETR should replace the MLEC, arts 16 and 17, leaving the decision to the discretion of each jurisdiction, possibly with the advice of the UNCITRAL secretariat.[19] However, jurisdictions that have enacted the MLEC, arts 16 and 17 should consider replacing them with the MLETR to benefit from a more comprehensive and modern legislative framework.[20]

From a practical perspective, electronic transferable records issued under the MLETR may comply with the requirements of the MLEC, arts 16 and 17 and vice versa. Consequently, jurisdictions that have enacted the MLEC, arts 16 and 17 may implement these provisions by using MLETR-compliant electronic transferable records management systems and services.

Certain jurisdictions that enacted the MLEC without its arts 16 and 17 included, nevertheless, transferable documents and instruments in the scope of application of the enacting law, be it at the onset or because of a later amendment. Since such laws give limited (for example, Jordan)[21] or no (for example, Mauritius)[22] guidance on the use of electronic transferable records, MLETR adoption seems particularly desirable to provide an adequate level of legal certainty and predictability.

2.1.2. Other UNCITRAL Legislative Texts on Electronic Commerce

The UNCITRAL Model Law on Electronic Signatures (MLES)[23] establishes criteria for the equivalence between electronic and hand-written signatures, as well as rules of conduct for assessing the duties and liabilities of the signatory, the party relying on the signature, and trusted third parties such as providers of cryptographic certificates. Because of its scope, the MLES may be considered a precursor of the UNCITRAL Model Law on the Use and Cross-border Recognition of Identity Management and Trust Services (MLIT).

sections have been adopted in eleven provinces and territories; see, eg: the Electronic Commerce Act 2000 of Ontario, s 23 (SO 2000, chap 17). The two missing provinces are New Brunswick and Quebec, the latter being the only Canadian province or territory that has not enacted the MLEC.

[19] UNGA, 'Report of the United Nations Commission on International Trade Law Fiftieth Session' (2017) UN Doc A/72/17, para 114.

[20] This was done in Bahrain by repealing art 20 of the Legislative Decree no 28 of 2002 with respect to Electronic Transactions (see ch 4, section 4.1).

[21] Electronic Transactions Law, arts 18–20, Law No 15 of 2015 (applicable to financial instruments but not to transport documents).

[22] Electronic Transactions Act 2000, s 4, Act No 23 of 2000, as amended by Act No 9 of 2015.

[23] UNCITRAL, *Model Law on Electronic Signatures with Guide to Enactment* (New York, United Nations, 2002).

MLES, art 3 provides an example of an explicit rule mandating technology neutrality of electronic signatures. MLES, art 6 embraces a 'two-tier' approach to electronic signatures that gives legal effect to all forms of electronic signatures and attaches additional legal consequences, such as presumptions on origin and integrity of the signed data message, to those signatures that satisfy more requirements. It also foresees the identification of those sophisticate signatures before their use. This mechanism foreshadows the approach taken in the MLIT, based on a combination of ex ante designation of reliable services and ex post determination of reliability.

The interaction between the MLETR and UNCITRAL provisions on electronic signatures and other trust services goes beyond the explicit reference to electronic signature contained in the MLETR, art 9. Those provisions are directly relevant for MLETR implementation as electronic transferable records management systems rely on trust services for the issuance and circulation of the records.

The United Nations Convention on the Use of Electronic Communications in International Contracts[24] is the first and only treaty dealing with cross-border aspects of the use of electronic transactions, including electronic signatures.[25] It contains provisions on legal recognition of electronic communication and on functional equivalence with the paper-based notions of 'writing', 'signature' and 'original' that legally enable cross-border electronic exchanges. It also complements other treaties applicable to international commercial transactions that contain form requirements by providing functional equivalence rules to satisfy those requirements with the use of electronic means. By doing so, the ECC avoids the need to formally amend those treaties, some of which have many state parties. Moreover, the ECC updates and complements certain provisions of the MLEC. For this reason, several states have enacted the substantive provisions of the ECC into their legislation on electronic transactions.[26]

The ECC, art 2, para 2 excludes transferable documents and instruments from the scope of application of the Convention. This provision was used as the starting point for defining the scope of application of the MLETR.

The UNCITRAL Model Law on Automated Contracting (MLAC)[27] complements the MLEC and the ECC on the use of automated systems (also referred to

[24] United Nations Convention on the Use of Electronic Communications in International Contracts (adopted 23 November 2005, entered into force 1 March 2013) 2898 UNTS 3 (ECC).

[25] On the ECC, see: AH Boss and W Kilian (eds), *The United Nations Convention on the Use of Electronic Communications in International Contracts: An In-depth Guide and Sourcebook* (Frederick, Md, Kluwer Law International, 2008); KW Chong and JS Chao, 'United Nations Convention on the Use of Electronic Communications in International Contracts: A New Global Standard' (2006) 18 *Singapore Academy of Law Journal* 116; L Castellani, 'The United Nations Convention on the Use of Electronic Communications in International Contracts at Ten: Practical Relevance and Lessons Learned' (2016) 3 *Journal of Law, Society and Development* 132.

[26] The list of these jurisdictions is available on the status page of the MLEC on the UNCITRAL website under footnote (e). Some 35 states have enacted domestically the ECC, while the number of state parties to the Convention is about 20.

[27] UNGA, 'Report of the United Nations Commission on International Trade Law Fifty-seventh Session' (2024) UN Doc A/79/17, Annex IV.

as 'smart contracts') in the various stages of the contract's lifecycle. Automated systems are deterministic or non-deterministic systems capable of carrying out actions without the necessary review or intervention of a natural person. The MLAC does not require the use of any particular technology, method or system to carry out automation, in line with the principle of technology neutrality and unlike the frequent association of smart contracts with the use of distributed ledger technology.

The MLAC, art 5 gives legal recognition to the contracts concluded or performed with the use of automation and to related actions. The MLAC, art 6 gives legal recognition to contractual terms concluded solely in computer code, and to the incorporation in contracts of information that changes periodically or continuously ('dynamic information'). These two provisions may be relevant for implementing the MLETR, art 6, which enables the inclusion of dynamic information in electronic transferable records.

The MLAC, art 7 contains rules on the attribution of actions carried out by automated systems, which is preferably done according to the procedure agreed by the parties. The MLAC, art 8 addresses unexpected (or, rather, expected but undesirable) outputs that may occur when using non-deterministic algorithms.

2.1.3. Electronic Documents

UNCITRAL texts on electronic commerce drafted under a functional equivalence approach do not explicitly refer to the notion of an 'electronic document' though they contain provisions on electronic contracts. It is assumed that such a notion may be determined with reference to substantive law texts.[28] On the other hand, reference to specific documents may be found in UNCITRAL texts that adopt a medium-neutral approach (and therefore contain both substantive law and provisions on the use of electronic means) like the United Nations Convention on the Contracts for the International Carriage of Goods Wholly or Partly by Sea[29] and the UNCITRAL – Unidroit Model Law on Warehouse Receipts.[30]

This does not mean that UNCITRAL texts on electronic commerce are irrelevant for the digitalisation of commercial documents: on the contrary, this is one of their main goals. But their effect takes place through functional equivalence rules and other provisions that do not affect the substantive law of each document.

[28] The notion of 'substantive law' in UNCITRAL texts on electronic commerce refers to the law applicable to the paper-based document and that, by way of their enactment, becomes applicable also to the electronic document. This notion is relevant for texts based on a functional equivalence approach. Texts based on a medium-neutral approach also contain substantive law rules. The notion of 'substantive law' in this context has no relationship with the notion of substantive law as opposed to procedural law.

[29] See section 2.2 below.

[30] See ch 4, section 4.2.1.

The use of documents in electronic form presupposes confidence in their legal effect and enforceability. The examination of the validity of an electronic document requires a three-step process: (i) legal characterisation of the data message as a specific type of document; (ii) verification of its compliance with any applicable form and content requirement; and (iii) assurance of the qualities of the data message. To determine the type of document (for example, contract for sale of goods; promissory note) it is necessary to consider the content of that document and the intention of the parties, as ascertained by applying the relevant interpretation rules. Once the type of document has been identified, it is possible to determine the applicable substantive law and any requirement of form (for example, in writing; signature) and content (for example, the identification of the type of goods sold; the amount of money due) that are applicable irrespective of the use of electronic or paper medium. Finally, trust services or other methods may be used to provide assurance of the quality of the data message (for example, its origin and integrity).

Although UNCITRAL has not done so, it is possible to envisage a rule that applies the principle of legal recognition (or non-discrimination) to electronic documents. This rule has proven useful when giving legal effect to commercial documents,[31] and legislators may consider its inclusion in electronic transactions laws enacting UNCITRAL model laws.

2.2. Other UNCITRAL Texts: Carriage of Goods by Sea

UNCITRAL has carried out significant work on uniform laws for contracts for the carriage of goods by sea.[32] The United Nations Convention on the Carriage of Goods by Sea (the 'Hamburg Rules')[33] was the first UNCITRAL text in the field. Article 14, para 3 of the Hamburg Rules recognises that the signature on the bill of lading may be made by electronic means. The commentary clarifies that electronic means may be used if not inconsistent with the law of the country where the bill of lading is issued. Moreover, article 1, paragraph 8 of the Hamburg Rules clarifies that '"Writing" includes, inter alia, telegram and telex'.[34] A discussion was held

[31] Tribunale di Milano, 16 October 2016, *Graficad Sas in Liq v Marcello Salvadori*, Case no 11402/2016, CLOUT Case no 2054, applying art 46 of the Regulation (EU) No 910/2014 of the European Parliament and of the Council of 23 July 2014 on electronic identification and trust services for electronic transactions in the internal market and repealing Directive 1999/93/EC [2014] OJ L257/73 (eIDAS).

[32] For an introduction to this area of work of UNCITRAL, see: V Bath, 'UNCITRAL and International Carriage of Goods by Sea' in R Gulati, T John and B Köhler (eds), *The Elgar Companion to UNCITRAL* 541.

[33] United Nations Convention on the Carriage of Goods by Sea (adopted 31 March 1978, entered into force 1 November 1992) 1695 UNTS 3 (Hamburg Rules).

[34] See also Caprioli, 'La Loi-type' (2023), 473.

during the travaux préparatoires of the Hamburg Rules on the secure identification of the sender of a telegram.[35]

The Hamburg Rules do not contain any explicit reference to electronic bills of lading although suggestions were made in that regard.[36] Interestingly, the United Nations Convention on the Liability of Operators of Transport Terminals in International Trade,[37] which complements the Hamburg Rules, foresees explicitly in its art 4, para 3 the possibility of issuing a document acknowledging receipt of the goods in electronic form according to the electronic data interchange (EDI) format.[38] These elements may be useful to prove that the use of electronic bills of lading is compatible with older treaties on carriage of goods by sea; it would however be excessive to expect that those texts contain a fully-fledged legal treatment of electronic bills of lading, as the use of those documents was not widely accepted in business practice, and there was limited awareness of the related requirements. Legally enabling the use of electronic bills of lading and other transferable records has been a long learning process that underwent several steps before MLETR adoption.

UNCITRAL worked again on this topic when preparing the United Nations Convention on the Contracts for the International Carriage of Goods Wholly or Partly by Sea (the 'Rotterdam Rules').[39] Similar to the Hamburg Rules (but with broader scope and different policy approaches), the Rotterdam Rules are a comprehensive treaty on the rights and obligations of the parties to a contract for the carriage of goods by sea and on the documents related to that contract.

One of the goals of the Rotterdam Rules is to enable the use of electronic bills of lading, which are referred to as 'negotiable electronic transport records' (Rotterdam Rules, art 1(19)). This goal was one of the main reasons for UNCITRAL to start work in this field.[40] The Rotterdam Rules achieve that goal by adopting a

[35] United Nations, *Conference on the Carriage of Goods by Sea (Hamburg, 6–31 March 1978) Official Records* (New York, United Nations, 1981), paras 59–61.

[36] United Nations, 'Analysis of comments and proposals by Governments and international organizations on the draft Convention on the Carriage of Goods by Sea, and on the draft provisions concerning implementation, reservations and other final clauses prepared by the Secretary-General' (10 November 1977) UN Doc A/CONF.89/8, para 35 (comment by the International Chamber of Commerce).

[37] United Nations Convention on the Liability of Operators of Transport Terminals in International Trade (adopted 19 April 1991, not in force).

[38] While this document may be a warehouse receipt, it is unclear whether it could be transferable.

[39] United Nations Convention on the Contracts for the International Carriage of Goods Wholly or Partly by Sea (adopted 11 December 2008, not in force) (Rotterdam Rules). The Rotterdam Rules attracted significant attention from maritime law scholars at the time of their adoption. See, eg: T Fujita, M Sturley and G van der Ziel, *The Rotterdam Rules: The UN Convention on Contracts for the International Carriage of Goods Wholly or Partly by Sea*, 2nd edn (London, Sweet & Maxwell, 2020); A von Ziegler, J Schelin and S Zunarelli (eds), *The Rotterdam Rules 2008: Commentary to the United Nations Convention on Contracts for the International Carriage of Goods Wholly or Partly by Sea* (Alphen aan den Rijn, Wolters Kluwer, 2010).

[40] UNCITRAL, 'Transport law: possible future work' (31 March 2000) UN Doc A/CN.9/476, para 2. See also: N Gaskell, 'Book Review' (2013) 27 *Australia & New Zealand Maritime Law Journal* 42, 43, for a description of several circumstances and issues influencing the preparation of the Rotterdam Rules.

medium-neutral approach that applies the same substantive rules to electronic records and paper-based documents.

Chapter 3 of the Rotterdam Rules, on electronic transport records, contains artis 8, 9 and 10, respectively giving legal recognition to the use of such records, providing basic guidance on the procedures for their use and regulating the replacement of negotiable electronic transport records with paper-based negotiable transport documents and vice versa. The basic elements contained in the Rotterdam Rules, art 9 may reflect the model prevailing at the time of preparation of the treaty, which was based on contractual agreements, to which all concerned parties had to consent, and the use of central registries. Additional elements on issuance, control, and transfer of control of electronic transport records may be found in various provisions of the Rotterdam Rules such as art 1(21) and (22).[41] These provisions were drafted by a joint group of experts and submitted to the consideration of the Working Group.[42]

Because the Rotterdam Rules adopt a medium neutral approach, they do not contain any functional equivalence rule. However, in doing so they may sometimes depart from UNCITRAL electronic commerce standards. For instance, the Rotterdam Rules, art 3 indicates that certain communications must be made in writing or electronically, if the parties agree on the use of electronic means. However, it does not require that electronic communications should be available for future reference, as would usually be required to achieve functional equivalence with the written form requirement. Similarly, the Rotterdam Rules, art 38 requires that a transport document should be signed by the carrier. The signature may be electronic provided it identifies the signatory and indicates the carrier's authorisation of the issuance of the electronic transport record, which is the specific function pursued by the carrier's signing of an electronic bill of lading. However, this definition may not encompass signatures used for endorsing an electronic transport record.

The relationship between the MLETR and the Rotterdam Rules is a double one: on the one hand, certain provisions of the Rotterdam Rules have influenced the corresponding provisions of the MLETR; on the other hand, the MLETR may be useful for implementing the Rotterdam Rules, as indicated by UNCITRAL, including by filling in any gaps.[43]

Moreover, when preparing the MLETR there was full awareness of the need to ensure compatibility with the Rotterdam Rules. One issue arose with respect

[41] M Alba Fernández, 'Electronic Commerce Provisions in the UNCITRAL Convention on Contracts for the International Carriage of Goods Wholly or Partly by Sea' (2009) 44 *Texas International Law Journal* 387. Art 50 of the Rotterdam Rules deal with the notion of 'right of control' but that notion relates generally to control of the transported goods and is not specific to electronic bills of lading.

[42] UNCITRAL, 'Transport Law: Preparation of a draft instrument on the carriage of goods [wholly or partly] [by sea]. Proposed revised provisions on electronic commerce' (24 March 2005) UN Doc A/CN.9/WG.III/WP.47.

[43] UNGA, 'Report of the United Nations Commission on International Trade Law Forty-fourth Session' (2011) UN Doc A/66/17, para 235.

to then draft art 15 of the MLETR on the issuance of multiple originals. That provision, which had been inserted to accommodate a business demand for giving explicit legal recognition to the practice of issuing multiple original electronic transferable records, indicated that multiple originals could be issued when substantive law allowed issuance for transferable documents. This provision was seen as problematic for maritime law as it would perpetuate the deprecated practice of issuing multiple originals, which could lead to multiple claims for the same performance. The Rotterdam Rules, art 36, para 2(d) recognises the possibility of issuing multiple originals of a negotiable transport document, but the Rotterdam Rules are silent on the issuance of multiple electronic negotiable transport records. The Comité Maritime International (CMI) submitted to UNCITRAL a detailed discussion of why the Rotterdam Rules recognised explicitly the use of multiple original paper-based negotiable transport documents but should be interpreted as being incompatible with the issuance of multiple original electronic transport records.[44] However, the interpretation suggested by the CMI may violate the medium-neutral approach underlying the Rotterdam Rules as different rules would apply depending on the medium used. Draft art 15 of the MLETR on multiple originals was eventually deleted.

In general, as noted, the relationship between the Rotterdam Rules and the MLETR is of compatibility and complementarity.[45] The details for implementing the Rotterdam Rules are to be found in national law or contractual agreements. Interaction with the MLETR could occur when the MLETR is enacted as national law or when its operative provisions are incorporated in contractual agreements, including rulebooks and other terms and conditions for the use of electronic transferable records management systems. MLETR rules could provide, for instance, guidance on the notion of control of an electronic transferable record as well as on steps for the replacement of an electronic record with a paper-based document.[46] On the other hand, those who believe that a statement at the treaty level is needed

[44] UNCITRAL, 'Draft Model Law on Electronic Transferable Records – Compilation of comments by Governments and international organizations' (25 April 2017) UN Doc A/CN.9/921/Add.1.

[45] See the analysis of M Goldby, 'Can the Rotterdam Rules co-exist with laws based on the MLETR?' in CMI, *The Rotterdam Rules Convention* (Antwerp, CMI, 2024) 91, concluding that 'While the approaches of the [Rotterdam Rules] and the MLETR are distinct, the analysis in this paper demonstrates that the distinction stems from their different purposes, not from any divergence in principle' (at 99), and that any electronic bill of lading that satisfies the MLETR would also satisfy the Rotterdam Rules, so that the additional requirements of the MLETR could usefully complement the Rotterdam Rules. See also L Fosgaard, *The Transfer of Rights in a Digitalised Age* (Aalborg, Aalborg Universitetsforlag, 2023), ch 4 'The Rotterdam Rules and its interaction with the MLETR'. However, a document prepared in 2022 for a Dutch public consultation on legislative provisions enabling the use of electronic bills of lading seemed to consider the adoption of the MLETR as alternative to the adoption of the Rotterdam Rules (the consultation paper is available at www.internetconsultatie.nl under 'elektronisch vervoerbestand'). This approach was eventually not taken up: see the discussion of the Dutch draft legislation in ch 4, section 4.1.

[46] A Møllmann, *Delivery of Goods Under Bills of Lading* (Abingdon, Oxon, Routledge, 2017), ch 7, 197; I Magklasi, *The Rotterdam Rules and International Trade Law* (Abingdon, Oxon, Routledge, 2018), para 4.10.1.

to achieve full predictability on the legal status of electronic bills of lading will find that declaration in the Rotterdam Rules and promote their adoption accordingly.

The Rotterdam Rules have not yet entered into force, and it is difficult to predict when that will happen. Given the significant codification effort behind them, the Rotterdam Rules have been utilised as a source of inspiration for the modernisation of maritime law, for instance in Germany and Spain.[47]

2.3. Other Uniform Texts: eCMR

In current commercial practice, the only broadly used transport document commonly recognised as a document of title is the bill of lading involving a maritime leg. UNCITRAL is working on a negotiable cargo document that does not require carriage by sea.[48] However, certain transport documents that are not transferable are also relevant for electronic transferable records implementation due to their widespread commercial use and modalities of circulation.

The Convention on the Contract for the International Carriage of Goods by Road (CMR)[49] defines the obligations of the parties to a contract for carriage of goods by road, namely the sender and the carrier, and sets the requirements for the consignment note, which is a related document. The consignment note is not negotiable and is not a document representing goods.[50] The Additional Protocol to the CMR concerning the Electronic Consignment Note (eCMR)[51] allows the issuance and use of consignment notes in electronic form.[52] The CMR and the eCMR have attracted significant support from states, especially in Europe and neighbouring regions.

The eCMR deals with a non-negotiable and non-transferable transport document and therefore its application does not interfere with that of the MLETR. However, digitalisation of trade documents should ideally take place according to the same standards and in fully interoperable digital trade ecosystems to enable seamless dataflows. Because of that, electronic transferable records management systems should handle also electronic non-transferable records such as air and sea waybills, straight bills of lading[53] and consignment notes.

[47] See ch 4, section 4.1, under the respective state name.

[48] See ch 4, section 4.2.2.

[49] Convention on the Contract for the International Carriage of Goods by Road (adopted 19 May 1956, entered into force 2 July 1961) 399 UNTS 189 (CMR).

[50] However, the CMR, art 1, para 5 gives states the option 'to authorize the use in transport operations entirely confined to their territory of consignment notes representing a title to the goods'.

[51] Additional Protocol to the Convention on the Contract for the International Carriage of Goods by Road concerning the Electronic Consignment Note (adopted 20 February 2008, entered into force 5 June 2011) 2762 UNTS 23 (eCMR).

[52] For an introduction to the eCMR, see: J Putzeys, 'Adapting the CMR to the Electronic Age' (2006) 11 *Uniform Law Review* 530.

[53] MLETR, Explanatory Note, para 21.

The UNCITRAL Secretariat contributed to the drafting of the eCMR, and certain UNCITRAL provisions have significantly influenced the corresponding ones of the eCMR.[54] This is the case for the definitions of 'electronic communications' and 'electronic signature' contained in the eCMR, art 1 and the circumstances relevant for presumption of reliability listed in the eCMR, art 3, para 1. Moreover, the eCMR, art 4, para 2 establishes a requirement of 'integrity' of the electronic consignment note that includes the ability to detect any supplement or amendment to the note. It is also foreseen that the electronic consignment note may be replaced with a paper-based one (eCMR, art 5, para 1(f)) though the details for the change of medium are left to contractual agreements.

The conditions for managing electronic consignment notes listed in art 5 of the eCMR may be closely compared to those set out in the MLETR for managing electronic transferable records, regardless of the negotiability of the document. The parties to the contract of carriage must agree upon these conditions to implement the eCMR:

(a) The method for the issuance and the delivery of the electronic consignment note to the entitled party (eCMR, art 5, para 1(a)); this method needs to provide assurance of singularity and control of the electronic consignment note;
(b) An assurance that the electronic consignment note retains its integrity (eCMR, art 5, para 1(b)), which corresponds to the requirement in the MLETR, art 10, para 1(b)(iii);
(c) How the party entitled to the rights arising out of the electronic consignment note may demonstrate that entitlement (eCMR, art 5, para 1(c)), which relates to how transfer of control is carried out;
(d) The way in which confirmation is given that delivery to the consignee has been effected (eCMR, art 5, para 1(d)), which also relates to how transfer of control is carried out;
(e) The procedures for supplementing or amending the electronic consignment note (eCMR, art 5, para 1(e)), which are related to the notion of integrity in the MLETR as well as to the MLETR, art 16, on amending the electronic transferable record; and
(f) The procedures for the possible replacement of the electronic consignment note by a consignment note issued by different means (eCMR, art 5, para 1(f)), which may be implemented by meeting the requirements of the MLETR, arts 17 and 18, on change of medium.

These common elements are not unexpected given the shared goal of MLETR and eCMR to prevent multiple claims for the same goods based on the same document.

[54] See, eg: UN Economic Commission for Europe, 'Analysis of the provisions of Article 5 to the eCMR protocol' (26 July 2022) UN Doc ECE/TRANS/SC.1/GE.22/2022/2, paras 3–7, on the relationship between art 5 of the eCMR and the Rotterdam Rules.

While the eCMR entered into force in June 2011, its implementation is ongoing. A group of experts has been set up to work on the operationalisation of the eCMR, art 5.[55] One issue to be addressed is interoperability among the services of different providers.

While there was not yet any in-depth discussion on coordinating implementation of the eCMR and of the MLETR, possibly also because of differences in market structure between carriage of goods by sea and by road,[56] the need for all electronic transport documents to comply with the European Union (EU) Electronic Freight Transport Information (eFTI) Regulation[57] may promote the use of common standards that facilitate convergence in the EU digital trade and transport ecosystem and, possibly, beyond. In that perspective, a MLETR-compliant transferable records management system should also be able to manage electronic consignment notes issued under the eCMR.

2.4. National Legislation Predating the MLETR

Few national laws enabling electronic transferable records existed when UNCITRAL started work on the MLETR, and even fewer shared the approach and fundamental principles of the UNCITRAL project. Moreover, the use of electronic transferable records based on those laws was limited to specific documents and instruments and to national use.

Legislation from Japan, the Republic of Korea and the United States of America (US) was considered during the MLETR drafting process. The Japanese and the Korean laws were used to identify the steps in the lifecycle of an electronic transferable record. Some US law core notions were further elaborated in light of the fundamental principles underlying UNCITRAL texts on electronic commerce. The illustration of these laws may be useful to appreciate certain features of the MLETR, including in contrast with those earlier laws.

2.4.1. Japan

Some jurisdictions have adopted laws regulating the use of electronic promissory notes in dedicated registries. Japan has been an early adopter of such legislation.

The Japanese Electronically Recorded Monetary Claims Act (ERMCA)[58] establishes a type of electronic transferable record, called Electronically Recorded

[55] ibid para 1.
[56] ibid para 10.
[57] Regulation (EU) 2020/1056 of the European Parliament and of the Council of 15 July 2020 on Electronic Freight Transport Information [2020] OJ L249/33 (eFTI).
[58] Act No 102 of June 27, 2007, as amended; Order for Enforcement of the Electronically Recorded Monetary Claims Act, Cabinet Order No 325 of October 22, 2008; Enforcement Regulation of the

Monetary Claim (ERMC), which exists only in electronic form and to which therefore the principle of functional equivalence does not apply.[59] Functionally, the ERMC is a promissory note in electronic form. The different name reflects the decision to create a new type of transferable instrument not to interfere with the operation of the Convention Providing a Uniform Law for Bills of Exchange and Promissory Notes.[60] Hence, the ERMCA contains both the substantive law applicable to the ERMC and the provisions enabling its use in electronic form, including those relating to the oversight of ERMC management system operators.

Despite this fundamental difference, the ERMCA and the MLETR have several elements in common. For instance, the arguments supporting the creation of the ERMC also apply to the dematerialisation of promissory notes. Those arguments focus on the desirability of offering to business, especially SMEs, safe and efficient access to credit at reduced cost. In particular, the attractiveness of ERMC may reduce the use of non-assignable account receivables, and hence improve overall cashflow management, including of less creditworthy companies.[61] Moreover, the electronic nature of the monetary claim may facilitate its securitisation and exclude the possibility of double assignments, and the involvement of both obligor and obligee in the issuance of the ERMC may provide additional assurance of its existence and value.

The ERMCA foresees the use of registries to manage the ERMC.[62] The substantive law applicable to the ERMC is generally aligned with the law applicable to transferable instruments and includes bona fide protection of the third-party holder. Thus, the ERMC may be assigned, given as a guarantee, and pledged. Presentation for payment is automated without need for giving notice.

Unlike paper-based bills and notes, the ERMC may be split, which, for instance, allows payments to multiple secondary suppliers. This feature may simplify the management of more complex financing schemes such as lump-sum settlement facilities, where a financing institution pays subcontractors in exchange of an ERMC issued by the main contractor and assigned by the subcontractor, and securitisation of syndicated loans.

Electronically Recorded Monetary Claims Act, Cabinet Office and Ministry of Justice Order No 4 of October 22, 2008.

[59] See ch 3, commentary on the MLETR, art 3.

[60] Convention providing a Uniform Law for Bills of Exchange and Promissory Notes (adopted 7 June 1930, entered into force 1 January 1934) 143 LNTS 257. The issue is discussed in UNCITRAL, 'Legal Issues Relating to the Use of Electronic Transferable Records' (27 September 2013) UN Doc A/CN.9/WG.IV/WP.125, and gave rise to a possible exception to the scope of application of the MLETR (see ch 3, commentary on the MLETR, art 1).

[61] K Katayama, 'Electronic Claims: A Japanese Financial Innovation' (2008) Nomura Research Institute Lakyara vol 33.

[62] See the ERMCA, art 2, para 3: 'The term "registry" in this Act means a book in which monetary claims record is recorded, and which is prepared by an electronic monetary claim recording institution using a magnetic disk (including media specified by order of the competent ministry as being capable of securely recording certain matters by means equivalent to those of a magnetic disk)'. It is unclear whether this definition could encompass the use of distributed ledger technology and of tokens.

About half of the articles of the ERMCA deal with the requirements and oversight of the ERMC management system operators, called Electronic Monetary Claim Recording Institutions (EMCRI). EMCRI are licensed entities.[63]

There are different views on whether, and to what extent, the ERMCA has met expectations. A tax incentive has been given to promote the use of ERMC, and EMCRI are active and seem to be consolidating. However, certain limits of the ERMCA approach seem to emerge, such as the possible creation, by mandating the use of licensed registry operators, of data silos isolated from the trade finance ecosystem, which hinders their integration in end-to-end digitalisation as well as their cross-border use. Moreover, the ERMCA was designed primarily for national use. Attempts have been made to export the business model and related technology.[64] However, the legal transplant may need more than transferring technology and business practices.

2.4.2. Republic of Korea

At the time of the drafting of the MLETR, the Republic of Korea was the only jurisdiction with legislation enabling both the use of electronic bills of lading and the use of electronic promissory notes. This was done with separate acts.

Article 862 of the Commercial Act of the Republic of Korea gives legal recognition to the use of electronic bills of lading.[65] Issuance and circulation of the bill of lading shall take place through the designated registry. The legal effects of electronic and paper-based bills of lading are the same. The details for the implementation of this provision are contained in a Regulation.[66]

The Regulation confirms that only an entity designated by the Minister of Justice may operate the electronic bills of lading management registry. The operations of the registry should cover the lifecycle of the bill of lading, including conversion to paper and archiving. The registry should use 'certified digital signatures' as defined in the Digital Signature Act, art 2, para 3,[67] whose substance corresponds to that of the MLES, art 6, para 3. Article 3 of the Regulation specifies the technical, financial and legal requirements for designating a registry operator. One requirement pertains to carrying an insurance policy to cover damages to users arising from wilful or negligent acts.

[63] There are a few operators, which may be part of banking groups, see, eg: Mizuho Electronic Monetary Claim Recording Co. Moreover, the Japanese Bankers Association obtained a licence for its EMCRI, Densai.net Co, in pursuit of the goal of supporting financing of SMEs.

[64] Japan International Cooperation Agency, 'Collaboration Program with the Private Sector for Disseminating Japanese Technology for Electronically Recorded Monetary Claims Service Project Completion Report' (2019).

[65] It was enacted with Act No 8581 of 3 August 2007. Article 863 of the Commercial Act allows the issuance of a sea waybill in electronic form.

[66] Regulation on the Implementation of the Provisions of the Commercial Act Regarding Electronic Bills of Lading, adopted with Presidential Decree No 20829 of 20 June 2008, amended.

[67] Act No 5792 of 5 February 1999, amended.

Article 6 of the Regulation provides guidance on the content of the electronic bill of lading, which includes: the consent of the parties to its use; the inclusion of the same particulars contained in the paper-based bill of lading; the indication of the place of receipt or the place of delivery of the shipment (when different from the ports of loading and unloading, which are annotated as particulars); the electronic signature of the carrier or its agent; and the applicable standard terms and conditions. Importantly, users need to pre-register with the registry operator to access the registry.

The mechanism for the transfer of the electronic bill of lading illustrates the operation of the registry: the holder of the bill informs the registry operator of its intention to endorse the bill; the operator enters the details of the transfer in the registry and informs the transferee accordingly (Regulation, art 8).[68]

Interestingly, one main motivation for giving legal effect to electronic bills of lading in the Republic of Korea was to achieve the complete dematerialisation of trade documents for paperless trade facilitation.[69] This may explain the policy choices underlying the electronic bills of lading management system, which focus on domestic elements. For instance, the applicable law is the law of the Republic of Korea. Under Korean law, the certified digital signatures needed to operate in the system may be issued only to companies registered in the Republic of Korea. Accordingly, it is unclear if and how a commercial operator established outside the Republic of Korea may register in the system. However, the commercial use of electronic bills of lading is inherently transnational: the main users of the current system are therefore Korean corporations shipping goods to controlled companies overseas.

The approach followed in the Korean law is not based on functional equivalence. For instance, it is doubtful that transfer of an electronic bill of lading by delivery alone is possible. By requiring the use of licensed operators, the system is not technology- and model-neutral. These features may discourage interaction with foreign traders both on the technical plan, due to lack of interoperability, and on the legal plan, as the law does not recognise electronic bills of lading issued under foreign law, which may be common.[70]

The legislation of the Republic of Korea had some influence on the formulation of certain provisions relating to specific steps in the lifecycle of electronic

[68] Additional details on the provisions of the Presidential Decree are contained in UNCITRAL, 'Present and possible future work on electronic commerce' (15 April 2010) UN Doc A/CN.9/692, paras 30–46. See also the electronic bills of lading portal at www.eblkorea.or.kr.

[69] For the technical framework, see the website of the uTradeHub initiative at www.utradehub.or.kr as well as www.eblkorea.or.kr. For the legislative framework, see the Electronic Trade Facilitation Act, Act No 7751 of 23 December 2005, amended.

[70] For a comparison between the Korean legislation on bills of lading and the MLETR, see: SB Choi, 'Compliance of Electronic Bill of Lading Regulation in Korea with Model Law on Electronic Transferable Records' (2019) 23 *Journal of Korea Trade* 68. South Korean carriers are testing the use of electronic bills of lading issued by MLETR-compliant management systems, possibly based on the understanding that South Korean law does not preclude the issuance of electronic bills of lading under foreign law.

transferable records contained in the first set of draft provisions of the MLETR.[71] However, those provisions have been significantly revised according to the functional equivalence approach.

The Korean legislation on electronic promissory notes, called the Issuance and Distribution of Electronic Bills Act,[72] has several elements in common with that on electronic bills of lading. However, the practical impact of the two laws is significantly different.

The Electronic Bills Act refers, for substantive law, to the Bills of Exchange and Promissory Notes Act;[73] and for the law of electronic transactions, to the Framework Act on Electronic Documents and Transactions,[74] which is based on UNCITRAL texts, especially the MLEC. Therefore, electronic promissory notes (called 'electronic bills') must fulfil the same information requirements as paper-based ones unless the Electronic Bills Act specifies otherwise. Differences include the maximum maturity of an electronic bill, set at one year, and the impossibility of issuing an electronic bill as a blank bill (Electronic Bills Act, art 6, paras 5 and 6). Moreover, an electronic bill may not be endorsed more than 20 times (Electronic Bills Act, art 7, para 5). The limit to the number of endorsements is aimed at mitigating the risk of a snowball effect in the event of mass insolvencies. It is possible to endorse the bill in part, but its payment must be in full. The presentation for payment on the due date of the electronic bill is automated.

The critical elements in the management of the electronic bills are the identification of the parties and of the bill through unique identifiers (Electronic Bills Act, art 6, paras 2–4 and Enforcement Decree, art 8) and the preservation of all of the transactions relating to the bill (Electronic Bills Act, art 16 and Enforcement Decree, art 13).

The Electronic Bills Act foresees the appointment of an operator managing the electronic bills management system that must meet the requirements specified in the Enforcement Decree, art 3. The current operator is the Korea Financial Telecommunications and Clearings Institute.[75] Prior registration is needed to access the electronic bills management system, as is the use of an 'officially certified digital signature' as defined in the Digital Signature Act, art 2, para 3.

The use of electronic bills is mandatory for larger companies (Electronic Bills Act, art 6, para 2). This rule is aimed at increasing tax compliance, one of the goals of the Electronic Bills Act, together with a reduction in the cost and an increase in the efficiency of managing promissory notes.

[71] UNCITRAL, 'Draft provisions on electronic transferable records' (4 March 2013) UN Doc A/CN.9/WG.IV/WP.122.

[72] Act No 7197 of 22 March 2004, amended, see especially Act No 9651 of 8 May 2009 (Electronic Bills Act), and Enforcement Decree of the Issuance and Distribution of Electronic Bills Act, Presidential Decree No 18637 of 31 December 2004, amended (Enforcement Decree).

[73] Act No 5009 of 6 December 1995, amended, see especially Act No 10198 of 31 March 2010.

[74] Act No 6614 of 19 January 2002, amended.

[75] The operator maintains a website dedicated to this service at www.unote.kr.

As indicated, the Electronic Bills Act and the Korean legislation on bills of lading share several features. Both laws require the use of licensed operators and refer to national standards for electronic signatures, which means that the management systems are accessible only to commercial operators based in the Republic of Korea. However, the use of electronic bills in the Republic of Korea is much more common than that of electronic bills of lading. The difference between the two documents seems to lie in the prevailing domestic use of promissory notes as opposed to the prevailing cross-border use of bills of lading, so that limits to international use do not have the same impact on the former as they have on the latter. Moreover, certain policy concerns related to the use of promissory notes by large businesses to the detriment of smaller enterprises may not apply to bills of lading.

2.4.3. United States of America

United States law and UNCITRAL texts on electronic commerce have historically had a close relationship. In particular, the Uniform Electronic Transactions Act (UETA), adopted in 1999 by the National Conference of Commissioners on Uniform State Law and subsequently enacted in all States (except New York) and several territories, shares the same fundamental principles as the MLEC. The UETA is complemented at the federal level by the Electronic Signatures in Global and National Commerce (ESIGN) Act of 2000,[76] which is also based on the same principles as the MLEC. Commonality of principles may be traced to the interaction between the preparation of US legislation, namely the work of the Subcommittee on Electronic Commercial Practices of the American Bar Association, and of the MLEC.[77] Moreover, UETA and ESIGN have influenced certain provisions of the ECC.

A similar relationship may be established between various US provisions and the fundamental traits of the MLETR: the transferable record must be unique (ie in MLETR language, 'singular') and identifiable (as requires the MLETR, though US law refers to the notion of 'single authoritative copy' as an equivalent of 'holdership', which is a notion unknown to the MLETR). Moreover, under US law the transferable record must: (i) identify the person claiming control as the person to whom the record was issued or most recently transferred; (ii) be under the control of the person in control; and (iii) be alterable only with the permission of the person in control, which are requirements that operatively correspond to the notion of 'control' in the MLETR.

[76] 15 US Code, Chapter 96. For a comparison of the provisions of ESIGN and UETA, see: Smedinghoff, 'The Legal Requirements' (2005) 757.

[77] See, eg: UNCITRAL, 'Draft uniform rules on the legal aspects of electronic data interchange (EDI) and related means of trade data communication' (1992) UN Doc A/CN.9/WG.IV/WP.57, Annex I, draft art 6, para 6.

US law provisions relevant for electronic transferable records may be found in the Uniform Commercial Code (UCC) Article 7 (on security interests in chattel papers, for example, promissory notes, but not the papers themselves) and UCC Article 9 (on electronic transferable documents, ie warehouse receipts and bills of lading) as well as in UETA and ESIGN.[78]

Historically, the notion of control was first used in UCC § 8-106, on control of investment securities, drafted in 1994. However, that provision has few elements in common with more recent notions of control.[79] UCC § 9-105 (Control of Electronic Chattel Paper) indicates that a secured party has control of electronic chattel paper if a system reliably establishes that secured party as the assignee of the chattel paper.[80] It then identifies the following conditions that presume reliable control ('safe harbour rule'): the existence of a 'single authoritative copy' of the record which is 'unique, identifiable and unalterable'; the identification of the secured party as the person in control (referred to as 'assignee' of the record); the control (referred to as 'communication and maintenance') by the secured party or its designated custodian; the ability to transfer control and to identify non-authoritative copies as such; the ability to readily identify amendments to the authoritative copy as authorised or unauthorised.

UCC § 7-106(a) (Control of Electronic Document of Title) indicates that 'a person has control of an electronic document of title if a system employed for evidencing the transfer of interests in the electronic document reliably establishes that person as the person to which the electronic document was issued or transferred'.[81] UCC § 7-106(b) specifies the conditions for presuming reliable control in a manner similar to UCC § 9-105, with minor clarifications, for instance by indicating that a copy of the electronic document of title or a change in its control may be made only with the consent of the person in control.

According to UCC § 7-105, an electronic document of title may be reissued on paper if the person in control 'surrenders' control and the paper-based document contains a statement that it is issued in substitution for the electronic document. The provision also specifies that the effect of the change of medium is that the electronic document ceases to have any effect or validity; and that the holder of

[78] For recent UCC developments on digital assets, see ch 3, at 3.3.7.

[79] On the evolution of the notion of 'control' see: H Gabriel, 'The Concept and Necessity of "Control" in the Use of Emerging Technologies in Commercial Transactions' (2023) 28 *Uniform Law Review* 257. For a comparison between UCC Article 7 and the MLETR, see: Stephenson Harwood LLP in collaboration with Infocomm Media Development Authority (IMDA), 'TradeTrust-enabled Electronic Bills of Lading: A Legal and Practical Analysis of Their Use in Global Trade' (2023), section 7.

[80] As defined in UCC § 9-102, a chattel paper is 'a record or records that evidence both a monetary obligation and a security interest in specific goods […]'. The notion of control has been developed bearing in mind the needs of the finance industry to ensure priority of security interests in electronic chattel papers, see: TE Plank, 'A New System of Electronic Chattel Paper: Notification of Assignment' (2019) 71 *South Carolina Law Review* iss 1, art 6, scholarcommons.sc.edu.

[81] Gabriel, 'The Concept and Necessity of "Control"' (2023) 260, identifies this as the core provision on control in US law, explaining that the provision points at the outcome rather than at the method to be followed, and that it fits well with the use of centralized registries prevailing at the time of its adoption, while accommodating the development of other technologies.

the paper-based document warrants to all subsequent concerned parties that it was the person in control at the time of the change of medium. Similar conditions apply to the reverse change of medium from paper to electronic. Article 7 of the UCC inspired the MLETR, arts 17 and 18 on the change of medium.

Section 16 of the UETA sets a general rule establishing that a party 'ha[d] control of a transferable record if a system employed for evidencing the transfer of interests in the transferable record reliably establishes that person as the person to which the transferable record was issued or transferred'. That general rule is complemented by a description of specific conditions that, when met, satisfy the general rule, and therefore are associated with a presumption of control of a transferable record. Similar provisions may be found in section 201 of E-SIGN[82] that, on the one hand, is applicable as federal law but, on the other hand, is restricted to notes related to a loan secured by real property.

US law has seen uneven implementation in business practice. While UCC Article 9 is widely used,[83] as is the legislation on warehouse receipts for certain types of commodities, the use of electronic bills of lading is rare and recent. Moreover, cheques do not fall under any of the provisions mentioned above and therefore cannot be issued electronically.[84]

This summary of selected US law provisions highlights the influence of those provisions on the MLETR, namely the requirements of its functional equivalence rules despite the fact that US law is not based on a functional equivalence approach and the notion of control. While useful elements may be drawn, it is important to bear in mind that the MLETR is to be interpreted in light of the principle of autonomous interpretation of uniform law and without reference to or influence of any domestic law provision (so-called 'homeward trend').[85] This applies in particular to the notion of control, which in US law may have meanings beyond functional equivalence with possession.[86]

US law on electronic transferable records is particularly complex as it intersects state and federal law as well as various types of transferable documents and instruments, or the security interests therein. Nevertheless, it may be said that it is generally compatible with the MLETR[87] and compliant with its underlying

[82] 15 US Code § 7021 – Transferable records.

[83] Gabriel (n 79) 262, illustrating the use of tokens in the real estate mortgage market (as opposed to the used of centralised registries for cotton warehouse receipts).

[84] Under US law, checks may be deposited remotely by transmitting images instead of the paper-based original and may be presented electronically through the check truncation procedure foreseen in the Check 21 Act. Check truncation is done at the time of presentation when the check ceases to be a negotiable instrument. For more information, see: B Geva, 'From Paper to Electronic Order: The Digitalization of the Check in the USA' (2015) 4 *Penn State Journal of Law & International Affairs* 96.

[85] See ch 3, commentary on the MLETR, art 3.

[86] Gabriel (n 79) 262–265. For instance, application of control to digital assets may not take place on the basis of the principle of functional equivalence because those assets exist only in electronic form.

[87] For a similar conclusion with respect to the United Kingdom Electronic Trade Documents Act 2023, see: M Goldby, 'The Electronic Trade Documents Act 2023 and the 2003 Amendments to Article 7 of the Uniform Commercial Code: Do They Do the Same Thing?' (2024), ssrn.com.

fundamental principles with regard to the commercial documents it applies to (promissory notes, bills of lading, warehouse receipts[88]).

2.5. Contractual Frameworks

A panorama of the legislation enabling the use of electronic transferable records predating the adoption of the MLETR includes solutions based on purely contractual agreements. Because of the contractual nature, those solutions may fulfil the functions of evidencing the contract of carriage of goods and the receipt of the goods but cannot replicate the transferability and negotiability of the bill of lading. Such a limitation arises from the principle of privity of contract, providing that third parties cannot be bound by contracts they did not subscribe to. In short, contract-based commercial documents may reproduce some functions of a bill of lading, but are not a bill of lading, and accordingly the law of bills of lading does not apply to them: more generally, contract-based commercial documents in electronic form are not electronic transferable records.[89] Yet, contractual frameworks have played a role in promoting digitalisation of transport documents and may continue to do so in legacy settings.

Contractual frameworks often foresee the use of a centralised registry to issue and transfer the document among participating parties. Centralised registries usually require prior identification of the parties that access them. Moreover, the use of centralised registries may limit interoperability, including by requiring use of proprietary software. This approach may give rise to concerns about possible customers' lock-in by service providers.[90]

Contractual frameworks leverage on the English law notions of 'attornment' and 'novation'. Attornment is a common law notion often used in real estate law to make a tenant acknowledge the rights of a new landlord after the property has been sold. Novation is a Roman law notion that is used also in common law and that permits terminating a contract and concluding a new contract on the same terms but between different parties.

The parties must subscribe to a rulebook prepared by the registry operator to access the registry. The rulebook typically fulfils several functions: it sets up

[88] The United States Warehouse Act (7 USC 241, originally enacted in 1916) also applies to warehouse receipts. The US Department of Agriculture maintains Regulations for this Act that foresee a licensing system for electronic warehouse receipts providers.

[89] *Delphi-Delco Elecs Sys v M/V Nedlloyd Europa*, 324 F Supp 2d 403 (SDNY 2004), 424: '[T]he Sea way-bill, unlike a traditional bill of lading, is not a document of title; it functions merely as a non-negotiable receipt that may also serve as the contract of carriage.' See also: LS Niv, 'Electronic Express Sea Waybill as Perceived in Sea-Land Service, Inc v Lozen International, LLC and Later Case Law' (2013) 30 *Arizona Journal of International and Comparative Law* 507.

[90] On the 'membership requirement' as a main obstacle to the widespread use of electronic bills of lading, see: I Ioannou, 'Is Enabling Legislation Sufficient to Promote the Uptake of Electronic Paperless Trading Systems?' (2023) NUS Centre for Maritime Law Working Paper No 23/04.

the legal mechanism for the transfer of the contract-based electronic document; it spells out rights and obligations of the registry operator and of the users of the system; it designates English law as the applicable law and contains a dispute resolution clause.

MLETR enactment provides a statutory basis for the use of electronic transferable records and therefore avoids the need to rely on contractual agreements as the legal basis for this purpose. In most cases, rulebooks remain in use because of their other functions, ie outlining the rights and obligations of the parties, and providing a choice of law and a choice of forum for dispute resolution. The choice of law clause also further clarifies the intention to issue the document under a certain legal regime (for example, English law or the law of Singapore).

The Baltic and International Maritime Council (BIMCO) Electronic Bills of Lading Clause 2014 (the 'BIMCO Clause') was designed to facilitate the use of such contractual frameworks, namely, to reduce the use of letters of indemnity because of the unavailability of paper-based bills of lading. The BIMCO Clause is supposed to operate in conjunction with – and be contractually incorporated in – a charterparty. The first paragraph of the BIMCO Clause gives the owner and the charterer the possibility to use electronic bills of lading, if so wished, with the same legal effect as their paper-based equivalents (but within the limits of party autonomy). The second paragraph of the BIMCO Clause requires owners to subscribe to a service provided by a provider approved by the International Group of Protection and Indemnity Clubs, and at the cost of the charterer. The third clause excludes damages arising from the use of electronic systems from those covered by the International Group of the Protection and Indemnity Clubs on behalf of the owners.[91]

The Comité Maritime International (CMI) Rules on Electronic Bills of Lading[92] (CMI Rules) represent another example of contractual framework for electronic bills of lading. Adopted in 1990, the CMI Rules do not presuppose the subscription of a rulebook or the exclusive use of a registry. Moreover, the CMI Rules do not displace the applicable legal regime, be it national or international. The CMI Rules, building on the technical and legal framework used for EDI systems, prescribe the use of a 'private key', which is not however defined only with regard to cryptographic means, but 'means any technically appropriate form, such as a combination of numbers and/or letters, which the parties may agree for securing the authenticity and integrity of a transmission' (CMI Rule 2).

[91] See www.bimco.org for further information.
[92] Available at comitemaritime.org.

3

The UNCITRAL Model Law on Electronic Transferable Records

The attempts at enabling the use of electronic transferable records, especially electronic bills of lading, described in chapter two did not reach sufficient acceptance, especially at the international level, for legal, technical, and business reasons.

With regard to legal matters, absent dedicated legislation, some jurisdictions may allow in principle the issuance of electronic transferable records, but do not provide sufficient guidance on how to do so in a reliable manner. Other jurisdictions may allow issuance of electronic transferable records only when private parties are involved but not for regulatory and compliance purposes, for example submission of information to customs. Yet other jurisdictions may follow a more formal approach and require a specific statutory statement on the validity of electronic transferable records. Case law is rare and provides little additional insight.[1]

From a technical perspective, the use of centralised registries, coupled with the perception that parties may be locked-in to a particular registry, has discouraged clients' buy-in. Moreover, requirements to use certain technology may hinder cross-border dataflows, increase compliance costs, and ultimately discourage digital uptake.

Finally, commercial operators are generally cautious in embracing innovation, given that this entails rethinking business processes and abandoning legacy procedures, with significant investment in technical and human resources. The involvement of possible competitors as service providers may also limit buy-in.

To overcome those obstacles, it is necessary to adopt a new approach aimed at establishing open digital trade ecosystems. The adoption of modern uniform legislation is required to achieve that goal.

[1] *Glencore International AG v MSC Mediterranean Shipping Co SA and Another* [2015] EWHC 1989 (Comm) is cited, at least to some extent, as a relevant precedent. However, the procedures followed for the delivery of the containers in this case (ie sharing of the container electronic release code in a mailbox accessible by many employees) would not be considered a reliable method under the UNCITRAL Model Law on Electronic Transferable Records (MLETR). See the case note by M Goldby, 'What is needed to get rid of paper? A new look at delivery orders' (2015) 21 *The Journal of International Maritime Law* 5.

3.1. The Drafting Process of the MLETR

The MLETR is the result of several years of work of the United Nations Commission on International Trade Law (UNCITRAL), namely, its Working Group IV, which has been active for decades on electronic commerce matters. The desirability of work on electronic transferable records was first suggested at a colloquium held at the request of UNCITRAL in New York on 14–16 February 2011[2] to identify suitable work topics in the area of electronic commerce.[3] Among the various topics discussed at the colloquium, the Commission prioritised the preparation of a uniform legislative text, enabling the use of transferable documents and instruments[4] in electronic form.[5] Initial discussions focused on establishing functional equivalence rules for the paper-based notions of 'possession' and 'delivery', which play a central role for the issuance and circulation of transferable documents and instruments. The adoption of a functional equivalence approach at the same time required and ensured that the uniform legislative text would not modify the relevant substantive law applicable to transferable documents and instruments.

From the onset, it was clear that the result of the work would be a legislative text, with a preference for a model law to combine flexibility in enacting the uniform text and predictability based on sufficient guidance. This preference acknowledged the achievements of model laws in promoting the harmonisation and modernisation of international trade law.[6]

The alternative option was the preparation of a treaty, possibly in the form of a protocol to the United Nations Convention on the Use of Electronic Communications in International Contracts (ECC). That protocol would include the functional equivalence rules needed to enable the use of electronic transferable records and remove the exclusion of transferable documents and instruments from the scope of application of the ECC. The treaty option was in line with the fact that certain transferable documents and instruments (ie bills of lading;[7] bills

[2] UNGA, 'Report of the United Nations Commission on International Trade Law Forty-second Session' (2009) UN Doc A/64/17, para 343.

[3] UNCITRAL, 'Present and Possible Future Work on Electronic Commerce' (21 March 2011 and 22 March 2011) UN Doc A/CN.9/728 and Add.1.

[4] The term 'transferable document or instrument' is used in the law of the United States of America (US), according to which transferable instruments refer to money, while transferable documents refer to goods: UNCITRAL, 'Legal Issues Relating to the Use of Electronic Transferable Records – Proposal by the Governments of Colombia, Spain and the United States' (3 August 2012) UN Doc A/CN.9/WG.IV/WP.119, paras 1–3.

[5] UNGA, 'Report of the United Nations Commission on International Trade Law Forty-fourth Session' (2011) UN Doc A/66/17, para 238.

[6] On the evolution of uniform commercial law and the rise of model laws at the detriment of treaties, see L Castellani, 'Uniform Law and the Production and Circulation of Legal Models' in G Low (ed), *Convergence and Divergence of Private Law in Asia* (Cambridge, Cambridge University Press, 2022) 7, 10–11.

[7] International Convention for the Unification of Certain Rules of Law Relating to Bills of Lading (adopted 25 August 1924, entered into force 2 June 1931) 120 LNTS 155 (Hague Rules); Protocol to Amend the International Convention for the Unification of Certain Rules of Law Relating to Bills of

of exchange and promissory notes;[8] cheques[9]) fall under the scope of treaties. However, with the exception of bills of lading, the cross-border use of those treaties is limited. The treaty option was eventually set aside for possible future consideration based on the uptake of the MLETR and the evolution in business practices. Such delay would also make it possible to fine-tune functional equivalence rules based on evolving practice, if needed.

The Working Group started its deliberations with a comprehensive overview of the relevant issues supported by comparative law analysis.[10] For the reasons already discussed,[11] pre-existing laws could be used only to a limited extent as models for the MLETR.

Because of the need to discuss in-depth general issues, a first set of draft provisions could only be prepared after a few Working Group sessions had taken place.[12] That first draft set was significantly revised to closer align the provisions with the functional equivalence approach. Several articles referred to specific events in the lifecycle of the electronic transferable records. Those provisions were eventually deleted to avoid infringing substantive law and replaced with more general provisions based on functional equivalence. Provisions on the obligations of third-party service providers were also deleted.

The Working Group completed its work in November 2016, thus allowing for circulation of the draft model law with an explanatory note to elicit comments by states and other concerned organisations for consideration by UNCITRAL at its 50th session, held in July 2017, when the MLETR was adopted.[13]

3.2. The MLETR

3.2.1. General Provisions

Chapter I of the MLETR contains provisions of general application, as opposed to functional equivalence rules (contained in Chapter II), provisions relating to

Lading (adopted 23 February 1968, entered into force 14 February 1984) 1985 UNTS 127 (Hague-Visby Rules); United Nations Convention on the Carriage of Goods by Sea (adopted 31 March 1978, entered into force 1 November 1992) 1695 UNTS 3 (Hamburg Rules).

[8] Convention Providing a Uniform Law for Bills of Exchange and Promissory Notes.

[9] Convention Providing a Uniform Law for Cheques (adopted 19 March 1931, entered into force 1 January 1934) 143 LNTS 355.

[10] UNCITRAL, 'Legal Issues Relating to the Use of Electronic Transferable Records' (8 September 2011) UN Doc A/CN.9/WG.IV/WP.115; UNCITRAL, 'Legal Issues Relating to the Use of Electronic Transferable Records' (17 August 2012) UN Doc A/CN.9/WG.IV/WP.118 and Add.1. The legislative history of the MLETR is summarised in Section E of the Explanatory Note. The travaux préparatoires of the MLETR are available on the UNCITRAL website.

[11] See ch 2, section 2.4.

[12] The first set of draft provisions is contained in UNCITRAL, 'Draft Provisions on Electronic Transferable Records' (4 March 2013) UN Doc A/CN.9/WG.IV/WP.122.

[13] In accordance with United Nations rules and practice, the text of the MLETR and its Explanatory Note are available at no cost on the UNCITRAL website in the six official languages of the United Nations.

the use of electronic transferable records (contained in Chapter III) and provisions on the cross-border use of electronic transferable records (contained in Chapter IV).[14]

Articles 1 and 2 of the MLETR define what an electronic transferable record is, thus determining the scope of application of the Model Law. The MLETR, arts 3 and 4 contain rules, respectively, on the autonomous interpretation of law of uniform and supranational origin and on the possible effects of party autonomy that are commonly found in UNCITRAL texts. The MLETR, art 5 sets out a rule relating to the enabling nature of the Model Law, which is common in UNCITRAL texts on electronic commerce. The MLETR, art 6 clarifies that electronic transferable records may contain information available only in electronic form. Finally, the MLETR, art 7 explicitly recognises the legal validity of electronic transferable records.

Article 1. Scope of application

1. *This Law applies to electronic transferable records.*
2. *Other than as provided for in this Law, nothing in this Law affects the application to an electronic transferable record of any rule of law governing a transferable document or instrument including any rule of law applicable to consumer protection.*
3. *This Law does not apply to securities, such as shares and bonds, and other investment instruments, and to [...].*

The MLETR applies to electronic transferable records, which are defined in the MLETR, art 2 as electronic records that are equivalent to transferable documents and instruments, ie that incorporate the right to delivery of goods or payment of money.[15] These documents and instruments are identified in applicable substantive law and include: bills of lading; bills of exchange; promissory notes; and cheques. Warehouse receipts, consignment notes, air waybills and certificates of

[14] On the MLETR in general, see L Fosgaard, *The Transfer of Rights in a Digitalised Age* (Aalborg, Aalborg Universitetsforlag, 2023); Y Guo, *Legislation on Electronic Transferable Records: the 'Singularity' Problem and Solution* (Beijing, Beijing University Press, 2019); É Caprioli, 'La Loi-type de la CNUDCI sur les documents transférables électroniques : analyse et perspectives' (2023) *Journal du droit international 'Clunet'* 465; L Castellani and G Finocchiaro, 'The UNCITRAL Model Law on Electronic Transferable Records: Introduction and Overview' (2023) *European Review of Private Law* 955; H Gabriel, 'The UNCITRAL Model Law on Electronic Transferable Records' (2019) 24 *Uniform Law Review* 261; A Madrid Parra, 'Contenido Esencial de la Ley Modelo de la CNUDMI/UNCITRAL sobre Documentos Transmisibles Electrónicos' (2018) 48 *Revista Aranzadi de derecho y nuevas tecnologías* 19; MB Oluwabunmi, and J Henning, 'Beyond the Centennial of the Hague Rules: Assessing the UNCITRAL Model Law on Electronic Transferable Records (MLETR)' (2025) 30 *The Journal of International Maritime Law* 163; Z Šafranko, 'The Notion of Electronic Transferable Records' (2016) III *Intereulaweast* 1. See also the relevant parts of M Goldby, *Electronic Documents in Maritime Trade: Law and Practice*, 2nd edn (Oxford, Oxford University Press, 2019).

[15] For a general introduction to the law of negotiable instruments (as transferable instruments may also be named, and which include promissory notes, bills of exchange and cheques, but not transport documents and warehouse receipts), see P Ellinger, 'Chapter 4. Negotiable Instruments' in K Zweigert and U Drobnig (gen eds), *International Encyclopedia of Comparative Law*; J Ziegel (ed), *Vol IX: Commercial Transactions and Institutions* (Leiden, Brill, 2000), in particular paras 97–105 for a discussion of the work of UNCITRAL in this area and other harmonisation efforts. These UNCITRAL texts were seldom discussed during the preparation of the MLETR due to their limited acceptance.

insurance may also fall within this definition, as well as less common documents such as crop receipts. Letters of credit may fall within the definition of transferable document and instrument if transferable under national law.[16]

Conversely, the MLETR does not apply to documents or instruments that, although usually transferable, are not transferable in the case at hand (for example, a straight non-negotiable bill of lading, or a crossed non-endorsable cheque) because of the parties' agreement.[17] However, this does not prevent the use of the same management system to handle both electronic transferable records and any other electronic record. In fact, possession of certain non-transferable documents may still be necessary to demand performance.[18] Moreover, the use of a single electronic records management system may avoid fragmentation and creation of data silos, reduce costs, increase user friendliness, ensure data quality and consistency, facilitate data-sharing, and improve overall governance of the business process. Also, it would be highly inefficient to determine which electronic transferable records management system should be used based on the parties' agreement, which may occur after the issuance of the electronic transferable record, thus requesting a change of system during the circulation of the record that may inconvenience multiple involved parties.

The MLETR may be enacted with respect to a specific transferable document or instrument or to a set of documents and instruments. This policy choice is made considering commercial needs and the level of business and technological readiness.[19] The decision to apply the MLETR to all transferable documents and instruments supports the creation of a comprehensive interoperable digital trade ecosystem. In jurisdictions where different approaches to the management of certain electronic transferable records are already implemented (for example, registries for electronic promissory notes in China, Japan, and the Republic of Korea), additional work may be needed to ensure interoperability between legacy systems and MLETR-compliant applications.

[16] Explanatory Note, para 28(a). This statement may need coordination with arts 38 and 39 of the Uniform Customs and Practice for Documentary Credits (UCP 600), which deal with transferability. See ch 4, section 4.2.3, for the application of the UCP to electronic records. On the relationship between the MLETR and letters of credit, see A Davidson, 'The Digitalisation of Transferable Documents and Instruments in International Trade' (2018) 22 *Documentary Credit World* 27; K Takahashi, 'Blockchain Technology for Letters of Credit and Escrow Arrangements' (2018) 135 *Banking Law Journal* 89. For further considerations on letters of credit in electronic form, M Nezhad, S Rashidian and C Botta, 'Revolutionizing Trade Finance: Leveraging the Power of Blockchain and AI in Electronic Letters of Credit' (2024) 29 *Uniform Law Review* 87.

[17] Transferability refers to the ability to transfer the title with the document, while negotiability relates to the ability to transfer the title unaffected by possible claims of certain other parties. The MLETR addresses transferability but not negotiability, which is dealt with in substantive law.

[18] For this reason, straight bills of lading are considered electronic trade documents in the Electronic Trade Documents Act 2023 (see ch 4, section 4.1).

[19] Sometimes the law permits the use of a specific transferable document or instrument in electronic form subject to the adoption of adequate regulations. This is, for instance, the case of electronic bills of lading in Australia (Carriage of Goods by Sea Act 1991, s 22) and New Zealand (Contract and Commercial Law Act 2017, s 323).

Even when the legislative intent is to apply MLETR to all transferable documents and instruments, it may be useful to list those documents and instruments. The experience with enacting MLETR shows that there may be many such documents and instruments, some of which are being used only in specific business cases and are not well-known even among commercial lawyers (see below). On the other hand, in less developed legal systems there may be limited awareness of transferable documents and instruments generally, as domestic law does not exist or is not applied.

The practical implementation of the MLETR to each document and instrument may vary significantly due to several reasons. Bills of lading are used in diverse trade ecosystems, often involving several jurisdictions and both private and public actors. The broad scope of the MLETR may be particularly suited to encompass all actors. Other documents may be traded mostly domestically, which greatly simplifies their management. For instance, warehouse receipts are usually managed in registries, which could also be commodity- and location-specific. In the latter case, MLETR implementation may take place according to well-tested solutions. However, the importance of building an open and interoperable trade ecosystem should not be underestimated: for instance, an electronic warehouse receipt may contain important information on the production and transportation of a commodity, including compliance with environmental, social and governance standards. That information needs to recorded continuously and directly from the source. Hence, the electronic registry for warehouse receipt management should guarantee interoperability and compliance with MLETR standards.

The MLETR, art 1, para 2 embodies a fundamental principle underpinning all UNCITRAL texts on electronic commerce, ie non-interference with substantive law. The notion of 'rule of law' captures any possible source of law, not just statutes. The reference to consumer protection was inserted given the importance of the matter to certain jurisdictions. However, transactions carried out with electronic transferable records usually do not involve consumers, except possibly for cheques.

The MLETR, art 1, para 3 expressly excludes from the scope of application of the Model Law 'securities, such as shares and bonds, and other investment instruments'. This ensures that the MLETR does not affect the well-established legal framework for such instruments. A similar, but more articulate exclusion may be found in the ECC, art 2, para 1(b). The MLETR streamlined provision reflects a scope of application significantly narrower than that of the ECC.

The MLETR, art 1, para 3 accommodates additional carve-outs from the scope of application of the MLETR. These are documents and instruments that, although transferable, do not fall under the scope of the MLETR, for instance because they already have a complete set of legal rules, or because the MLETR would interfere with existing practice, which may be well-established and based on the use of specific solutions (for example, central registries for electronic promissory notes). As noted, experience with MLETR enactments highlighted the existence in some jurisdictions of transferable documents and instruments of sectoral use that may be little known outside the specific business and legal community.

Another set of possible exceptions pertains to the compatibility between the MLETR and pre-existing treaties dealing with transferable documents and instruments. As noted,[20] since the 1970s there has been increasing awareness of the possibility of using electronic bills of lading. The issue seems more debatable for finance documents. If the Convention Providing a Uniform Law for Bills of Exchange and Promissory Notes and the Convention Providing a Uniform Law for Cheques (the Geneva Conventions) are deemed incompatible with the use of electronic records,[21] the application of the MLETR to the documents and instruments falling under the scope of the Geneva Conventions may result in the violation of a treaty obligation. In that case, it may be necessary to pass separate legislation establishing a new type of transferable instrument existing only in electronic form, and therefore unrelated to the Geneva Conventions. This view has led to the adoption of the Electronically Recorded Monetary Claims Act in Japan.[22] Alternatively, updating the Geneva Conventions may require a dedicated treaty such as a protocol to the ECC covering electronic transferable records.[23]

The incompatibility argument is based on the observation that the use of electronic means was unforeseen in the 1930s (although electronic communication devices such as the telegraph, the teleprinter and the telex were already in use), and that the Geneva Conventions refer not only to the notions of 'writing' and 'signature' but also to features of the physical paper-based document such as 'face' and 'back', as well as its physical attachments such as the 'allonge'. Additional arguments may arise from the transposition of the Geneva Conventions in national law: for instance, German law[24] refers to the notion of 'Urkunde' that is interpreted as requiring the paper medium, but that may be different from the notions of 'instrument' and 'titre' in the Geneva Conventions that it purports to translate.[25]

The opposite view is based on the absence of an explicit obligation to use paper, and therefore the possibility to satisfy information requirements with the use of electronic means provided functional equivalence rules are satisfied. That liberal interpretation supports business needs to use electronic transferable records, while business practice using paper-based instruments under the Geneva Conventions is waning. Moreover, there seems to be little doubt that bills of lading issued under the Hague Rules may be in electronic form, even though the Hague Rules predate

[20] See ch 2, section 2.2.

[21] See the various arguments compiled in UNCITRAL, 'Legal Issues Relating to the Use of Electronic Transferable Records' (27 September 2013) UN Doc A/CN.9/WG.IV/WP.125.

[22] See ch 2, section 2.4.1.

[23] See section 3.1 above.

[24] Wechselgesetz of 21 June 1933, as amended.

[25] However, national law is not part of the treaty and should not influence the uniform interpretation of that treaty.

the Geneva Conventions. Hence, a conclusion in favour of the compatibility between Geneva Conventions and other older treaties, on the one hand, and the MLETR, on the other hand, seems preferable. Insisting on alleged form requirements in venerable texts does not do justice to their drafters, whose goal was to promote trade and not to hinder it.

Finally, the MLETR does not apply to electronic transferable records that have no paper-based equivalent, ie that exist only in electronic form. This exclusion is because the operation of the principle of functional equivalence presupposes the existence of a substantive law applicable to paper-based documents. If a transferable record exists only in electronic form, its law must contain both the substantive law governing the electronic transferable record and the provisions enabling its use in electronic form. In practice, however, the latter provisions may be similar to the rules contained in the MLETR. For instance, core provisions such as the MLETR, arts 10 and 11 may be used to ensure singularity and control over electronic transferable records existing only in electronic form.[26]

> ***Article 2. Definitions***
>
> *For the purposes of this Law:*
>
> *'Electronic record' means information generated, communicated, received or stored by electronic means, including, where appropriate, all information logically associated with or otherwise linked together so as to become part of the record, whether generated contemporaneously or not;*
>
> *'Electronic transferable record' is an electronic record that complies with the requirements of article 10;*
>
> *'Transferable document or instrument' means a document or instrument issued on paper that entitles the holder to claim the performance of the obligation indicated in the document or instrument and to transfer the right to performance of the obligation indicated in the document or instrument through the transfer of that document or instrument.*

The MLETR, art 2 contains only definitions specific to the use of electronic transferable records. Other relevant definitions, such as those of 'electronic signature' or of 'information system', may be found in pre-existing UNCITRAL texts on electronic commerce. The various definitions should be read harmoniously considering complementarity and interaction between the MLETR and those pre-existing texts. If the jurisdiction enacting the MLETR has not priorly enacted any UNCITRAL text on electronic commerce, it may consider adding definitions from those texts.

The definition of 'electronic record' refers to electronic means, which is a term to be understood in light of the notion of 'data message' underpinning UNCITRAL texts to ensure a technology neutral approach (see, for example, ECC,

[26] UNCITRAL, 'Draft Model Law on Warehouse Receipts' (20 November 2023) UN Doc A/CN.9/WG.I/WP.133, contains an example of legislation drafted both under the medium-neutral and under the functional equivalence approaches. The document was prepared to assist UNCITRAL Working Group I in considering the approach to be taken in the Model Law on Warehouse Receipts.

art 4(c)). The electronic record is a record made of data messages using electronic, magnetic, optical and any other similar means.[27] To encompass records stored on distributed ledgers, the definition of 'electronic record' refers to 'information logically associated with or otherwise linked together so as to become part of the record'. The term 'logically' refers to computer and not human logic,[28] ie that the record should be connected by software or similar means and not only by human reasoning.

As noted,[29] the definition of 'transferable document or instrument' aims to encompass all paper-based documents and instruments that incorporate the right to delivery of goods or payment of money.[30] The notion of transferable document or instrument and its legal treatment may vary across legal traditions and jurisdictions. In common law jurisdictions, the law may deal separately with each transferable document and instrument, while in civil jurisdictions a single set of rules may apply to all transferable documents and instruments.[31]

The substantive law of these documents and instruments is based on treaties, model laws and standard contractual agreements, and is to some extent uniform.[32] With regard to instruments, an influential model in common law countries is the United Kingdom (UK) Bills of Exchange Act 1882. Civil law countries have been influenced by the Geneva Conventions. In the maritime law field, the Hague Rules or the Hague–Visby Rules are the most commonly applied treaty. To preserve such uniformity, the dematerialisation of transferable documents and instruments should take place on the basis of uniform legal rules.

Whether a commercial document or instrument is a transferable document or instrument for the purposes of the MLETR will depend on the substantive law of the enacting state, which may itself not always be clear on this point. The principle of numerus clausus, which applies especially in civil law jurisdictions, is relevant to carry out that determination. According to this principle as applied to transferable documents and instruments, the types and main features of transferable documents and instruments are limited and must be pre-determined by statute. Hence, a document or instrument must be identified or, at least, treated as such

[27] As to the content of the record, the technical standard of the International Organization for Standardization (ISO) ISO 15489, on 'Records Management', defines records as information that 'an organization or individual produces, receives or maintains as evidence or information in the course of carrying out its legal obligations or in the conduct of its business' (ISO 15489-1: 2001, 3.15).

[28] Explanatory Note, para 35.

[29] See the commentary on the MLETR, art 1 in this section.

[30] From a terminological standpoint, 'documents' may pertain to goods while 'instruments' may pertain to money. The legal effect of these documents and instruments may vary: in some legal systems they may transfer title to property of goods and money, and not just possession subject to valid transfer of title. The term 'document of title' is used in this context but is also used for documents transferring possession only, which may be confusing.

[31] The unitary legal treatment in civil law countries is evidenced in the use of a single term (Wertpapiere in German; effets de commerce in French; titulos valores and títulos de crédito in Spanish; titoli di credito in Italian).

[32] For details on the codification of the law of transferable instruments, see B Geva and S Peari, *International Negotiable Instruments* (Oxford, Oxford University Press, 2020), 11–15.

in a statute. Party autonomy may not be used to create a new type of transferable document or instrument. If the substantive law of the relevant jurisdiction applies the principle of numerus clausus to documents of title, electronic transferable records may not be used to create by agreement new types of transferable documents or instruments. This approach gives legal certainty, especially to subsequent holders; it may however limit innovation in trade finance.

The notion of transferability in the MLETR is therefore a function and not a substantive law concept.[33] National law will define that concept, together with the related notion of negotiability, which presupposes transferability but goes beyond it by granting additional legal effects such as non-opposability of certain exemptions from performance. The MLETR is content with defining an electronic transferable record as the functional equivalent of a transferable document or instrument, as clarified by the interaction of the MLETR, arts 2 and 10.[34]

Article 3. Interpretation

1. *This Law is derived from a model law of international origin. In the interpretation of this Law, regard is to be had to the international origin and to the need to promote uniformity in its application.*
2. *Questions concerning matters governed by this Law which are not expressly settled in it are to be settled in conformity with the general principles on which this Law is based.*

The MLETR, art 3 aims to ensure the uniform interpretation of the MLETR by requiring interpretation in accordance with the provisions of the MLETR and the uniform general principles it is based on, without recourse to national law. To do so, it is however necessary to identify those general principles, which are not explicitly listed.

The MLETR, art 3, para 1 sets forth the principle of autonomous interpretation of uniform law in line with the settled UNCITRAL wording. This principle, which was first formulated in the Convention on the Limitation Period in the International Sale of Goods, art 7,[35] acknowledges that the adoption of a uniform legal text is not sufficient per se to achieve legal uniformity, as the interpretation and application of uniform law may be influenced by domestic legal notions (so-called 'homeward trend').[36] It is therefore necessary to ensure that interpretation and application are uniform. This goal may be achieved by establishing a court tasked with the review of all relevant decisions. However, the establishment of such a

[33] O Cachard, 'UNCITRAL Model Law on Electronic Transferable Records: The missing link towards e-shipping?' in B Soyer and A Tettenborn (eds), *Disruptive Technologies, Climate Change and Shipping* (Abingdon, Oxon, Informa Law from Routledge, 2022), 32.

[34] Which may however give 'an uncomfortable impression of circular reasoning': Cachard, 'UNCITRAL Model Law' (2022) 34.

[35] Convention on the Limitation Period in the International Sale of Goods (adopted 14 June 1974, amended 11 April 1980, entered into force 1 August 1988) 1511 UNTS 3.

[36] F Ferrari, 'Autonomous Interpretation Versus Homeward Trend Versus Outward Trend in CISG Case Law' (2017) 22 *Uniform Law Review* 244.

court would have significant implications in terms of budgetary requirements, of acceptance of shared jurisdictional functions between national and supranational courts, and of coordination between national and supranational proceedings.[37] Hence, UNCITRAL formulated the solution found also in the MLETR, art 3, para 1, which is based on a special rule of interpretation: the judge and the arbitrator must consider the uniform nature of the text and give due consideration to the necessity to promote and maintain its uniform interpretation. This means that it is desirable to take into account foreign decisions interpreting and applying the relevant uniform provision, and to give them persuasive value in light of the overarching goal to promote legal uniformity.

The need for autonomous interpretation applies to MLETR and other model laws in the same manner and for the same reasons that it applies to treaties: the application of MLETR across borders would be frustrated in case of divergent interpretations. Moreover, the substantive law of transferable documents and instruments is already largely uniform, and such uniformity should be preserved.

The mechanism contained in the MLETR, art 3, para 1 presupposes the ability to access foreign decisions. Several databases compile decisions applying uniform commercial law. Case law on UNCITRAL texts on electronic commerce may be found in the Case Law on UNCITRAL Texts (CLOUT) database, maintained by the UNCITRAL Secretariat.[38] Some decisions reported in CLOUT interpret provisions that are found in pre-existing UNCITRAL texts and the MLETR, such as those for functional equivalence with the paper-based notions of writing and signature, and are therefore relevant also for MLETR interpretation and application. Moreover, the principle of autonomous interpretation has been extensively interpreted and applied with respect to the United Nations Convention on Contracts for the International Sale of Goods, art 7, para 1,[39] and the related case law is available also in consolidated form.[40]

Unlike similar provisions in other UNCITRAL texts,[41] the MLETR, art 3, para 1 does not contain a reference to promoting the observance of good faith in international trade. This is because the principle of good faith has a specific meaning in the context of transferable documents and instruments, and such reference might lead to unintended interference with substantive law.[42] On the other hand, the first

[37] A dedicated court has been established in the European Union and in the Organisation pour l'Harmonisation en Afrique du Droit des Affaires. For further considerations, see R David, 'Le droit continental, la Common Law, et les perspectives d'un jus commune européen' in M Cappelletti (ed), *New Perspectives for a Common Law of Europe/Nouvelles perspectives d'un droit commun de l'Europe* (Leiden, Brill | Nijhoff, 1978–2024) 113.

[38] CLOUT is available at uncitral.un.org.

[39] United Nations Convention on Contracts for the International Sale of Goods (adopted 11 April 1980, entered into force 1 January 1988) (CISG) 1489 UNTS 3.

[40] UNCITRAL, *Digest of Case Law on the United Nations Convention on Contracts for the International Sale of Goods* (United Nations, Vienna, 2016) commentary on art 7.

[41] See, eg, CISG, art 7, para 1.

[42] UNCITRAL, 'Report of Working Group IV (Electronic Commerce) on the work of its fifty-third session' (20 May 2016) UN Doc A/CN.9/869, paras 28–30.

sentence of this paragraph is not found in other UNCITRAL texts. Its purpose is to highlight the uniform and supranational nature of the MLETR enactment.

The MLETR, art 3, para 2 contains a rule on autonomous gap-filling by way of interpretation. Its purpose is to ensure that there is no recourse to national law also when filling any gap in the MLETR, so as to preserve its uniform and autonomous interpretation. The provision is inspired by the CISG, art 7, para 2, but without reference to private international law as a supplementary source, which was deemed inappropriate in a model law.

The general principles on which the Model Law is based are not the principles underpinning the substantive law of each transferable document and instrument but are specific to electronic transactions law and are common to other UNCITRAL texts on electronic commerce. These general principles include the fundamental principles of legal recognition of the use of electronic means, technology neutrality and functional equivalence.[43]

The principle of legal recognition of the use of electronic means is set out in the MLETR, art 7, para 1. The principle of technology neutrality is not formulated in specific provisions but is reflected throughout the text of the Model Law. One consequence of the application of this principle is, the MLETR being model-neutral, that it may be implemented using registries, tokens and distributed ledgers, or any other technical solution. Chapter II of the Model Law deals with functional equivalence rules.

A closely related principle underpinning UNCITRAL texts on electronic commerce, including the MLETR, and related to their enabling nature is the principle of non-interference with substantive law (or 'least interventionist' principle). The term 'substantive law' refers to the law applicable to the 'substance' of the commercial transaction or document, ie the law that applies to that transaction or document regardless of the form of the contract or of the document. In the case of the MLETR, this is the law applicable to the transferable document or instrument corresponding to the electronic transferable record: for example, in case of an electronic bill of lading, the law applicable to bills of lading issued on paper.[44] As a result, the same substantive law applies to the contract or document regardless of the medium used. For instance, the MLETR does not contain a provision on how to take security interests on electronic transferable records, as the law on security interests should provide that guidance regardless of the medium used.[45] On the other hand, the UNCITRAL – International Institute for the Unification of Private Law (UNIDROIT) Model

[43] See ch 2, section 2.1.1.

[44] Explanatory Note, para 24.

[45] Explanatory Note, para 108. However, additional guidance may be needed to address emerging technologies, for instance for taking security in tokenised electronic transferable records: H Gabriel, 'The Future of the Transnational Law of Security Rights: The Emergence of Security Rights in Electronic Data' (2024) 29 *Uniform Law Review* 244, 249–251. For a discussion of relevant issues predating the MLETR, see M Dubovec, 'The Problems and Possibilities for Using Electronic Bills of Lading as Collateral' (2006) 23 *Arizona Journal of International and Comparative Law* 437.

Law on Warehouse Receipts (MLWR)[46] provides additional guidance on how to take security interests on electronic warehouse receipts (which are a type of electronic transferable records), as the MLWR is a medium-neutral text, ie contains both substantive law and rules on enabling the use of electronic transactions.[47]

Thanks to the joint operation of the principles of non-interference and of functional equivalence, the MLETR enactments do not need to reproduce all the substantive provisions applicable to the paper-based transferable document or instrument.

The principle of non-interference applies not only to commercial law, but to any law of enabling or regulatory nature. For instance, laws on data privacy and data protection, and on cross-border data transfer, also apply, according to their own scope of application, to data contained in electronic transferable records.[48] Other examples of regulations relevant for MLETR implementation include: financial regulations, for example, on access to credit and trade financing; regulations on the legal effect of trust services, including oversight of providers; and regulations on customs operations, including interaction with the single window.

Another fundamental principle common to other UNCITRAL texts on electronic commerce is that of the voluntary use of electronic means, which is contained in the MLETR, art 7, para 2. This principle derives from the enabling nature of UNCITRAL texts, which do not set any new regulation.

These general principles received an interesting judicial application in a case from Colombia regarding a specific type of electronic transferable records.[49] Colombia has established a registry (RADIAN registry) for the management of certain electronic transferable records, called electronic invoices, that is not based on the MLETR.[50] Colombia has also adopted a Law on Electronic Commerce based on the UNCITRAL Model Law on Electronic Commerce (MLEC).[51] In this case, one party claimed the payment of a sum of money based on electronic invoices allegedly evidenced by screenshots. The judge indicated that the reference of the Law on Electronic Commerce to the general principles underlying the MLEC such as non-discrimination, technology neutrality and functional

[46] UNGA, 'Report of the United Nations Commission on International Trade Law Fifty-seventh Session' (2024) UN Doc A/79/17, Annex I.

[47] See ch 4, section 4.2.1.

[48] In the framework of the process of consideration of a bill on electronic bills of lading (see ch 4, section 4.1.7), the Dutch Data Protection Authority (Autoriteit Persoonsgegevens) was asked to comment on data privacy and data protection aspects of that bill, and issued on 9 January 2024 a letter of no comment. The letter is available at www.autoriteitpersoonsgegevens.nl. Moreover, electronic transferable records may contain personally identifiable information whose transmission is subject to special rules when in electronic form but not on paper. In that case, anonymisation techniques may be used to transmit the information in a manner that complies with regulation.

[49] Juzgado Primero Civil Municipal de Ibagué – Tolima, 26 February 2024, Radicación: 73001-40-03-001-2023-00612-00, *Rentaequipos SAS v La Constructora El Pomar SAS.*

[50] Registro de factura electrónica de venta considerada título valor (RADIAN) established with Decreto 1154 of 20 August 2020.

[51] Ley 527 of 18 August 1999.

equivalence had to be interpreted in a broad sense and included UNCITRAL texts adopted after the MLEC. Regarding electronic transferable records, that reference to general principles was to be interpreted as incorporating also the MLETR requirements of singularity, control, and integrity, and of use of a reliable method according to a relative standard. The judge noted that the use of the RADIAN registry could satisfy the MLETR requirements, and added that, based on the principle of technology neutrality, those standards could also be satisfied with the use of other systems. In deciding the case, however, the judge indicated that screenshots did not provide any evidence of the use of reliable methods in managing electronic transferable records.[52]

An additional set of relevant general principles apply to all UNCITRAL texts. This set includes the principle of party autonomy contained in the MLETR, art 4 and the principle of uniform and autonomous interpretation of the MLETR contained in the MLETR, art 3, para 1. Finally, the principle of good faith as a general principle of international trade law (and as opposed to the notion of good faith specific to transferable documents and instruments), although not mentioned in the MLETR, may also be considered a general principle applicable to the MLETR.[53]

Article 4. Party autonomy and privity of contract

1. *The parties may derogate from or vary by agreement the following provisions of this Law: [...].*
2. *Such an agreement does not affect the rights of any person that is not a party to that agreement.*

The principle of party autonomy enables the parties to a contract to derogate from or vary the provisions of the law. Party autonomy is a general principle underpinning commercial law, including UNCITRAL texts.[54] However, this principle has found different application in each UNCITRAL text on electronic commerce, varying from allowing broad derogation to setting strict limits to its operation.

The MLEC, art 4 permits varying by agreement the provisions relating to communication of data messages and preserves the possibility of varying by agreement any substantive law provision that already allows doing so. Article 5 of the UNCITRAL Mode Law on Electronic Signatures (MLES) allows the parties to derogate from or vary any provision of the MLES unless the derogation would violate any law of mandatory application (for example, on special signature requirements such as notarisation). The ECC, art 3 indicates that the parties may exclude the application of the Convention or derogate from or vary any of

[52] The decision may also provide guidance on the application of arts 26 and 27 of the Ley 527, which enact in Colombian law the MLEC, arts 16 and 17 on electronic transferable transport documents.

[53] Explanatory Note, para 42.

[54] See, for instance, the CISG, art 6. In UNCITRAL texts, the principle of party autonomy may find limits in certain provisions of the treaties on carriage of goods by sea (eg, Hamburg Rules, art 2, para 2).

its provisions: however, party autonomy does not extend to setting aside statutory requirements.[55] The UNCITRAL Model Law on the Use and Cross-border Recognition of Identity Management and Trust Services (MLIT) does not contain a specific provision on which provisions may be varied or derogated from, although it identifies core obligations that service providers may not opt out of, thus recognising a certain degree of party autonomy.

The variety of legislative choices reflects different policy concerns and understanding of the extent to which party autonomy may derogate from substantive law. Possibly, these are variations of the same fundamental rule: party autonomy operates in those cases when it already does so with respect to paper-based documents, and the parties to a contract may not derogate from functional equivalence rules or modify their requirements. Moreover, derogation cannot affect third parties in good faith.

The MLETR, art 4, para 1 contains an open-ended statement on party autonomy that leaves the identification of the provisions that the parties may derogate from or vary, if any, to the enacting jurisdictions. This compromise solution accommodates different, and sometimes conflicting, considerations. It acknowledges that party autonomy is a fundamental commercial law principle but limited by rules of mandatory application. It also preserves the detailed guidance on party autonomy offered by the substantive law of transferable documents and instruments.

The practical importance of party autonomy in the MLETR is to acknowledge the ability of the parties to develop innovative solutions. For instance, the MLETR, art 12 enables parties to agree on the reliability of the methods used when choosing an electronic transferable records management system. However, the effectiveness of any such agreement does not extend to third parties, as indicated in the MLETR, art 4, para 2, which refers to the principle of privity of contract that limits the effects of party autonomy to the parties of the contractual agreements.

Given that functional equivalence rules are outside the reach of party autonomy, it is not surprising that domestic enactments of the MLETR often omit this provision and leave the matter entirely to the substantive law applicable to transferable documents and instruments. In this manner, party autonomy operates in the same manner with regard to electronic transferable records and to transferable documents and instruments.

Article 5. Information requirements

Nothing in this Law affects the application of any rule of law that may require a person to disclose its identity, place of business or other information, or relieves a person from the legal consequences of making inaccurate, incomplete or false statements in that regard.

The MLETR, art 5 is an application of the general principle that the MLETR, like other UNCITRAL texts on electronic commerce, does not affect substantive law,

[55] Explanatory Note to the ECC, para 85.

namely obligations to disclose information. This provision is inspired by the ECC, art 7 and buttresses the principle contained in the MLETR, art 1, para 2 with regard to information requirements. Similar considerations apply to any other regulatory requirement.

This obligation is different from the obligation of the issuer of the electronic transferable record to comply with information requirements contained in the substantive law of the transferable document or instrument under the MLETR, art 10, para 1(a). Similarly, the obligation to identify the person in control is separate from any obligation to provide identification information under other law.[56]

Article 6. Additional information in electronic transferable records

Nothing in this Law precludes the inclusion of information in an electronic transferable record in addition to that contained in a transferable document or instrument.

The electronic medium is intrinsically different from the paper-based one. To conceive an electronic document as a mere transposition of the corresponding paper-based one means missing out on the opportunities offered by digital means. These opportunities arise from the ability to share, reuse, and analyse data. To take full advantage of those opportunities, the electronic transferable record should contain as much information as possible. Some of that information may be available only in electronic form. The MLETR, art 6 indicates that the Model Law does not preclude the inclusion of information that exists only in electronic form in an electronic transferable record.

A first set of information that is only available electronically is metadata, ie data that describes other data, specifically, the electronic transferable record.

A second set of information that is only available electronically is information about contract automation. Contracts may be concluded and performed in electronic form, and commercial documents in electronic form may contain clauses that are executed automatically, ie without the need for review or input of a human person. For example, an electronic promissory note may be presented for payment upon its due date by programming the management system to send a payment request to the bank of the debtor without the need for clerical work.[57]

A third set of information available only electronically is information generated by oracles. Oracles are physical or digital objects that generate data. The data generated by oracles may change periodically or continuously,[58] and may be used in contract automation. To perform automation by using data generated by

[56] See commentary on the MLETR, art 11, para 1(b).

[57] See the examples provided in J Lampič and I Ng, 'An Analysis on the Application of the UNCITRAL Model Law on Electronic Transferable Records on Contract Automation and Metadata' in AM Lopez Rodriguez, MD Green and ML Kubica (eds), *Legal Challenges in the New Digital Age* (Leiden, Brill, 2021) 45. For additional information on the legal treatment of the use of automation in contracts, see the comment to the UNCITRAL Model Law on Automated Contracting (ch 2, section 2.1.2).

[58] This type of data is referred to as 'dynamic data' in para 58 of the Explanatory Note.

oracles, the data should be reliable. Trust services may be used to give assurance of the desirable level of reliability.

For instance, the execution of a contractual clause requiring partial payment of goods when the cargo arrives at the port of destination may be automated by linking the global positioning system information of the ship carrying the goods, the electronic bill of lading covering the goods, and the account from where the payment is to be made. This means that payment is not only immediate but also independent of human input. This may have business consequences as the party who may delay payment until the paper documents are received would have to pay immediately. Also, this may require careful coordination with the timing of the inspection of the goods. These matters should be dealt with in contractual agreements on payment terms and acceptance of goods.

The use of electronic transferable records may help to satisfy certain legal obligations such as the requirement to make available a translation of the content of the transferable document or instrument in the national language.[59] The electronic transferable record management system may be programmed to automatically generate that language version and make it available to the relevant parties whenever a party with place of business or another connecting factor with one such jurisdiction is involved. While a translation in a foreign language of standard terms and conditions of a paper-based document is possible, the electronic form allows the instant inclusion in the electronic transferable record of a pre-approved translation of annotations and any other information.

For evidentiary and other purposes, the methods used to manage information that exists only in electronic form should meet the standards for functional equivalence with the notions of writing and signature, which apply to the whole electronic transferable record. Dedicated technical standards for the use of oracles and for contract automation are emerging. Information existing only in electronic form should be preserved in case of conversion from electronic to paper medium pursuant to the MLETR, art 18.

The MLETR, art 6 does not affect the obligation set in the MLETR, art 10, para 1(a) to comply with substantive law information requirements applicable to the specific type of document, including any prohibition to include specific information.

[59] See, eg, art 31 of the Law No 24 of 2009 on National Flag, Language, Emblem and Anthem of Indonesia, and the decision of the Indonesian Supreme Court No 601 K/Pdt/2015 of 31 August 2015 that declared an international loan agreement invalid due to the lack of a translation in Bahasa: L Gama, *Recueil des cours de l'Académie de La Haye, Vol 406, Les principes d'UNIDROIT et la loi régissant les contrats de commerce* (Leiden, Brill, 2020) 198–199; A Suyudi and HS Budi, 'Reconsidering the Mandatory Use of Indonesian Language in Private Commercial Contract' (2022) 2 *Global Legal Review* 2, 185, ojs.uph.edu; J Purba, 'Ratio Decidendi, Agreement, Against the Decision of MA No 601K/PDT/2015 in the Case of Agreements that do not use Indonesian' (2021) 21 *Jurnal Penelitian Hukum De Jure* 517. For Türkiye, see art 2 of the Law on the Compulsory Use of Turkish Language in Economic Enterprises, Law No 805 of 1926.

Article 7. Legal recognition of an electronic transferable record

1. *An electronic transferable record shall not be denied legal effect, validity or enforceability on the sole ground that it is in electronic form.*
2. *Nothing in this Law requires a person to use an electronic transferable record without that person's consent.*
3. *The consent of a person to use an electronic transferable record may be inferred from the person's conduct.*

The MLETR, art 7, para 1 enshrines the well-known principle of legal recognition of (or non-discrimination against) the use of electronic transferable records. This fundamental principle, which was first set out in the MLEC, art 5 with regard to data messages, ensures that an electronic transferable record is not denied legal recognition only because of its electronic nature.[60] The principle does not in itself assure that the electronic transferable record will be given legal recognition, as other circumstances, including lack of compliance with functional equivalence requirements, may affect its validity.

The MLETR, art 7, para 2 sets forth the principle that the use of electronic transferable records under the MLETR is voluntary. This principle applies to the use of all electronic transactions (see the ECC, art 8, para 2).

In many jurisdictions, paper and electronic medium may co-exist to facilitate transition to the digital world while not excluding any stakeholder. Legislators may decide to exempt electronic transferable records from stamp duties to encourage digital buy-in. However, they may also decide to mandate the use of electronic transferable records for certain types of users.[61] This may be done, for instance, to increase regulatory oversight of commercial operations.

For a variety of reasons, including digital literacy, caution should be used in mandating the use of electronic transferable records to all users. With regard to legislative drafting, if the use of electronic transferable records is made mandatory it is necessary to ensure that the substantive law of the transferable document or instrument remains applicable through functional equivalence provisions or, alternatively, that a law is drafted establishing electronic transferable records that exist only in electronic form.

Consent by a person to the use of electronic transferable records may be implicit in the conduct of the person, as indicated in para 3. In practice, the expression of consent to the use of electronic transferable records may vary significantly with the type of application and technical solution.[62] Consent may be indicated by a person specifically accepting the terms and conditions contained in the rulebook of the

[60] A similar provision is contained in the eIDAS, art 46, which grants legal recognition to all electronic documents and therefore, arguably, also electronic transferable records.

[61] In the Republic of Korea, the use of electronic promissory notes is mandatory for commercial societies that meet certain capital or assets requirements: art 6-2 of the Issuance and Distribution of Electronic Bills Act, Act No 15022 of 31 October 2017 (see ch 2, section 2.4.3).

[62] See also Caprioli, 'La Loi-type' (2023) 484.

electronic transferable records management system operator or incorporated in the terms and conditions contained in or linked to the electronic transferable record. In other cases, such as when tokens are used, consent may be implicit when a person takes control of the electronic transferable record.

Whether use of a system by a person entails implicit acceptance by that person of the terms and conditions of the operator of the system is a matter of contractual interpretation. It should also be noted that usually electronic transferable records are exchanged among commercial operators who have advanced knowledge of business practices and who are able to ascertain the consequences of taking control of the records.

3.2.2. Provisions on Functional Equivalence

The MLETR legally enables the use in electronic form of existing paper-based transferable documents and instruments by establishing the requirements for achieving functional equivalence of certain legal notions applicable to paper-based transferable documents and instruments. As noted,[63] the principle of functional equivalence presupposes the existence of a law applicable to paper-based documents, referred to as 'substantive law', which contains form and other requirements presupposing the use of paper.[64]

Although it is often said that these and other functional equivalence rules provide for functional equivalence with certain form requirements, it should be stressed that the equivalence is not with the form requirements themselves, but with the function they fulfil. The functional approach does not aim to replicate paper-based documents in the electronic domain, but to achieve the functions pursued with the use of paper-based documents.

The MLETR contains four functional equivalence rules that are necessary to legally enable the use of electronic transferable records: two predate the MLETR; and the other two are new. The pre-existing rules provide for the notions of 'writing' and 'signature' and often are already in force in MLETR-enacting jurisdictions. In that case, the application of existing rules may be extended to electronic transferable records and the MLETR, arts 8 and 9, which contain these rules, do not need to be enacted.

The new functional equivalence rules refer to the notions of 'transferable document and instrument' and of 'possession'. These provisions lie at the core of the Model Law: without them, a law cannot be considered a MLETR enactment.

The application of the principle of functional equivalence is not the only possible manner to legally enable the use of electronic transferable records. One

[63] Comment to the MLETR, art 46.

[64] For the requirements of a bill of lading, see L Zhu and X Pan, 'A Conceptual Analysis of the Electronic Bill of Lading' (2021) 4 *Journal of Business Law* 336.

alternative solution consists of extending the notion of possession to intangible goods, which is the approach adopted in the United Kingdom.[65] This solution aims to achieve equivalence with the notion of possession and not with its functions. Another option is the creation and use of transferable records existing only in electronic form, ie that have no paper-based equivalent.[66]

The adoption of an approach alternative to functional equivalence does not mean that the provisions of the MLETR should be disregarded. On the contrary, the notions of 'control', 'singularity' and 'integrity' as well as the circumstances relevant for assessing the reliability of the method may be used to determine how an electronic transferable record should circulate regardless of the reference to functional equivalence.[67] The broad adoption of these rules is particularly important to ensure legal recognition and technical interoperability across documents, systems and jurisdictions.

> ***Article 8. Writing***
>
> *Where the law requires that information should be in writing, that requirement is met with respect to an electronic transferable record if the information contained therein is accessible so as to be usable for subsequent reference.*

Substantive law sometimes explicitly requires the use of the written form for transferable documents and instruments. In other cases, the use of the written form is implied based on business practice as well as certain prescriptions such as the indication of information on the front or the back of the paper document.

The MLETR, art 8 sets forth the requirements for the functional equivalence between written and electronic form based on the well-known provision contained in the MLEC, art 6, para 1. Writing allows for the recording of information on a durable medium that makes it available for future reference. Hence, the written form requirement is met when the information in electronic form is accessible 'to be usable for subsequent reference'. This means that the data message should be accessible. For instance, if the file is corrupt, the memory support is lost, or the software used is obsolete and the file cannot be read, the standard is not met. This provision has been interpreted and applied in judicial decisions: about 15 cases related to it may be found in the CLOUT database.

The words 'usable for subsequent reference' include cases when information may only be used for computing processing.[68] In other words, the information does not need to be intelligible to humans, provided it is accessible and usable by a machine. This enables the transition from documents to data: trade-related information is exchanged automatically and is, at request, presented to humans. Often, presentation to humans occurs according to a layout that mimics the paper-based document. However, the existence of a human-readable electronic

[65] See ch 4, section 4.1.12.
[66] See ch 3, section 3.3.1.
[67] See the comment to the Electronic Trade Documents Act 2023 in ch 4, section 4.1.12.
[68] Guide to Enactment of the MLEC, para 50.

document is not needed to achieve functional equivalence between written and electronic form.

The MLEC, art 6, para 2 specifies that the rule for functional equivalence between the written and electronic form applies both when the law requires writing and when the law simply provides consequences for the information not being in writing. This provision has not been reproduced in the MLETR, art 8. This, however, does not create misalignment between the two model laws because the MLETR generally assumes that any reference to a legal requirement relevant for a functional equivalence rule includes cases when the law provides consequences for not meeting that legal requirement.[69]

The written form requirement should be distinguished from other form requirements, such as signatures and original versions, which are also relevant for the MLETR.

Because of the widespread adoption of the MLEC, many jurisdictions have already adopted a rule on the functional equivalence between the written and electronic form, often by enacting the MLEC, art 6 in their electronic transactions law. In those cases, the MLETR, art 8 may not need to be adopted and the application of the provision enacting the MLEC, art 6 may be extended to electronic transferable records. This drafting option may be preferable especially if the MLETR is enacted as an additional chapter of an existing electronic transactions law, and not as a discrete piece of legislation. When doing so, the legislator needs to take into consideration that the requirements to determine reliability of a method may be set out differently when applicable to electronic transferable records[70] and to other data messages. To maintain uniformity in the notion of reliable method, it is desirable to apply the MLETR provisions on determination of reliability to all forms of electronic records.

Article 9. Signature

Where the law requires or permits a signature of a person, that requirement is met by an electronic transferable record if a reliable method is used to identify that person and to indicate that person's intention in respect of the information contained in the electronic transferable record.

The notion of an electronic signature is prominent in electronic transactions law. Provisions on electronic signatures are commonly found in national law even in the absence of an electronic transactions law. However, there are different understandings of 'electronic signature'. Significant differences may exist between technical notions of electronic signatures based on the use of particular standards, methods or technologies; legal notions, which may or may not be technology neutral; and common parlance, which may include expressions such as 'signing into a system' (ie requesting credentials validation to access a system).

[69] Explanatory Note, para 67.
[70] See the MLETR, art 12.

Every UNCITRAL legislative text on electronic commerce contains a provision on electronic signatures, and two model laws – the MLES and the MLIT – deal extensively with the matter.[71] In UNCITRAL texts, electronic signatures were first considered under the angle of providing a functional equivalence rule for handwritten signatures. Lately, the MLIT added to that perspective the consideration of electronic signatures as a trust service, ie a service that provides assurance of data quality regardless of the existence of a legal requirement to sign, and therefore independent of the functional equivalence approach.[72]

Signatures are of great practical importance also in transferable documents and instruments, where they are used for issuance and transfer.[73] The MLETR, art 9 provides a functional equivalence rule for electronic signatures used in conjunction with electronic transferable records that requires the use of a reliable method for the identification of the signatory and for the indication of the signatory's intention with regard to the signed message. The reliability of the method used is to be assessed according to the general reliability standard contained in the MLETR, art 12.

The MLETR, art 9 follows the formulation contained in the ECC, art 9, para 3(a), which refers to the notion of 'party's intention' (as opposed to the notion of 'person's approval' contained in the MLEC, art 7 and the MLES, art 6, para 1) to better capture the fact that paper-based signatures do not always express approval of the signed document but may satisfy other functions such as knowledge of content or witnessing. The actual content of the intention associated with the electronic signature must be ascertained on a case-by-case basis in light of the terms in which the intention is expressed and any other relevant circumstance. The method used should clearly indicate the intention of the party, both in terms of expression of the intention itself (along the lines of a statement such as: 'I sign in order to express this intention' and of consent to embrace that intention (that is to say, signifying that 'by performing this action, I am aware I am signing').[74]

The identification of the signatory usually takes place based on credentials: for instance, a financier may be able to access an electronic transferable documents management system to dispose of an electronic transferable record by inserting

[71] See comment to the MLIT, art 16.

[72] In the MLIT electronic signatures are explicitly qualified as a type of trust services. Nevertheless, the MLIT, art 16, on electronic signatures, is drafted as a functional equivalence rule similarly to the MLETR, art 9.

[73] Law or commercial practice may call for the use of a signature; see the illustration of the use of signatures in bills of lading in S Girvin, 'Evidentiary Aspects of Transport Documents and Electronic Transport Records under the Rotterdam Rules' (2010) 2 *European Journal of Commercial Contract Law* 109, 115–116. For the relevance of the notion of signature in determining the originality of transferable instruments, see art 17 of UCP 600, as qualified by para A27 of the International Standard Banking Practice (ISBP) 821, and by the eUCP, art e3(b)(iv) ('Definition of electronic signature').

[74] T Smedinghoff, 'Article 9: Form Requirements', in AH Boss and W Kilian (eds), *The United Nations Convention on the Use of Electronic Communications in International Contracts: An In-depth Guide and Sourcebook* (Frederick, Md, Kluwer Law International, 2008), 136, 153.

a smart card in a reader and inputting a number provided by an authenticator. The reliability of the method used for identification generally depends on the level of reliability of the trust service used and on the level of assurance of the underlying identity management scheme.[75]

Signatories do not need to be identified in the electronic transferable records with their legal name, as the MLETR recognises the use of pseudonyms provided that the identity of the signatory may be otherwise ascertained. For commercial law purposes (for example, the record is transferred to bearer), full identity information may not be disclosed to the other parties involved in the electronic transferable record if so wished. Signatories may however need to be identified with their real identity for compliance purposes.

The ECC, art 9, para 3(b)(ii) contains a safety clause to ensure that whenever it is possible to identify the signatory of an electronic communication and to ascertain its intention with respect to the signed communication, that signatory may not repudiate the signature because of the signature's unreliable method. That provision, which applies only to electronic signatures in the ECC, has been included in the MLETR, art 12(b) so that it would apply to all instances of use of a reliable method under the Model Law.

The MLETR is compatible with the adoption of a 'two-tier' approach, thus allowing the use of electronic signatures that are associated with legal presumptions ('designated electronic signatures' according to the MLIT, arts 16 and 23).[76] This issue is related to the accreditation of electronic transferable records management systems operators.[77]

Accordingly, those jurisdictions that have already enacted the MLES, art 6 may apply that provision and its 'two-tier' approach also to electronic signatures issued in connection with an electronic transferable record. This means that electronic transferable records signed with sophisticate electronic signatures may benefit from presumptions of origin and integrity.

The MLETR, art 9 does not deal explicitly with cross-border recognition of the legal effects of electronic signatures issued or used abroad. However, the MLETR, art 19, para 1, on non-discrimination of foreign electronic transferable records, applies also to electronic signatures. As a result, the place of issuance or use of the electronic signature is irrelevant for the assessment of the reliability of the electronic signature.

In practice, formal recognition of a foreign electronic signature may be achieved by virtue of a general reciprocity agreement, or of a cross-certification agreement between a foreign certification service provider and a provider accredited in the country where the signature needs to be recognised, or any other similar

[75] On these notions, see ch 5, commentary on the MLIT, art 10, and ch 6, commentary on the MLIT, art 22.

[76] See the commentary on these articles, respectively, in chs 5 and 6.

[77] See the commentary on the MLETR, art 12 in this chapter.

arrangement. These legal mechanisms are foreseen in domestic laws but have found limited practical application due to their being time- and resource-intensive.[78]

The matter may be addressed more expeditiously by choosing the law applicable to the electronic signature, which would usually be the same law applicable to the electronic transferable record, or by agreeing contractually on the validity and effect of electronic signatures, if possible.

The considerations on the application of any existing functional equivalence rule on the notion of writing apply to electronic signatures as well. Hence, the MLETR, art 9 does not need to be enacted when a rule on electronic signatures already exists in the enacting jurisdiction and the application of that rule is extended to electronic transferable records.

On the other hand, and quite importantly, legislation on electronic signatures that is not compatible with the general principles underlying UNCITRAL texts on electronic commerce may need to be amended to allow the implementation of the MLETR. This is particularly true with regard to cross-border recognition of electronic signatures and the principle of technology neutrality.

Article 10. Transferable documents or instruments

1. *Where the law requires a transferable document or instrument, that requirement is met by an electronic record if:*
   - (a) *The electronic record contains the information that would be required to be contained in a transferable document or instrument; and*
   - (b) *A reliable method is used:*
     - (i) *To identify that electronic record as the electronic transferable record;*
     - (ii) *To render that electronic record capable of being subject to control from its creation until it ceases to have any effect or validity; and*
     - (iii) *To retain the integrity of that electronic record.*
2. *The criterion for assessing integrity shall be whether information contained in the electronic transferable record, including any authorized change that arises from its creation until it ceases to have any effect or validity, has remained complete and unaltered apart from any change which arises in the normal course of communication, storage and display.*

Possession of a transferable document or instrument allows the identification of the person entitled to claim performance, and its delivery with or without endorsement permits the transfer of that entitlement. However, possession and delivery are legal notions that presume the existence of tangible media, which is typically paper. A main obstacle to the use of transferable documents and instruments in electronic form is to reproduce possession and delivery in a virtual environment. The MLETR, arts 10 and 11 address this issue by setting requirements to achieve

[78] See UNCITRAL, *Promoting Confidence in Electronic Commerce: Legal Issues on International Use of Electronic Authentication and Signature Methods* (Vienna, United Nations, 2009) for guidance on cross-border recognition mechanisms for electronic signatures. See also ch 8 on mechanisms for cross-border recognition of trust services, including electronic signatures, in the MLIT.

equivalence with the functions pursued by the notions of possession and delivery of a paper-based transferable document or instrument. The requirements are providing the information necessary for the transferable document or instrument, and using a reliable method to ensure singularity, control, and integrity of the electronic transferable records. These functional equivalence rules apply only to transferable documents and instruments and are not generic functional equivalence rules to be used whenever the law refers to possession and delivery.

Generic functional equivalence rules for possession and delivery were not discussed during the preparation of the MLETR as the scope of work was limited to transferable documents and instruments. Similarly, the UK Electronic Trade Documents Act 2023 (ETDA 2023), s 3(1) declares that: 'A person may possess, indorse and part with possession of an electronic trade document'. A question on the ability to possess intangibles may arise with regard to certain digital assets existing only in electronic form, such as crypto-assets. However, functional equivalence rules do not apply to those assets precisely because they exist only in electronic form.

The electronic transferable record must contain all the information that is required to give legal validity and effect to the corresponding transferable document or instrument (MLETR, art 10, para 1(a)). These information requirements are set in substantive law. This rule derives from the fact that the MLETR does not modify substantive law, which applies equally to paper-based and electronic documents. The need to reproduce required information does not extend to those 'physical formalities', ie requirements such as the need to record information on the front or the back of the document, which presuppose the use of paper. Requirements regarding information placement on paper-based documents do not apply to electronic transferable records by their own nature. In practice, the electronic transferable records management system designers may decide to reproduce visually the paper-based document and to place the information where it should be placed on a paper document for easier human reading.

The inclusion of this information permits the identification of the specific type of transferable document or instrument, which triggers the application of the relevant substantive law. Moreover, the electronic transferable record may contain any additional information that may be included in the paper-based document or instrument under substantive law and commercial practice, and any additional information that may be available only in electronic form.

The second condition for achieving functional equivalence between an electronic transferable record and a paper-based transferable document or instrument is comprised of four elements: (a) the use of reliable methods; to (b) identify the electronic transferable record ('singularity'); (c) render it capable of being subject to control throughout its lifecycle; and (d) retain its integrity.

The MLETR, art 12 provides further guidance on the reliability of the methods used. As for the other three elements, singularity focuses on the existence of a single claim, control relates to the relationship between the record and the person in control, and integrity deals with recording all events occurring during the record's lifecycle. Singularity, control, and integrity operate jointly to ensure that it is not possible to: issue more than one electronic transferable record entitling the same performance; transfer control of that record without the consent of the person in control; and alter that record against the will of the person in control. If these three conditions are met, there is assurance that the electronic transferable record is the 'original' record issued for that transaction and relevant to demand the performance contained therein. Thus, the joint operation of these conditions may address the 'double spending' problem.

Singularity

The singularity requirement mandates the identification of an electronic transferable record from the moment of its issuance as the record that is transferable and relevant for the given commercial transaction. The function pursued is not the existence of a single record, but the existence of a single claim for the obligation evidenced in the electronic transferable record. This is expressed by using the definite article 'the', which has been preferred to the use of the qualifier 'authoritative' or similar that could have been misunderstood as a statement on the validity of the electronic transferable record under substantive law.[79]

The identification of the electronic transferable record is a matter of fact: the electronic transferable records management system must allow the identification of such a record as well as its separation from other records. More precisely, the electronic transferable records management system shall ensure that only one electronic record is identified and identifiable as the electronic transferable record relevant for that commercial transaction. Singularity is a factual circumstance that must be maintained throughout the lifecycle of the electronic transferable record. The management system should prevent reproducing the electronic transferable record unless allowed by law or agreement. The Explanatory Note juxtaposes the notion of singularity to that of uniqueness (ie assurance of impossibility to reproduce), which may be technically impossible to guarantee.[80] While impossibility to reproduce may technically not be assured, the system should have in place at least commercially feasible safeguards in line with applicable technical and business standards.

The notion of singularity does not forbid the issuance of multiple originals, if allowed under substantive law. This matter has been discussed with respect to the interaction between the MLETR and the Rotterdam Rules.[81] However, two clarifications on this point seem useful. First, the MLETR does not apply the notion of 'original', 'authentic' or similar to electronic transferable records: the quality of originality is achieved by fulfilling all functional equivalence requirements and thus providing access to information as reliable as it would be when contained in an original paper-based document. Second, issuance of multiple electronic

[79] The definite article does not exist in Chinese and Russian, and therefore the official text of the MLETR, art 10, para 1(b)(i) in those languages differs; see Explanatory Note paras 96–97.
[80] Explanatory Note, paras 81–82.
[81] See the discussion in ch 2, section 2.2.

transferable records for the same obligation (ie multiple 'originals') does not necessarily entail the issuance of multiple records: for example, different persons may be in control of a different 'original' of the same electronic transferable record. Technology may ensure that the record circulates according to the intended rules, including with the consensus of all persons in control of an 'original' if so required. If multiple originals are issued, all original electronic transferable records shall be identified as such.

Singularity may be achieved with adequate technical means, including the use of distributed ledger technology, as the composite nature of an electronic transferable record does not prevent its identification as the relevant singular record. To that end, the definition of 'electronic record' in the MLETR, art 2 refers to 'information logically associated with or otherwise linked together so as to become part of the record, whether generated contemporaneously or not'. Non-Fungible Tokens (NFTs) are a blockchain-based technology that may offer higher assurance of the impossibility of reproducing the token. Hence, the use of NFTs, which are by design identifiable in an unequivocal manner, may be a suitable manner to satisfy the singularity requirement.[82]

Control

Control is a factual circumstance that relates to the relationship between the person in control and the electronic transferable record in a manner akin to the relationship between the holder and the paper-based transferable document or instrument. Control is achieved when the functions pursued with possession, such as benefitting from the electronic transferable record, disposing of that record, and excluding others from its disposal, are achieved.

Like singularity and integrity, control applies throughout the lifecycle of the electronic transferable record. The starting moment of control is the creation of the electronic transferable record (as opposed to the subsequent moment of the issuance of the record, which is when it becomes transferable).[83]

[82] Blockchain technology is often used to manage electronic bills of lading. One technical solution relies on storing only selected information on the blockchain: for an illustration involving non-fungible tokens, see J Krebs, 'The Technological Practicality of Electronic Bills of Lading and Non-Fungible Tokens' (2023) 20 *Manchester Journal of International Economic Law* 34, mostly discussing the notion of control in the UK Electronic Trade Documents Act 2023 (ETDA 2023). For a technical and legal description of a blockchain-based framework for electronic transferable records, see Stephenson Harwood LLP in collaboration with INFOCOMM Media Development Authority, 'TradeTrust-enabled Electronic Bills of Lading: A Legal and Practical Analysis of Their Use in Global Trade' (2023), paras 3.13–3.18. TradeTrust uses NFTs to represent title, while the data component (eg, the information needed to comply with the requirements of the transferable document or instrument) is stored off-chain. See also the illustration by 2Tokens of the use case of a Non-Fungible Token (NFT) based bills of lading in the TradeTrust ecosystem at www.2tokens.org/bill-of-lading.

[83] However, the MLWR, art 6, para 1(b) refers to the later moment of issuance for the beginning of control (UNCITRAL, 'Report of Working Group I (Warehouse Receipts) on the Work of its Forty-first Session' (16 February 2024) UN Doc A/CN.9/1165, paras 33–34). This view may be based on the understanding that control is not needed unless the electronic transferable record may be transferred, which is the moment when the transferable document or instrument is considered perfected. The discussion

As for the end of control, the MLETR, art 10, para 1(b)(ii) specifies that the electronic transferable record does not need to be subject to control when it 'ceases to have any effect or validity'. This event should be understood as relating to the inability of the electronic transferable record to further circulate and it usually coincides with presentation for performance. Such record, even if archived, may however have evidentiary effect and validity. This is because the cessation of the transferability of the electronic transferable record transforms that record in an electronic record, and legal effects may continue to arise from the electronic record, for example, evidentiary ones. Accordingly, the terminated electronic record is subject to ordinary rules, namely on data retention and archiving.

The MLETR does not specify how presentation should take place, as this depends on the features of the electronic transferable records management system.[84]

The relationship between singularity and control is of complementarity. Singularity focuses on the existence of a claim evidenced by the electronic transferable record; control focuses on the attribution of the authority to benefit from and dispose of the electronic transferable record, including by transferring it. Singularity alone would not suffice if seen as a static notion, and control alone would not prevent the issuance of another electronic transferable record for the same obligation.[85]

Integrity

The notion of integrity is strictly related to that of original.[86] According to UNCITRAL provisions predating the MLETR, originality of a document is

is not new: see M Stella Richter, 'I titoli di credito nel nuovo sistema di diritto internazionale privato' (1996) Consiglio Nazionale del Notariato Studio n 1185/2, 10–11, for references to the debate that took place in the 1930s.

[84] See art 15, para 1 of the French Law n 2024-537, specifying that the presentation may be made by delivering the electronic transferable record at the electronic address indicated by the recipient (ie usually the debtor), or by making information allowing the access to the electronic transferable record available to the recipient.

[85] H Gabriel, 'The Concept and Necessity of "Control" in the Use of Emerging Technologies in Commercial Transactions' (2023) 28 *Uniform Law Review*, 257, 266–268, expresses doubts about the notion of control in the MLETR. These doubts reflect the position of the US delegation when drafting the MLETR, which favoured retaining the notion of control and deleting that of singularity. (The Chinese delegation had opposite views.) See also Gabriel, 'The Future of the Transnational Law of Security Rights' (2024) 254–256, explaining that 'control' is clearly defined in the UNIDROIT Principles on Digital Assets and Private Law (and in UCC Article 12) as 'that which provides the party having control the benefits of the asset to the exclusion of others', and that this approach is clearer than that of the MLETR. However, the MLETR does not define control because control is the functional equivalent of possession, which is, in turn, defined in each jurisdiction. The core definition of possession usually refers to the ability to enjoy the benefits of the asset to the exclusion of others. On the other hand, the UNIDROIT Principles on Digital Assets and Private Law and UCC Article 12 apply when no substantive law exists, and therefore may (and should) include a definition of control (see section 3.3.7).

[86] See Explanatory Note, paras 189–190, noting that the MLETR does not make explicit reference to the notion of 'original', whose functions are achieved by the operation of the various functional equivalence requirements.

achieved when there is reliable assurance of the integrity of the information contained in a data message from the time when it was first generated in its final form (MLEC, art 8; ECC, art 9, para 4), among other conditions. However, transferable documents and instruments normally circulate during their lifecycle and therefore their content will change, including with respect to the person in control. Hence, the notion of integrity of an electronic transferable record cannot refer to a fixed point in time but must capture all changes. Accordingly, the MLETR, art 10, para 2 refers to maintaining the integrity of the information contained in the electronic transferable record during its entire lifecycle, and not just from the time of its creation. It is irrelevant whether the changes are legally significant or not, as this is a judgment that may require a lengthy investigation and specialised skills. The use of distributed ledger technology that offers higher assurance of data persistence could be useful in implementing this provision.

As usual in UNCITRAL texts, 'any change which arises in the normal course of communication, storage and display' is not considered a violation of integrity. This exception refers to modifications needed to implement technical solutions, which do not affect the legal value of the electronic transferable record.[87]

An issue relating to the end of the lifecycle of the electronic transferable record pertains to its loss or destruction. The MLETR does not contain a provision on such events. However, the issue was discussed during the preparation of the MLWR. The warehouse receipt may be a transferable document, and the substantive law of warehouse receipts provides detailed rules for the replacement of a lost or destroyed receipt. It is therefore necessary to provide similar rules for electronic warehouse receipts. The MLWR clarifies that the loss of any of the requirements for the issuance of an electronic warehouse receipt (which are the same as those for an electronic transferable record in the MLETR) amounts to loss or destruction of an electronic warehouse receipt.[88] It is also important to bear in mind that, while loss or destruction of a transferable document or instrument may involve negligence of the holder, loss or destruction of an electronic transferable record may involve negligence of the operator of the electronic transferable record management system, which often will limit contractually its liability to the fullest extent allowed by the law. In any case, replacement of a lost or destroyed electronic transferable record will likely require cooperation of the system operator, depending on the model chosen for the electronic transferable records management system. The observation applies also to issues such as providing evidence of the loss or destruction of the electronic transferable record.[89]

[87] Caprioli , 'La Loi-type' (2023) 490.

[88] UNCITRAL, 'Report of Working Group I (Warehouse Receipts) on the Work of its Forty-first Session', para 55.

[89] ibid para 57.

Article 11. Control

1. *Where the law requires or permits the possession of a transferable document or instrument, that requirement is met with respect to an electronic transferable record if a reliable method is used:*
   - *(a) To establish exclusive control of that electronic transferable record by a person; and*
   - *(b) To identify that person as the person in control.*
2. *Where the law requires or permits transfer of possession of a transferable document or instrument, that requirement is met with respect to an electronic transferable record through the transfer of control over the electronic transferable record.*

The MLETR, art 11 specifies the requirements to establish control, which is defined as the functional equivalent of possession, and to transfer control, ie to achieve functional equivalence with delivery.[90] This means that whenever the law refers to the notions of possession and delivery in connection with transferable documents and instruments, those notions may be transposed in an electronic environment by meeting the conditions set in the MLETR, arts 10 and 11. Accordingly, possessory remedies may be available to the person in control. In the digital space, possessory remedies are being used to recover stolen digital assets, but their use in relation to electronic transferable records seems untested.

Control consists of two factual conditions: establishment of exclusive control by a person and identification of the person in control. Establishment of exclusive control is, in turn, made of different elements. The electronic transferable records management system must not only enable the person entitled to exercise control to do so, but also exclude other persons from exercising control, and enable the person in control to transfer the control to the intended recipient.

The notion of 'control' under the MLETR is different from the notion of control under other laws relating to digital trade, such as the US Uniform Commercial Code (UCC), Article 12.[91] In the MLETR, 'control' is meant to achieve in the electronic environment the functions of possession and to attach the same legal consequences.[92]

Reference to a person in control does not prevent joint control: multiple persons may exercise control jointly for the same purpose. Moreover, different persons may exercise control for different purposes (for example, control for the purpose of claiming delivery of the goods represented by an electronic bill of lading and control for the purpose of a security interest in those goods). A person

[90] On the notion of 'control, see Rodríguez Delgado, JP and Albors Cano, J, 'El "control (exclusivo)" como concepto equivalente a la función posesoria en el conocimiento de embarque electrónico' in Pulido Begines JL, Alba Fernández M and Rodríguez Delgado JP (coords), Liber Amicorum: Estudios de Derecho de la Navegación Marítima en Homenaje al Prof José Luis Gabaldón (Madrid, Dykinson, 2024) 603–643.

[91] C Pejovic and U Lee, 'Towards Global Legal Recognition of Electronic Trade Documents: Control or Possession?' (2024) 59 *Texas International Law Journal* 101.

[92] For a different view, Gabriel, 'The Concept and Necessity of "Control"' (2023).

may exercise control over the electronic transferable records on behalf of another person, when admissible under substantive law. Control may also be attributed to a third party in execution of a court order (for example, to exercise judicial custody on the electronic transferable record).

In the case of documents comprising more than one part, the different parts may circulate separately until the law requires or the parties agree that they be reunited. This is the case of electronic warehouse receipts issued under the dual system, which are made of the warehouse receipts proper and the pledge bond or warrant. The use of electronic means allows monitoring closely the circulation of both parts, which is not possible for paper-based documents.

Transfer of control has the same legal effects as delivery of the paper-based transferable document or instrument. It is important to stress that, unlike for contract-based systems, the MLETR does not foresee novation in case of transfer of control over the record.

The identification requirement does not affect the transfer of electronic transferable records by delivery only ('to bearer'). Anonymity for commercial law purposes is possible in the electronic environment. At the same time, the identification of the person in control allows storing and sharing identity information as appropriate. This feature allows increasing compliance compared to the paper-based world where anonymity may be absolute. For instance, if a criminal investigation is carried out on possible illegal trade (for example, goods exported in violation of sanctions), the investigating authority may ask for the identification of the persons in control despite the electronic transferable record circulating as a bearer instrument.

The identification requirement is also compatible with the use of pseudonyms, which are common in blockchain technology.[93]

3.2.3. Use of Electronic Transferable Records

Chapter III of the MLETR contains provisions relating to the use of electronic transferable records. The MLETR, art 12 contains the standard for assessing the reliability of the methods used. This standard applies to all MLETR provisions referring to the use of a reliable method. The MLETR, arts 13, 14, 15 and 16 provide guidance on how to deal with certain events occurring in the lifecycle of electronic transferable records, and on how to provide information on time and place in conjunction with the use of an electronic transferable record. Finally, the MLETR, arts 17 and 18 set the procedures for change of medium.

[93] Explanatory Note, para 117. For an application, see Stephenson Harwood LLP, *TradeTrust-enabled Electronic Bills of Lading*, paras 3.24.2 and 4.9.2, explaining that in TradeTrust only the link between the NFT representing title and the digital wallet proving identity information is stored on-chain, but not the identity information itself.

Article 12. General reliability standard

For the purposes of articles 9, 10, 11, 13, 16, 17 and 18, the method referred to shall be:

(a) As reliable as appropriate for the fulfilment of the function for which the method is being used, in the light of all relevant circumstances, which may include:

(i) Any operational rules relevant to the assessment of reliability;
(ii) The assurance of data integrity;
(iii) The ability to prevent unauthorized access to and use of the system;
(iv) The security of hardware and software;
(v) The regularity and extent of audit by an independent body;
(vi) The existence of a declaration by a supervisory body, an accreditation body or a voluntary scheme regarding the reliability of the method;
(vii) Any applicable industry standard; or

(b) Proven in fact to have fulfilled the function by itself or together with further evidence.

The reference to the use of reliable methods is common in UNCITRAL texts and is key to defining the notion of reliability. Reliability results ultimately in legal predictability: business operators need to be reassured that commercial transactions will have the intended legal effect and that the chances that the transactions may later be invalidated because of the use of an unreliable method are minimal. For this reason, the reliability assessment of an electronic transferable records management system is critical for its success.

However, business may also have an interest in maintaining flexibility in the choice of methods, systems and technologies, which is upheld through the principle of technology neutrality. Predictability and flexibility are two sides of the same coin: both are needed to ensure success of trade. In finding a careful balance between these two goals, it is important to consider international consequences, as too strict reliability standards may result in barriers to the recognition of foreign electronic transferable records. This debate is similar to that held on the use of reliable trust services and, before that, on the use of reliable electronic signatures.

Predictability and flexibility are reflected, respectively, in the ex ante (ie before use), and ex post (ie after use), approach to the assessment of reliability. Since UNCITRAL texts typically refer to the use of a reliable method as a condition to achieve functional equivalence, the distinction is relevant for the implementation of those texts. The decision to use ex ante, ex post or combined approaches is a policy choice that has significant implications for promoting the use of electronic communications. UNCITRAL texts have adopted either the ex post approach (MLEC, ECC, MLETR) or a combination of ex ante and ex post approaches (MLES, MLIT). Relying on the ex ante approach alone is discouraged as it may lead to violating technology neutrality and to introducing barriers to the use of electronic means.

The ex ante assessment presupposes the existence of an evaluation mechanism based on predefined standards. The designation of reliability is carried out with reference to methods used in a specific service, as a provider may use the same management system to deliver multiple services offering different levels of reliability. A governmental entity or a delegated authority carries out the evaluation. It may be possible to accommodate private arrangements (such as the use of voluntary accreditation schemes) and to implement forms of co-regulation or self-regulation. The result of the evaluation is the declaration of compliance with the predefined standards, to which certain legal consequences are attached. For instance, satisfaction of the conditions contained in the MLES, art 6, para 3, and art 7 attributes a rebuttable presumption of reliability to the electronic signature. Other laws may give an absolute presumption of reliability. The services designated as compliant with the predetermined standards are advertised in public lists.

The main advantage of the ex ante approach is legal predictability and certainty on the effects of the use of a designated method. That approach may be combined with a licensing requirement for service providers to further increase oversight. However, the ex ante approach may be costly, especially in the case of low value, high volume transactions. Over-reliance on ex ante designation may violate technology neutrality, create data silos, and ultimately hinder digital uptake, especially in smaller economies. Moreover, giving legal recognition exclusively to designated services may curb competition and violate the principle of technology neutrality.

The ex post assessment of reliability requires carrying out the evaluation only in case of dispute, ie after the method is used. The law may provide a list of non-exhaustive circumstances relevant for the evaluation. This is the case of the MLETR, art 12. Any contractual agreement may also play a significant role in the evaluation. The ex post assessment gives maximum choice of methods and technologies to the parties, allowing optimal allocation of resources. On the other hand, it may affect legal predictability and certainty as the determination operates retroactively so that, if the method is considered unreliable, the electronic transaction is considered invalid.

The two approaches may be combined in the so-called 'two-tier approach', according to which all methods that comply with the basic requirements for functional equivalence may be legally recognised, and those methods complying with additional requirements enjoy a rebuttable presumption. This mechanism may be found in the MLES, art 3 and art 6, paras 1 and 3, as well as in the MLIT.

Moreover, recent UNCITRAL texts contain a clause that prevents challenging the reliability of a method when the method has in fact fulfilled its function. This safety clause may be found in the MLETR, art 12(b).

The presence or absence of explicit guidance on reliability standards may reflect the prevalence of a civil law view, keen on a higher level of predictability, or of a common law view, careful to preserve a high degree of flexibility. The inclusion of a detailed general reliability standard is a major feature of the MLETR. The provision of guidance on the circumstances relevant to determine the reliability of a method is useful to build confidence in the legal effects of the management system that uses that method. A similar general standard was included in the

MLES, art 10, on trustworthiness of systems, procedures and human resources, but is not found in other UNCITRAL texts on electronic commerce, which generally refer to a standard 'as reliable as appropriate for the purpose [...] in the light of all the circumstances, including any relevant agreement' (ECC, art 9, para 3(b)(i)). It is generally understood that circumstances such as the value and frequency of the transaction, any custom or practice applicable to the specific field of trade or between the parties, the sophistication of the parties etc, will be relevant in determining whether the method used is reliable. It is critical to ensure that uniform parameters for assessment of reliability of the methods are used across documents, applications, systems and jurisdictions to promote legal recognition and technical interoperability.

Another manner to address reliability is to provide a detailed and binding technical description of acceptable systems, methods and procedures. This would likely lead to mandating the use of a limited number of products, which is an outcome that violates the principle of technology neutrality and, possibly, competition law, and hinders market uptake of future developments.

The reliability standard in UNCITRAL texts is generally understood as being relative, and not absolute, and this applies also to the notion of reliability in the MLETR. 'Relative' means that reliability should be measured against the concrete features of the relevant transaction (value, frequency, qualification of the parties, etc) and not in abstract against a theoretical framework. In practice, it may be easier to have a flexible and relative approach to the determination of the reliability of the method when carrying out an ex post determination than when carrying out an ex ante one, given that ex ante determinations may take into account only a limited number of variables such as the value of the transaction.

The MLETR, art 12 indicates two ways in which the reliability of the method used can be determined: (a) through a list of circumstances relevant for the ex post assessment; and (b) through a safety clause. This approach favours flexibility but does not provide guidance on which methods may be considered reliable before their use. To provide that additional guidance, two solutions can be considered: (a) the agreement of the parties; and (b) an ex ante mechanism to identify reliable methods, services and systems.

If a mechanism for ex ante assessment of electronic transferable records management services is not available, it may be possible to rely on presumptions attached to the trust services used in the management system that are presumed reliable under a similar assessment mechanism. Where available, trust services that enjoy the presumption of reliability, such as qualified services under the eIDAS Regulation,[94] may be reliable methods for electronic transferable records management. This is because notions such as control and integrity need to be

[94] Regulation (EU) No 910/2014 of the European Parliament and of the Council of 23 July 2014 on electronic identification and trust services for electronic transactions in the internal market and repealing Directive 1999/93/EC [2014] OJ L257/73 (eIDAS). Like other European Union Regulations, eIDAS is in force in all European Union Member States without need for transposition in national law.

implemented through technical solutions that rely on the use of trust services. For instance, transfer of control may be recorded with an electronic registered delivery service, and higher assurance of integrity may be achieved with electronic signatures that utilise public-key infrastructure and with blockchain technology.

The use of a reliable method is a requirement for achieving functional equivalence. Hence, the consequence of not using a reliable method is the invalidity of the electronic transferable record as it cannot be considered functionally equivalent to a transferable document or instrument. The electronic transferable records management system operator may be held liable for using an unreliable method; however, often the terms and conditions of use of the system limit the liability of its operator to the fullest extent possible. Between the parties, the agreement to use a certain system may be considered evidence of its assessment as reliable, at least implicitly. In such case, the parties dealing with the invalid electronic transferable record may not have recourse against each other for damages arising from the unreliability of the method used. On the other hand, those parties may take any substantive law action available when a transferable document or instrument is found invalid.

Reliability requirements may differ depending on the type of document and on the features of a transaction. By combining ex ante and ex post approaches, commercial operators may benefit from flexibility and predictability at the appropriate cost. Rulebooks and other agreements on terms and conditions of the service remain relevant to assess reliability and, ultimately, allocate liability between service provider, person in control, and other concerned parties.

The List of Relevant Circumstances

The MLETR, art 12(a) offers a list of circumstances that may be used in the ex post assessment of reliability. This list has become the object of significant scrutiny by commercial operators who have two seemingly conflicting goals: on the one hand, they do not want to be bound by technical prescriptions that may impose additional costs and stifle innovation; on the other hand, they wish to have clarity on the reliability of the methods used in the management system to avoid legal uncertainty.

The list contained in art 12(a) is neither exhaustive nor mandatory: additional circumstances may be taken into account, and the judge or the arbitrator are not bound by any item in the list. The circumstances listed in art 12(a) may be classified in broad categories.

The reference to 'operational rules relevant to the assessment of reliability' contained in art 12(a)(i) relates to those rules that are relevant for reliability (as opposed to all operational rules) and may include contractual agreements but also rules set by a regulatory body that are incorporated in the agreements. These rules may be relevant because in themselves they provide evidence of the use of reliable methods or because, if the operator has not complied with them, the system and its methods may be considered unreliable.

If blockchain technology is used, reference may be made to satisfying consensus mechanisms such as 'proof of work' (based on computational power) and 'proof of stake' (based on acceptance by a sufficient number of participants).

The references to 'the regularity and extent of audit by an independent body' (art 12(a)(v)) and 'the existence of a declaration by a supervisory body, an accreditation body or a voluntary scheme regarding the reliability of the method' (art 12(a)(vi)) relate to assessments, declarations or other guidance provided by third parties based on criteria of general application. The neutral source of such declarations makes them particularly trustworthy. Such references also indicate that the MLETR is compatible with the adoption of ex ante mechanisms for assessing reliability. Article 12(a)(iv), (v) and (vi) is inspired by similar provisions contained in the MLES, art 10.

The references to 'the assurance of data integrity' (art 12(a)(ii)), 'the ability to prevent unauthorized access to and use of the system' (art 12(a)(iii)) and 'the security of hardware and software' (art 12(a)(iv)) refer to technical features of the system. The ability to prevent unauthorised access to and use of the system is a condition to establish exclusivity of control of electronic transferable records according to the MLETR, art 10(1)(b)(iii). On the other hand, the reference to 'assurance of data integrity' applies to all instances when a reliable method is used, and is not limited to control.

Last, but not least, art 12(a)(vii) refers to 'any applicable industry standard'. The commentary specifies that such standards are preferably international,[95] and this should ensure cross-border recognition and interoperability of electronic transferable records. The same commentary foresees that 'the use of international standards may promote the emergence of a common notion of reliability across jurisdictions', which is becoming true thanks also to the efforts of the private sector (see at the end of this section). However, the reference to industry standards shall not be interpreted in a manner that may violate the principle of technology neutrality or affect competition.

Third-Party Reliability Assessment

Third-party reliability assessment of an electronic transferable record management service may have a significant impact on the acceptance of that service by business. An illustration is provided by the role of the International Group (IG) of the Protection and Indemnity (P&I) Clubs in approving electronic bills of lading management systems and services. National P&I Clubs provide to their members liability coverage for maritime-related risks, such as cargo loss and damage. They adhere to the IG P&I Clubs. Approval of a form of bill of lading by the IG P&I Clubs is generally needed to provide cargo insurance coverage.

[95] Explanatory Note, para 135.

Moreover, P&I Clubs cover liabilities arising in respect of the carriage of cargo only if the electronic bills of lading management service used is approved by the IG P&I Clubs prior to the issuance of the bill of lading. This requires an evaluation of the reliability of the method used. Because of the frequent choice of English law in bills of lading, IG P&I Clubs approved systems must comply with the requirements of the ETDA 2023.[96] This entails the incorporation of a reference to that Act in the rulebooks of the service providers. The IG P&I Clubs have over time approved several electronic management systems (called 'paperless trading systems'), many of which consider themselves MLETR-compliant. Insurance coverage does not extend to liabilities arising from the use of the electronic system as it is limited to liabilities that would have also arisen with the use of paper-based bills of lading.

The increasing uptake of electronic bills of lading by the maritime sector has led IG P&I Clubs to change requirements and the process for approving management systems as of February 2025. Electronic transferable records management systems are deemed reliable if: (a) they only manage electronic bills of lading that are subject to a governing law which gives legal recognition to them as equivalent to paper bills of lading (such as MLETR, ETDA 2023 and UCC Article 7); and (b) are 'evidenced as' reliable. Reliability should be evidenced by 'an audit by an independent body; or a declaration by a supervisory, regulatory or accreditation body or applicable voluntary scheme; or applicable industry standards'. Alternatively, it is possible to seek individual approval of systems that are not deemed reliable and which meet several conditions.[97] The IG P&I Clubs maintain on their website a public list of systems that are deemed reliable and of systems that are otherwise considered reliable, including those approved before the change in policy.

In the banking sector, a similar role may be played by the audits and assessments carried out by third parties in the ordinary course of business. Moreover, electronic transferable records management system operators support the adoption of voluntary standards that provide additional guidance. Thus, voluntary and third-party assessments may play a significant role in determining the reliability of the methods used. However, the effectiveness of such assessments may be limited in those jurisdictions that require the use of particular trust services or attach legal consequences to the use of those trust services (such as the use of advanced and qualified trust services in the European Union).

The Agreement of the Parties

The MLETR, art 12(a) does not list the agreement of the parties as a relevant circumstance. A suggestion to include this item was not accepted due to the concern

[96] Electronic Trade Documents Act 2023, c 38.

[97] For more details, see 'International Group Requirements for Electronic Trading System Providers' and 'International Group Approvals: Process for E-bill System Providers' on the IG P&I website www.igpandi.org.

that parties could elude contractually the application of any mandatory rule.[98] This concern reflects the tension underlying UNCITRAL texts between regulation and party autonomy, with continental European countries and other civil law jurisdictions more supportive of the former, and the US and other common law jurisdictions of the latter.

Insofar as reliability requirements are not mandatory, the agreement of the parties on the use of procedures, technologies and products may play a prominent role in assessing reliability. This could be done, for example, by subscribing to a rulebook or by otherwise accepting the terms and conditions of use of the electronic transferable records management system.

The agreement of the parties may also be inferred otherwise. For instance, in *Claremont 24-7 Pty Ltd v Invox Pty Ltd (No 2)*,[99] the judge found that the practice of exchanging emails established between the parties was evidence that the parties had consented to the use of email as a method to meet the signature requirement, ie as a reliable signature method.[100]

Reliability Assessment: Options in MLETR Implementation

Like other UNCITRAL texts on electronic commerce, the MLETR does not provide guidance on the technical aspects of reliability. This is done to preserve the technology neutral approach and to respect the mandate of UNCITRAL, which does not cover technical matters. On the other hand, the efforts of the private sector in identifying reliable standards for MLETR implementation are meaningful and ongoing.

The increasing adoption of the MLETR has raised significant practical interest in defining a 'reliable method' and, more generally, a 'reliable electronic transferable records management system'. One business view is that established service providers should be able to prove without excessive hurdles the reliability of the methods used in delivering their services. In short, the MLETR does not raise the reliability bar compared to what the industry considered reliable before its introduction.[101] That view complements the opinion that the MLETR, art 12 provides a general standard for the assessment of the reliability ex post that is not meant to be higher or more difficult to prove than that of a commercially viable electronic transferable records management system.

At an early stage, service providers (or their clients) may prepare legal and technical reports to illustrate how their services utilise reliable methods. However, reliability self-assessment based on company-specific technical standards alone may not suffice. Widely accepted standards should be made available to avoid

[98] Explanatory Note, paras 138–139.

[99] Supreme Court of Western Australia, No CIV 1108 of 2015, [2015] WASC 220, CLOUT case 1832.

[100] See below in this section for more details of this case.

[101] Global Trade Review, 'Industry Perspectives: Reliable Systems – Are They Really Something New?' (10 January 2024) www.gtreview.com.

national and regional fragmentation. It seems preferable to leave to the private sector the development of these technical standards, which may be used in self-regulatory mechanisms or, when government authorities wish to be involved, co-regulatory mechanisms. The International Chamber of Commerce (ICC) Digital Standards Initiative (DSI) is working on the definition of such standards (see below in this section).

However, the use of reliable methods, and, more generally, of trustworthy management systems does not address all issues of trust per se. Trade involves many actors and includes offline procedures. Trust is built by managing risk in each stage of the commercial transaction. In other words, 'a system is just one cog in the reliability chain': reliable business processes require quality assurance from all participants and in all components. This is not possible in the paper-based environment, which makes supply chains fragile and unreliable. The digital trade ecosystem allows cross-verification of information and proactive monitoring, which may result in more efficiency, higher compliance, and reduced costs.

Thus, the use of a reliable method in managing electronic transferable records should be seen in the broader framework of resilient supply chain management. Integrated management of information contained in different electronic commercial documents – or even establishing a single authoritative source of information for all those documents – may give a much higher assurance of reliability than paper-based practices. Business operators should consider advantages arising from a comprehensive and holistic digital supply chain management, of which a reliable electronic transferable records management system is one important component.

To further increase legal predictability, several jurisdictions (for example, Bahrain, Singapore) have enacted the MLETR under the 'two-tier' approach. In those cases, an entity is tasked with assessing that the services meet pre-determined standards and are therefore presumed reliable. The 'two-tier' approach is fully compatible with the MLETR. Moreover, this is the preferred approach in jurisdictions where legislation on trust services following the 'two-tier' approach is in force.

Each service provider may offer multiple services of varying quality. Hence, the object of the accreditation is the service that uses reliable methods, and not the service provider, which is the entity that applies for accreditation and manages it. Moreover, an electronic transferable record management system may manage multiple documents. Depending on legal requirements and business solutions, some or all, of the services provided (and, consequently, the documents handled) in the management system may be considered reliable. This determination must be carried out in each concrete case.

The introduction of a licensing system for electronic transferable records management system operators may at a first glance be seen as prudent as it allows vetting the reliability of their services. However, this approach may restrict competition, which could result in additional costs for users. Moreover, it may create barriers to cross-border exchanges, as foreign operators may not be able, or have sufficient market demand, to apply for a local licence. Finally, and importantly, this mechanism relies on the existence of technical standards for the assessment of reliability, which are under development: absent those standards, the licensing mechanism may not operate, which in fact prevents the use of electronic transferable records.

The MLETR does not provide explicit guidance on the circumstances relevant for listing services presumed reliable. UNCITRAL Working Group IV considered provisions on the obligations of electronic transferable records management system operators, on the criteria for their accreditation, and on their liability.[102] Those provisions were largely inspired by corresponding provisions in the MLES. While the provisions were eventually deleted in favour of a minimalist approach relying exclusively on the ex post assessment, they may provide guidance to jurisdictions interested in implementing a two-tier approach.

Additional obligations of the operators may arise from other law, such as contract law or extra-contractual liability law, and contractual agreements. Regarding contractual obligations, operators should:

(a) act in accordance with representations made with respect to policies and practices;
(b) exercise reasonable care to ensure the accuracy and completeness of all material representations that are relevant to the lifecycle of an electronic transferable record;
(c) provide reasonably accessible means to ascertain any limitation on the purpose or value for which the electronic transferable record may be used;
(d) utilise trustworthy systems, procedures and human resources in performing their services.

Those obligations, which are explicitly mentioned in the MLIT, arts 6 and 14, may also be relevant for the determination of reliability of electronic transferable records management systems that use trust services compliant with the MLIT.

Development of Technical Standards

Comprehensive digital transformation calls for significant work on improving policies, innovating technology and business processes, and reforming the law. This broader perspective needs to be kept in mind when implementing the MLETR: the adoption of the Model Law is a fundamental step but does not suffice alone to achieve the intended goals if not supported by other conditions, including the private sector's buy in.[103]

[102] UNCITRAL, 'Draft Provisions on Electronic Transferable Records' (4 March 2013) UN Doc A/CN.9/WG.IV/WP.122, arts 31–33.

[103] See ch 1, section 1.2.

The development of widely adopted technical standards for assessing the reliability of the methods used in managing electronic transferable records is of great importance to ensure the broad acceptance and sustainable use of those records. These standards are needed for both ex ante and ex post assessments. One approach to developing such standards relies on the existence of a dedicated national or regional mechanism. Progressive regional harmonisation may in turn foster development of global standards.

Technical standards should facilitate interoperability of both documents and data. This requires the ability to not only transfer data from one application to another, but also to maintain the data structure, so that data exchanges will be meaningful. Some technical standards relevant for MLETR implementation predate the Model Law.[104] Other technical standards are being developed to cater specifically to MLETR needs.[105]

One set of existing standards pertains to the quality of trust services used for managing electronic transferable records. The outcome of the application of a trust service designated as reliable – to use the terminology of the MLIT, art 23 – is associated with significant legal presumptions. For example, the use of a reliable electronic signature for the endorsement of a bill of lading will allow subsequent holders and related parties to presume that the identification of the endorser and the expression of its intention to endorse have been carried out with reliable methods. This presumption could apply across borders if appropriate mechanisms for the recognition of the effects of trust services are in place.

The identification of existing technical standards and the development of new ones is an important part of the mission of the ICC DSI initiative.[106] ICC DSI and the World Trade Organization (WTO) have compiled a comprehensive list of technical standards relevant for cross-border paperless trade.[107] Subsequently, ICC DSI prepared a publication on the data elements of seven fundamental commercial documents,[108] which was eventually expanded[109] to cover

[104] Eg, standards ISO 19626-1:2020, Processes, data elements and documents in commerce, industry and administration – Trusted communication platforms for electronic documents – Part 1: Fundamentals; and ISO 19626-2:2021, Processes, data elements and documents in commerce, industry and administration – Trusted communication platform for electronic documents – Part 2: Applications, reference explicitly UNCITRAL texts (albeit not the MLETR).

[105] ISO/WD 5909, Data interchange processes of blockchain based negotiable maritime bill of lading related to e-Commerce platform (under development).

[106] The ICC DSI maintains a website at www.dsi.iccwbo.org.

[107] WTO and ICC DSI, *Standards Toolkit for Cross-border Paperless Trade* (Paris, ICC, 2022). The standards listed include: foundational standards and identifier standards; standards for commercial transactions; transport and logistics standards; standards for official control documents, and interoperable digitalisation frameworks that support the exchange of electronic trade documents.

[108] ICC DSI, 'Key Trade Documents and Data Elements: Digital Standards Analysis and Recommendations' (2024). The seven documents are: warehouse receipts; certificates of origin; commercial invoices; packing lists; bills of lading; customs or goods declarations; and insurance certificates.

[109] ICC DSI, 'Key Trade Documents and Data Elements: Digital Standards Analysis and Recommendations – An Integrated Framework for Digitalising the Entire Supply Chain' (2024).

all 36 documents featured in the Cross-border Paperless Trade Toolkit.[110] After having mapped existing standards, ICC DSI prepared a digital trade reliability assessment tool.[111] The tool provides a template for self-assessment of reliability of the services offered and aims at building confidence in the satisfaction of the standard set in the MLETR, art 12 and in the use of electronic transferable records. The tool was prepared in partnership with the Digital Governance Council of Canada and with the involvement of service providers.

The Digital Container Standard Association (DCSA) promotes the development and adoption of technical standards for bills of lading and other commercial documents. DCSA membership includes nine of the top 10 ocean carriers in the world, representing approximately 70 per cent of global container trade. DCSA standards are open source, free to use, technology neutral and vendor agnostic. For example, DCSA has developed data and process standards for the submission of shipping instructions and the issuance of bills of lading,[112] and the track and trace standards, which aim to enable seamless communication between carriers and other supply chain participants.

DCSA standards contribute to achieving the pledge of the DCSA member carriers to issue 50 per cent of their bills of lading electronically by 2028, and 100 per cent by 2030. To pursue this goal, ICC DSI, DCSA and other partners have tasked the Future International Trade (FIT) Alliance with accelerating the adoption of electronic bills of lading across all sectors of the shipping industry based on common standards.

Another relevant private sector initiative is the Global Shipping Business Network (GSBN), a not-for-profit consortium including shipping lines, terminal operators, banks, application developers and other stakeholders. GSBN is actively promoting the use of blockchain technology for electronic bills of lading, including through tokenisation.[113]

Finally, the United Nations Centre for Trade Facilitation and Electronic Business (UN/CEFACT)[114] formulates technical standards and prepares guidance documents on paperless trade facilitation and other trade-related matters. A UN/CEFACT project aims at developing the semantic foundation to support MLETR implementation in trade finance in the broader context of the digital and green transformation for sustainable development and, more specifically, of trade documents digitisation.[115] In practice, this project identifies the entities involved

[110] WTO, United Nations Economic and Social Commission for Asia and the Pacific and UNCITRAL, *Cross-border Paperless Trade Toolkit* (Geneva, WTO, 2022).

[111] The tool is available at github.com/dgc-cgn/CAS-Digital-Trade-Documentation.

[112] The standards may be found at dcsa.org.

[113] See, eg, the work carried out with the Hong Kong Monetary Authority and other stakeholders on tokenisation of electronic bills of lading for trade finance in the framework of Project Ensemble.

[114] UN/CEFACT is a subsidiary intergovernmental body of the UN Economic Commission for Europe Committee on Trade.

[115] UN/CEFACT, *Buy/Ship/Pay Data Exchange Structures for Trade Finance Facilitation* (Geneva, United Nations, 2024).

in MLETR-based transactions and defines their roles, so that data models will be based on a common semantic. Uniformity in data models is necessary to enable data exchange and interoperability.

UN/CEFACT, upon proposal of Singapore, also prepared a white paper that offers guidance on the practical implementation of the MLETR, focusing on requirements of management systems for electronic bills of lading that use blockchain technology.[116]

The Safety Clause

The safety clause contained in the MLETR, art 12(b) reproduces the one contained in the ECC, article 9, para 3(b)(ii). The purpose of the safety clause is to prevent repudiation of a method that, albeit in theory unreliable, has achieved its function. Specifically, this clause allows joint consideration of the result of the application of the method and of other evidence, which may also relate to the use of non-electronic means. Without this provision, the ex post reliability test could lead to the undesirable result of invalidating an otherwise valid record (or communication, in the case of the ECC) on the grounds alone that in theory the method used was not as reliable as appropriate, and this may lead to exempting one party from its contractual obligations. The safety clause test may be referred to as 'reliability in practice', while the one in art 12(a) may be referred to as 'reliability in theory'.[117]

Case law indicates that this provision is effective in buttressing the evidential value of electronic transactions and in curbing frivolous litigation. This typically happens for transactions regarding assets whose disposal requires complying with form requirements, such as real estate, and where the intention of the party is clear because of the use of multiple communication channels, electronic and not. In *SM Integrated Transware Pte Ltd v Schenker Singapore (Pte) Ltd*,[118] one party asked to invalidate a contract concluded by an exchange of emails after a negotiation conducted by email, telephone and in person, on the basis that the emails did not meet the form required by Singaporean land lease legislation, including the signature of the person against whom the contract is to be enforced. The emails were not signed and did not contain the name of the author typed in the message body. The judge deemed that the signature requirement had been satisfied by the presence of the header indicating the author of the emails in the field '[From: sender's name]', which was sufficient to identify the author of the message together with other factors.

[116] UN/CEFACT, *Transfer of MLETR-Compliant Titles* (Geneva, United Nations, 2023).

[117] With reference to the ECC, see KW Chong and JS Chao, 'United Nations Convention on the Use of Electronic Communications in International Contracts: A New Global Standard' (2006) 18 *Singapore Academy of Law Journal* 116, 130, note 2.

[118] Singapore High Court, Suit No 594 of 2003, [2005] SGHC 58, CLOUT case 661.

Similarly, in *Claremont 24-7 Pty Ltd v Invox Pty Ltd (No 2)*, the parties had negotiated a lease of commercial premises exchanging several communications in oral, written and electronic form, including an offer to lease and a reply, sent by email, stating that the terms in the offer were 'acceptable to both parties'. However, before the court one party argued, among other things, that the lease agreement was unenforceable because it did not comply with the signature requirement set in the Statute of Frauds. The judge found that the relevant law required that the lease agreement be signed, and that the signature block in the email under the word 'sincerely' identified the party and indicated its intention in respect of the information communicated, thus meeting the requirements for functional equivalence between handwritten and electronic signatures. Moreover, the judge declared to be satisfied that the method used to sign was as reliable as appropriate for the purpose for which the email was communicated in light of all the circumstances, which included the parties' decision to communicate by email.

Likewise, in *Stellard Pty Ltd and Anor v North Queensland Fuel Pty Ltd*,[119] the Court explained that, although in an acceptance e-mail there was no identification of any person as the acceptor of the earlier offer, the identification of that person and of its intention could be established by further evidence, namely: various conversations; the offer e-mail; and the admission in the pleadings as to the originator of the e-mail that contained the acceptance of the offer. The Court recalled that under Australian law two methods to prove reliability (corresponding to those in the MLETR, art 12(a) and (b)) were available and concluded that the second method had been established.

To sum up, the safety clause is useful in countering frivolous litigation when the facts of the case and the intention of the parties may be clearly established. This is part of a widespread judicial trend that mitigates strict technological and form requirements in certain circumstances.

Article 13. Indication of time and place in electronic transferable records

Where the law requires or permits the indication of time or place with respect to a transferable document or instrument, that requirement is met if a reliable method is used to indicate that time or place with respect to an electronic transferable record.

Indicating time and place plays an important role in the substantive law of transferable documents and instruments. For instance, it is rather common for the law to require an indication of the date and place of issuance of the document or instrument, whose accuracy may also be relevant for trade financing.[120] Moreover, the accurate recording of the time of an endorsement may be critical to determine the correct sequence of the obligors in an action in recourse. In such cases, a time-stamping trust service may provide assurance of the relevant information.

[119] Supreme Court of Queensland, File No 11998 of 2014, [2015] QSC 119, CLOUT case 1546.

[120] See, eg, the reference to the date of issuance of the bill of lading in art 20 of the Uniform Customs and Practice for Documentary Credits (UCP) 600.

The MLETR, art 13 requires the use of a reliable method to indicate time and place in an electronic transferable record. The MLIT, art 18 identifies two main functions of timestamp trust service: (a) to indicate the time and date, including by reference to the time zone; and (b) to associate that time and date with the data message.[121] The use of time-stamping trust services presumed reliable may facilitate meeting the condition set out in the MLETR, art 13.

The parties might be able to agree on a conventional time and place rather than indicating the actual one if substantive law allows them to do.[122] In those cases, the electronic transferable records management system shall record the intention of the relevant parties alongside metadata indicating when the intention was recorded.

An issue closely related to the indication of time is the possible automation of certain functions triggered by time such as presentation for payment. The flexibility of the MLETR with respect to contract automation facilitates the adoption of such solutions. Automation may also refer to a place determined by oracles, ie third-party services relying on software and physical devices to collect and share information from the real world such as location or temperature. For instance, an electronic bill of lading may contain a link to the global positioning system of the ship whereon the container containing the goods covered by the bill has been loaded. However, in that case the oracle may refer to the location of the goods and not of the document itself.

Indication of place in an electronic transferable record may not coincide with the place of business of any relevant party, in particular the person in control. The latter notion, which is factual, may be relevant for the application of mandatory law.

Article 14. Place of business

1. *A location is not a place of business merely because that is:*
   - (a) *Where equipment and technology supporting an information system used by a party in connection with electronic transferable records are located; or*
   - (b) *Where the information system may be accessed by other parties.*

[121] See ch 7.

[122] For a discussion of the place of issuance of a bill of lading, see *Poralu Marine Australia Pty Ltd v MV Dijksgracht* [2023] FCAFC 147, at 77–80, upholding *Poralu Marine Australia Pty Ltd v MV Dijksgracht* [2022] FCA 1038, [2023] 2 Lloyd's Rep 18, explaining that the place of issuance of a bill of lading is where the document is stamped and signed; that the issuance of a bill of lading is a unilateral, not a bilateral act; and that the place of issuance of a bill of lading may be different from the place where the bill of lading is given to the shipper. With reference to electronic bills of lading, the judgment indicates that: 'Given that modern commerce is principally conducted by electronic communication in circumstances where the individuals concerned might, at any particular time, be just about anywhere, it would lead to intolerable uncertainty if the place of issue of a bill of lading depended on where a particular person was at any given time when they sent or received an email. In my view, the relevant document must be regarded as issued where it is stated in it to have been issued, and in the absence of such a statement then where it was in fact signed or authenticated.'. The judgment also notes that parties involved subsequently in the bill of lading need to rely on the place of issuance indicated in the bill of lading to promote legal certainty.

2. *The sole fact that a party makes use of an electronic address or other element of an information system connected to a specific country does not create a presumption that its place of business is located in that country.*

Commercial law usually provides general rules on the determination of the place of business, which may be different for physical and legal persons. Specific rules for transferable documents and instruments may also exist.

The MLETR, art 14, which is inspired by the ECC, art 6, paras 4 and 5,[123] indicates that certain circumstances related to the use of electronic transferable records management systems such as location of equipment and technology do not, per se, create presumptions relevant to determine the place of business. This is because the place of business in international trade law is generally a physical place from where trading activities are carried out. Moreover, modern technology (such as cloud computing and distributed ledgers) has no link with a fixed physical location.

The elements listed in the MLETR, art 14 may nevertheless be taken into consideration, often with other circumstances, in determining the place of business. In any case, prominence in determining the place of business should be given to the criteria set in substantive law.

Electronic transactions laws that incorporate the substantive provisions of the ECC often contain these rules. In that case, the MLETR, art 14 does not need to be enacted and the application of the existing provisions may be extended to electronic transferable records.

Article 15. Endorsement

Where the law requires or permits the endorsement in any form of a transferable document or instrument, that requirement is met with respect to an electronic transferable record if the information required for the endorsement is included in the electronic transferable record and that information is compliant with the requirements set forth in articles 8 and 9.

Delivery of the document with or without endorsement are the two modes of transfer of a transferable document or instrument. Transfer of control over an electronic transferable record, which is functionally equivalent to delivery of a transferable document or instrument, is dealt with in the MLETR, art 11, para 2. The MLETR, art 15 establishes the requirements for endorsing an electronic transferable record.

The endorsement of a transferable document or instrument is effected by indicating in writing the intention to endorse, together with any additional instruction, and signing the document. Hence, the MLETR, art 15 establishes that an electronic transferable record may be endorsed by complying with the requirements set out in the MLETR, arts 8 and 9, respectively on functional equivalence with writing and signatures. Prescriptions specific to the use of the paper medium, such

[123] See Explanatory Note to ECC, paras 116–121.

as an obligation to endorse on the back of the document, do not apply to electronic transferable records.[124]

The MLETR, art 15 deals only with form requirements of the endorsement: any instruction admissible in a paper-based document or instrument may be reproduced in an electronic transferable record, and any instruction not admissible on paper is also forbidden electronically.

> ***Article 16. Amendment***
>
> *Where the law requires or permits the amendment of a transferable document or instrument, that requirement is met with respect to an electronic transferable record if a reliable method is used for amendment of information in the electronic transferable record so that the amended information is identified as such.*

The lifecycle of a transferable document or instrument typically foresees recording on paper several events from issuance to presentation for performance. Similarly, such events should be recorded electronically as required by the MLETR, art 10, para 1(b)(iii). In practice, the electronic transferable records management system should not only record any amendment, but also identify who performed the amendment and record its date and time.

The MLETR, art 16 adds to the integrity requirement by demanding that all amendments be identified as such. Humans should be able to recognise the amended information directly or by using software. The purpose of this provision is to ensure that the person in control – or the person considering taking control – is aware of all events that may affect the obligation incorporated in the record.

Substantive law determines which party may amend the record, which parties should consent to the amendment, and which parties should be informed of it. The MLETR, art 16 does not apply to amendments of a purely technical nature that entail no legal consequence.

> ***Article 17. Replacement of a transferable document or instrument with an electronic transferable record***
>
> 1. *An electronic transferable record may replace a transferable document or instrument if a reliable method for the change of medium is used.*
> 2. *For the change of medium to take effect, a statement indicating a change of medium shall be inserted in the electronic transferable record.*
> 3. *Upon issuance of the electronic transferable record in accordance with paragraphs 1 and 2, the transferable document or instrument shall be made inoperative and ceases to have any effect or validity.*
> 4. *A change of medium in accordance with paragraphs 1 and 2 shall not affect the rights and obligations of the parties.*

[124] Electronic transferable records service providers may however decide to reproduce the layout of paper-based documents and instruments for easier human readability.

The legal treatment of the change of medium from electronic to paper and vice versa is a matter that has attracted interest. The ability to change medium is perceived as important to promote uptake of electronic documents, given that, in case of need, a clear path to revert to the paper-based document is available. The provisions on change of medium generally aim to prevent the circulation of two documents issued on a different medium related to the same obligation. Three steps are needed to achieve that goal: (a) preserving all information contained in the replaced document; (b) ensuring that the replaced document may not further circulate; and (c) transcribing the relevant information in the replacing document.

Thus, the Rotterdam Rules contain only three articles specifically dealing with electronic transport records, but one of them (art 10) deals with a change of medium. The conditions set out in that article are that: the holder shall surrender the document, or the record; the carrier shall issue a replacing document or record that includes a statement about the change of medium; and the replaced document or record shall cease to have any effect or validity. Some of these elements were transposed in the MLETR, arts 17 and 18.

However, certain assumptions on a change of medium have changed due to the progress in implementing electronic transferable records. It is now clear that, while the law should normally have provisions for change of medium both from paper to electronic and from electronic to paper,[125] the most relevant instance in business practice is the change from electronic to paper because one stakeholder is not willing or able to accept an electronic transferable record. That stakeholder may not be a person in control: for instance, a customs authority may require the paper-based original of a bill of lading. Moreover, double-spending remains a significant issue, but the management of multiple originals may be easier when the originals are in electronic form, as the system may be programmed to demand presentation of all originals in compliance with legal and contractual requirements.

The MLETR, art 17 requires the use of a reliable method to replace a transferable document or instrument with an electronic transferable record. The reliable method may be part of a procedure for impeding further circulation of the transferable document or instrument and storing it. While the MLETR does not require an annotation on the replaced document or instrument, this annotation may be useful. Substantive law identifies the parties that are entitled to request the change of medium and those parties who need to consent to it.

The replacing electronic transferable record should contain an annotation that a change of medium took effect. Upon issuance of the electronic transferable record, the transferable document or instrument may no longer circulate

[125] But see art 10 of the Ley N° 10069, Ley sobre letra de cambio y pagaré electrónicos, de 9 de noviembre de 2021, of Costa Rica, indicating that a promissory note or bill of exchange issued in or converted to the electronic form may not be replaced by a paper-based document.

and ceases to have any effect or validity. However, the statement on the replaced document ceasing to have effect should be qualified. The replaced document will continue to have effect with regard to the information it contains, including information unrelated to the transferable nature of the document or instrument: for example, a bill of lading contains the proof of the contract for carriage of goods and the evidence of the receipt of the goods. It is desirable to reproduce all the information contained in a transferable document and instrument in the electronic transferable record for ease of reference and to prevent issues with subsequent holders. Moreover, the information contained in the replacing record may provide critical evidence if the replaced document is inadvertently destroyed or lost. When the conversion is from paper to electronic medium, inclusion of all information should be technically and commercially feasible.

It should be stressed that the change of medium does not entail novation: the document is the same, as are the obligations reflected therein and any other legally relevant information recorded either on paper or with electronic means. For instance, the limitation period does not cease to run because of the change of medium. The legal continuity is clearly expressed in the MLETR, art 17, para 4, and the words 'ceases to have any effect or validity' contained in para 3 of that article must be interpreted as referring to the document on paper medium, as only the electronic transferable record may circulate after replacement. In short, the information contained in the replaced transferable document or instrument should be preserved for evidentiary purposes and has full effect as integrated with the subsequent events recorded in the electronic transferable record. The transferable document or instrument is one, but its information is contained in two different supports.

The consequences of such a rule must be mitigated when the information may affect subsequent holders of the document or instrument. Such information must be ascertainable from the replacing record.

In the view of UNCITRAL, failure to comply with the requirements for change of medium has the effect of rendering invalid both the replaced document and instrument, and the replacing record.[126] According to a different view, the failure to perform the change of medium does not prevent the creation of a new valid document.[127] While the latter solution may result in the circulation of two documents for the same obligation, it has the advantage of avoiding the opposite result of having no document at all, and it is in line with the least interventionist principle that underpins MLETR. Both arguments have merit, and to some extent the solution may depend on factual circumstances. A difference in legal traditions with respect to the issuance of documents of title, including the creation of new types, may also play a role.

[126] Explanatory Note, paras 169 and 178.

[127] Law Commission, *Electronic Trade Documents: Report and Bill* (Law Com No 405, 2022), paras 9.64–9.68.

Article 18. Replacement of an electronic transferable record with a transferable document or instrument

1. *A transferable document or instrument may replace an electronic transferable record if a reliable method for the change of medium is used.*
2. *For the change of medium to take effect, a statement indicating a change of medium shall be inserted in the transferable document or instrument.*
3. *Upon issuance of the transferable document or instrument in accordance with paragraphs 1 and 2, the electronic transferable record shall be made inoperative and ceases to have any effect or validity.*
4. *A change of medium in accordance with paragraphs 1 and 2 shall not affect the rights and obligations of the parties.*

The MLETR, art 18 mirrors the MLETR, art 17 for the reverse case of change of medium from electronic to paper-based. In general, the comments made with respect to the MLETR, art 17 also apply to the MLETR, art 18. It should however be noted that some information recorded in an electronic transferable record may not be reproduced on paper, or its reproduction may be impractical. The MLETR, art 6 refers to this information. Such information should be adequately preserved, for instance by using reliable electronic archiving services.[128] It is important that all information that may affect third parties be reproduced in the replacing document or instrument. Whether subsequent holders may, or are required to, access information stored only electronically is a matter that may depend also on facts and circumstances. In dealings among professionals, a note pointing at such need may be included on the document or instrument together with the annotation of the change of medium.

According to the MLIT, art 19, an electronic archiving trust service shall perform the following functions:

(a) make the information contained in the data message accessible so as to be usable for subsequent reference;
(b) indicate the time and date of archiving and associate that time and date with the data message;
(c) retain the data message in the format in which it was generated, sent or received, or in another format which can be demonstrated to detect any alteration to the data message after that time and date, apart from the addition of any endorsement and any change that arises in the normal course of communication, storage and display; and
(d) retain such information, if any, as enables the identification of the origin and destination of a data message and the time and date when it was sent or received.

These functions apply to all the information contained in an electronic transferable record.

[128] See also the considerations on long-term data preservation in UN/CEFACT, *Transfer of MLETR-Compliant Titles*, 18.

The information so preserved continues to have effect, as noted above, as the MLETR, art 18, para 3 refers only to further circulation of the replaced electronic transferable record.

One issue that the MLETR does not address is the possibility of issuing originals on mixed media. This may be useful when the parties to the transaction wish to use an electronic transferable record but need a paper-based original for specific purposes and intend to have two documents of title on different media circulating simultaneously. The Model Law does not affect either the use of multiple originals or the issuance of both a transferable document or instrument and an electronic transferable record where admissible under substantive law.[129] However, substantive law is likely to be silent on an issue that specifically involves electronic transferable records.[130] Judicial decisions may clarify the point.

3.2.4. Cross-border Recognition of Electronic Transferable Records

International recognition of electronic documents and data is critical for carrying out digital trade across borders. On the one hand, legal mechanisms are being set up to facilitate (for example, the MLIT) or regulate (for example, legislation on data privacy and data protection) dataflows, including commercial documents in electronic form. On the other hand, certain commercial documents are subject to well-settled private international law rules, and the general principle of non-interference with substantive law underlying UNCITRAL texts on electronic commerce, including the MLETR, demands that those rules should be preserved. It is therefore necessary to enable international recognition of both documents and data in electronic form. The mechanisms for cross-border assurance of data quality through the application of trust services will be discussed in the context of the MLIT.[131]

The consideration of international recognition of electronic transferable records is intertwined with that of the private international law rules applicable to transferable documents and instruments. A discussion of those aspects is starting, triggered also by the interest in enabling their use in electronic form.[132] It is however also necessary to bear in mind that electronic transferable records usually contain a choice of law clause because their management system requires

[129] Explanatory Note, para 191.

[130] However, the Explanatory Memorandum to the Dutch bill on electronic bills of lading (see ch 4, section 4.1.7) mentions the possibility of issuing multiple originals if there is a practical need to do so, akin to the practice for paper-based bills.

[131] See ch 8.

[132] B Geva and S Peari, *International Negotiable Instruments*; A Dickinson, 'Electronic Trade Documents and the Conflict of Laws in the United Kingdom' (2024) *Lloyd's Maritime and Commercial Law Quarterly* 56.

it. Relevant practical issues relate rather to the recognition and enforcement of the electronic transferable record abroad, especially if the recognising jurisdiction does not have legislation on electronic transferable records and if written form requirements are considered law of mandatory application ('ordre public').

At a general level, a first consideration pertains to the opposite views of private international law as an enabler of party autonomy, subject to limited exceptions, and of private international law as a tool to solve conflicts on the application of law between states.[133] The fundamental role that party autonomy plays in commercial law, which inspires the enabling nature of UNCITRAL texts, suggests support for the former view.

A second consideration regards the actual impact of enabling the choice of a law that explicitly recognises the use of electronic transferable records. The parties do not intend to circumvent the form requirement, but to take advantage of functional equivalence to carry out business according to modern practices and needs. This approach should therefore be seen with favour, as it brings benefits without disadvantages.[134]

A third consideration refers to existing private international law rules for negotiable instruments. These rules may contain references to paper-based notions. For instance, section 72 of the Bills of Exchange Act 1949 of Singapore refers to the law of the place of issue, acceptance, and indorsement as applicable law. Such references may be overcome if the parties agree on applicable law in the electronic transferable record or in the rulebook of the electronic transferable records management system. Alternatively, the transposition of certain notions in an electronic environment may be addressed with rules on the functional equivalence for paper-based notions, such as time and place of receipt, or with the use of trust services such as electronic delivery services.

Moreover, according to the Bills of Exchange Act 1949, s 72(1)(ii), 'where a bill, issued out of Singapore, conforms, as regards requisites in form, to the law of Singapore, it may, for the purpose of enforcing payment thereof, be treated as valid as between all persons who negotiate, hold or become parties to it in Singapore'.[135] This provision may facilitate legal recognition of MLETR-compliant electronic documents of title issued in jurisdictions that have not enacted the MLETR.

Addressing these issues may be an exercise carried out in the framework of the more general review of private international law applicable to negotiable instruments.[136]

[133] M Lehmann, 'Liberating the Individual from Battles between States: Justifying Party Autonomy in Conflict of Laws' (2008) 41 *Vanderbilt Journal of Transnational Law* 381.

[134] On the law governing the form of transferable instrument, see B Geva and S Peari, *International Negotiable Instruments*, 111–115, warning on the differences in form requirements between English law and uniform law.

[135] The provision reproduces the UK Bills of Exchange Act 1882, s 72(1)(b), and may be commonly found in the enactments of that Act.

[136] B Geva and S Peari, 'Which Law Applies to Negotiable Instruments?' *OUPblog* (4 July 2021) at blog.oup.com. The Hague Conference on Private International Law is carrying out work in this field under the work topic 'Law Applicable to Digital Tokens'.

The determination of the law applicable to cross-border recognition of electronic documents is a process that requires several steps. The first step is to characterise the document in light of the information contained therein as a specific type of transferable document or instrument. The second step is to identify the relevant private international law rules that apply to the document regardless of its medium. The third step is to verify whether existing private international law rules need adjustment due to the electronic nature of the document. For instance, the reference to the place of receipt of a contractual communication (which could be the place of delivery of a transferable document or instrument) as place of conclusion of the contract, and hence connecting factor, needs to be adjusted to the features of the online world. At a general level, personal connecting factors (such as the law of the transferor) may be better applied to electronic documents than territorial connecting factors, which may be particularly challenging when distributed ledgers and other decentralised or distributed technologies and applications are used.[137] Moreover, certain private international law rules, such as those contained in older laws on bills of exchange and promissory notes, may be outdated and unfit for application to electronic transferable records. Once the applicable law has been identified, it is possible to ascertain whether the electronic document is valid under the applicable law, and, if it is not, whether its invalidity may be cured.

These steps apply to the cross-border recognition of the legal effect of the document, and not of the underlying data, which may need to be provided separately with trust services. However, assurance of certain data qualities may be provided by complying with the substantive law requirements of the document. For instance, by using an electronic signature it is possible to satisfy a signature requirement and, at the same time, provide assurance of the document's origin and integrity.

This complex analysis may be simplified by the choice of applicable law as well as the application of a uniform legal regime to transferable documents and instruments.[138] The inclusion of a choice of law and choice of forum clause is common in certain transferable documents and instruments used across borders such as bills of lading. For instance the Swiss digital assets law[139] has amended the law on private international law to clarify that the law chosen in the electronic transferable record is the applicable one or, in the absence of a clear choice of law, the law of the place of business of the issuer, or of its habitual residence.[140]

[137] But see A Sanitt, 'Digital Assets and Applicable Law: in Defence of the Lex Situs' (2025) *Lloyd's Maritime and Commercial Law Quarterly* 82.

[138] In general, on party autonomy see A Schwartze, 'New Trends in Parties' Options to Select the Applicable Law? The Hague Principles on Choice of Law in International Contracts in a Comparative Perspective' (2015) 12 *University of St Thomas Law Journal* 87, 87–88.

[139] Loi Fédérale du 25 septembre 2020 sur l'adaptation du droit fédéral aux développements de la technologie des registres électroniques distribués.

[140] Art 106 of the Swiss Law, referring to art 145a. For comments, see P Favrod-Coune and K Belet, 'Conflict of Laws and Tokens in Swiss Private International Law' in A Bonomi, M Lehmann and S Lalani (eds) *Blockchain and Private International Law* (Leiden, Brill | Nijhoff, 2023) 673.

The choice of law clause may be found in the document itself or in the rulebook of the electronic transferable records management system.[141] If both the electronic transferable record and the rulebook contain a choice of law clause, the two clauses ideally should be aligned.

However, freedom of choice is limited: generally, when mandatory law applies; and particularly, when applied to property matters, as opposed to contractual matters. Property matters usually follow the principle of lex rei sitae, ie the law where the object of property is situated. Another area that may create concerns is the application of form requirements as mandatory rules, so that non-compliance with form requirements may lead to invalidity of the electronic transferable record. In general, form requirements in private international law follow the law applicable to the document or, especially if more favourable to preserve the validity of the document, the lex loci actus, ie the place where the legal act is executed.[142]

The above analysis applies to electronic transferable records, which are documents or instruments in electronic form linked to real-world goods or to sums of money. Hence, the goods represented in the records are tangible. Electronic transferable records are different from digital assets that are not linked to real-world assets and that might be considered an object of some form of property.[143]

Finally, domestic private international law is also relevant for determining jurisdiction.

Article 19. Non-discrimination of foreign electronic transferable records

1. *An electronic transferable record shall not be denied legal effect, validity or enforceability on the sole ground that it was issued or used abroad.*
2. *Nothing in this Law affects the application to electronic transferable records of rules of private international law governing a transferable document or instrument.*

As noted, transferable documents and instruments, especially when traded professionally, often contain a choice of law clause. That means that the electronic transferable record can be issued under a law that gives it legal recognition.[144] The electronic transferable record does not need to be issued in a place that recognises its use; the recognising jurisdiction may give it legal effect even if the law of the place of issuance or use is silent on electronic transferable records.[145] However, there may be instances when this cannot be the case: for instance, the electronic

[141] Law Commission, *ETDs in Private International Law: FAQs*, para 1.93 suggests otherwise, noting that 'in most jurisdictions, many aspects of domestic negotiable instruments law are mandatory private law, in the sense that parties cannot contract out of them and impose their own contractually agreed standards.' Form requirements are listed among those aspects. Accordingly, 'domestic courts will be unlikely to uphold a choice of foreign law and/or jurisdiction'. The conclusion is mitigated by noting the prominent role of commercial practice, and the very limited litigation in this field.

[142] H Heiss and S Drobnjak, 'Formal Requirements and Validity' in J Basedow and ors (eds), *Elgar Encyclopedia of Private International Law* (Cheltenham, Edward Elgar Publishing, 2017) 783.

[143] Gabriel, 'The UNCITRAL Model Law' (2019) 19, argues otherwise.

[144] B Geva and S Peari, *International Negotiable Instruments*, 215 indicate that party autonomy is considered in various jurisdictions the primary choice of law rule for bills of lading.

[145] For a different view, Caprioli , 'La Loi-type' (2023) 501.

transferable record contains no choice of law, or the choice of law is invalid or otherwise not enforceable in the recognising jurisdiction, or it refers to a law that is silent. Electronic transferable records management systems may be programmed to make a choice of law mandatory before issuing the record, thus avoiding uncertainty. It is also possible to envisage that in the light of the relevant circumstances of the features of the transaction (such as port of charge and discharge in case of carriage of goods by sea) the system may provide advice on the suitable laws to be chosen.

The MLETR does not contain a mechanism for cross-border recognition of electronic transferable records. However, the MLETR, art 19 removes certain obstacles to such recognition.

The MLETR, art 19, para 1 indicates that a foreign electronic transferable record may not be discriminated against based on its place of origin or of use. Accordingly, the reliability of the foreign electronic transferable record should be evaluated against the same reliability requirements used to assess a record issued and used in the MLETR-enacting jurisdiction where recognition is sought. This provision enables the recognition of electronic transferable records issued or used in jurisdictions that do not have any dedicated legislation. It is inspired by the MLES, art 12, para 1, which applies to electronic signatures and certificates.

The MLETR, art 19, para 2 reiterates that the MLETR does not affect the operation of private international law rules. This is in line with the general principle that the MLETR does not interfere with domestic law, be it the law applicable to the document or to the obligation contained therein.

As for the application of private international law, as noted above in this section, a multi-step analysis is required to identify applicable law, ascertain the validity of the document and provide assurance of the data contained therein.

As noted, when transferable documents and instruments contain a choice of law clause, the law of choice applies also to the form requirements of the document.[146] For instance, an electronic bill of lading may be issued under the law of a jurisdiction enacting the MLETR although neither port of origin nor port of destination are located in MLETR-enacting jurisdictions. The question is whether the choice of law clause will be upheld in the jurisdiction where recognition is sought, or whether it will be considered against public order, in particular because of the electronic form of the document. If the MLETR has been enacted in both originating and recognising jurisdiction, recognition of foreign electronic transferable records will be greatly facilitated. This is why jurisdictions

[146] However, Law Commission, *ETDs in Private International Law* (n 141), para 1.68, indicates that party autonomy generally does not apply to contract form requirements. This is true in the sense that form requirements may be considered a matter of ordre public, or mandatory law: but this may be subject to the agreement of all involved parties. Hence, for instance, the electronic form of the document may be upheld among private parties, but not with regard to a public entity or any party that had not consented to its use.

should consider adopting the MLETR even if their law is not chosen as applicable to an electronic transferable record.

As to data quality, relevant matters include whether the law of the recognising jurisdiction has a dedicated legal recognition mechanism for foreign trust services.[147] Such mechanisms are common in electronic transactions and electronic signatures law and may not be technology neutral or may require ex ante recognition. Moreover, special standards may apply to exchanges with public entities (for example, customs authorities).

Another layer of complexity may be added by the interaction between the traditional notions of private international law, on the one hand, and the use of distributed ledger technology, on the other hand.[148] For instance, references to the location of the electronic transferable record may not be applicable in case of use of distributed ledgers. This may provide an incentive to ensure that both the electronic transferable record and the terms and conditions for the use of its management system contain a choice of law clause. However, if the system uses a public and permissionless distributed ledger, it may not be possible for users to agree contractually on the applicable law at the system level, though it may remain possible at the record level. Hence, the issue of a lack of applicable law in relation to using blockchain may be relevant for the electronic transferable records management system (for instance, in the case of malfunctioning), but not for the records.

Different considerations apply to non-contractual issues such as title to assets, especially when special circumstances arise such as insolvency of a party. It must be seen in the concrete case whether the electronic form of the document poses additional challenges. If so, broad adoption of MLETR would likely assist in addressing them.

3.3. MLETR Complementary Matters

MLETR implementation is a work in progress that touches upon a range of issues. Reliability standards and private international law matters have attracted interest at an early stage.[149] However, certain relevant issues were not discussed during the preparation of the MLETR because they fell outside the mandate of UNCITRAL or of the Working Group, because of policy choices, or because they arose at a later stage. Additional legal and technical issues are a consequence of policy and business decisions.

[147] See ch 9.

[148] K Takahashi, 'Blockchain-based Negotiable Instruments: with Particular Reference to Bills of Lading and Investment Securities', in A Bonomi, M Lehmann and S Lalani (eds) *Blockchain and Private International Law* 494.

[149] S Green, 'Happy Birthday to the Electronic Trade Documents Act!' (2024) 23 *Trade Finance Talks* 50.

3.3.1. Electronic Transferable Records Existing Only in Electronic Form

An issue that has been regularly evoked during the preparation of the MLETR is its relationship with the so-called 'electronic transferable records existing only in electronic form'. These 'standalone' electronic transferable records are not based on the functional equivalence approach because they have no paper-based equivalent. A legislator may not wish to enable the electronic use of an existing transferable document or instrument and may create instead a new transferable document or instrument that exists only in electronic form. The principle of numerus clausus, which is often found in civil law jurisdictions, requires creation of new types of documents of title by statute (as opposed to creation by contract).[150]

Different views were expressed in Working Group IV on the inclusion of electronic transferable records existing only in electronic form in the scope of the MLETR. On the one hand, the MLETR is based on the functional equivalence principle, which presupposes the existence of a paper-based document. On the other hand, these electronic documents exist, sometimes predate the MLETR, and their law shares many features with the MLETR. Eventually, the desire to uphold the functional equivalence approach prevailed.[151]

The law creating a new type of electronic transferable record existing only in electronic form must be self-contained, in the sense that it should feature both the substantive law of the document and the provisions enabling its electronic use. The substantive law provisions often reproduce those of the corresponding paper-based document, sometimes with minor deviations due to the use of electronic means. The provisions enabling the use in electronic form may reflect the content of the provisions of the MLETR, but will be drafted akin to medium-neutral rules due to the impossibility of a functional equivalence approach. In other words, these provisions will set conditions for the validity of the transferable record without reference to form requirements for paper-based documents.[152]

From a practical perspective, the fact that an electronic transferable record exists only in electronic form does not pose peculiar challenges if the record is transferred in an open and interoperable ecosystem that complies with the reliability standards of the MLETR. However, issues may arise when the record must be traded in a segregated ecosystem, such as a dedicated central registry. This may be the case with certain equivalents of promissory notes that exist only in electronic form. Similar considerations apply to electronic transferable records issued under a law that adopts a medium-neutral approach.

[150] This is the reason behind the adoption of the Electronically Recorded Monetary Claims Act in Japan (see ch 2, section 2.4.1).
[151] Explanatory Note, para 23.
[152] See the MLWR for an example of medium-neutral drafting based on the MLETR.

3.3.2. Division and Consolidation

The possible insertion in the MLETR of a provision on division and consolidation was considered but Working Group IV eventually discarded it as the matter was considered to fall under substantive law. The issue has also been considered during the preparation of the MLWR. Here it was retained as the MLWR also contains substantive law provisions. The MLWR provisions may shed light on the treatment of these events during the lifecycle of any electronic transferable record as the operational steps are the same provided they are compatible with applicable substantive law.

The MLWR, art 27, dealing with partial delivery requires, among other things, surrendering the warehouse receipt to the warehouse operator, who shall note the partial delivery on the warehouse receipt and return the receipt to the holder. This procedure may be necessary for paper-based warehouse receipts, but may be simplified when electronic warehouse receipts are used as there is no need to transfer control as long as the request of the holder for partial delivery is recorded in the system and the warehouse operator annotates the partial delivery.

The MLWR, art 28, on split warehouse receipts requires, among other things, surrender of the original warehouse receipt. Upon issuance of the split warehouse receipts, the warehouse operator shall cancel the original warehouse receipt to prevent the simultaneous circulation of original and split documents. The same procedure would apply to electronic transferable records, noting that the original record would be electronically archived, and that a notation should be made on the split records if substantive law dates their legal effect back to the issuance of the original record.

3.3.3. Liability

The MLETR does not contain any provision on liability. The substantive law of the relevant transferable document or instrument determines the liability of the parties involved in the emission and circulation of the electronic transferable record.

Liability may also arise for managing electronic transferable records. At its 47th session Working Group IV considered a provision that referred to the liability of the operator for breach of contract or negligence and did not touch upon liability of other parties.[153]

The main source of liability for system operators is contractual, subject to the application of any mandatory law. As noted,[154] typical contractual obligations of

[153] UNCITRAL, 'Draft Provisions on Electronic Transferable Records' (4 March 2013) UN Doc A/CN.9/WG.IV/WP.122, draft art 33.

[154] See the discussion on 'Reliability Assessment: Options in MLETR Implementation' in relation to the MLETR, art 12 contained in section 3.2 of this chapter.

the operators may include: (a) acting in accordance with representations made by it with respect to its policies and practices; (b) exercising reasonable care to ensure the accuracy and completeness of all representations made by them; (c) providing reasonably accessible means to ascertain any limitation on the purpose or value for which the electronic transferable record may be used; (d) utilising trustworthy systems, procedures and human resources in performing its services. The liability may be limited when permitted under applicable law, which may be the law chosen by the parties or other mandatory law.

The liability of electronic transferable records management system operators may interplay with that of trust service providers, which may be subject to stricter liability regimes under laws such as the MLIT and the eIDAS Regulation (for example, on presumption of negligence and burden of proof). If the system operator also performs the functions of a trust service provider, both liability regimes may apply. When the operator is not a service provider, the affected user of an electronic transferable record may have separate recourse against the trust service provider (for example, as a relying party) regardless of the contractual arrangements between the operator and the service provider.

3.3.4. Enforcement of Electronic Transferable Records: Protest

An electronic transferable record may be presented for performance, but performance may not occur and the record may be dishonoured. If the performance relates to delivery of goods, the matter is usually litigated or arbitrated. If the performance relates to payment of a sum of money that is not honoured because of lack of funds, the creditor may initiate a procedure for protesting the electronic transferable record that may entail the assistance of a notary public or other public authority. Protest is required under the Geneva Conventions but is usually optional in common law systems.[155]

While the paper-based protest procedure is well-tested, there is no established practice for protesting electronic transferable records. International organisations representing notaries public and other concerned public authorities may take interest in developing uniform guidance on this matter.

The use of electronic transferable records raises the issue of the acceptance of the record by notaries public, bailiffs,[156] and any other concerned authority, and the compatibility of the format of the record with the one required for the protest. From a practical perspective, three options seem possible:

- to change medium and follow the procedure for protesting a paper-based document;

[155] B Geva and S Peari, *International Negotiable Instruments*, 21.
[156] The Swedish case Ö 5072-16 of 2 November 2017, discussed in ch 4, arose out of the refusal of the bailiff to deal with an electronic promissory note.

- to convert the format of the electronic transferable record to the one requested by the notary public effecting the protest; and
- to develop a solution that allows the notary public to use the original format of the electronic transferable record.

The first solution is based on the conversion of the electronic record into a paper-based document. For caution, the requirements of the MLETR, arts 17 and 18 may be followed, although after presentation and non-performance the electronic record may not be transferred any more under general rules, but only under the rules of protest.

The second solution foresees the conversion of the electronic record into a format that is acceptable for those involved in the protest procedure, ie notary public, bailiff, and, eventually, court.

The third solution envisages the adoption of a format that is compatible across all stages. This requires coordination of evidentiary and procedural rules with MLETR standards, which, in turn, may follow general rules on the application of trust services for data quality assurance.[157]

In general, evidence rules do not facilitate the submission as evidence of electronic transactions taking place during the ordinary course of business. This is understandable since traditionally evidence rules aim to maximise the reliability of the submission of the parties to ascertain the facts of the case. However, rethinking the issue from the data management perspective could greatly facilitate taking of evidence, discovery and related matters.

3.3.5. The Use of Blockchain

The use of blockchain and of other distributed ledger technology for MLETR implementation has attracted significant interest.[158] Several electronic transferable records service providers use blockchain technology, albeit in a different way.[159] For instance, some may store only critical information on the blockchain.

[157] For instance, art 634 of the Italian Civil Procedure Code admits electronic invoices managed in compliance with the law, including those exchanged in the national electronic invoice system, as written evidence of a credit for the purpose of obtaining an enforcement order.

[158] LSE Trade Policy Hub, 'Benefits of the Digitalisation of Trade Processes and Cross Border Barriers to Their Adoption, Final Report' (2023), 23, illustrates the use of blockchain in paperless trade. See also E Ganne, 'Blockchain's Practical and Legal Implications for Global Trade and Global Trade Law' in M Burri (ed) *Big Data and Global Trade Law* (Cambridge, Cambridge University Press, 2021) 128; S Wunderlich and D Saive, 'The Electronic Bill of Lading' in J Prieto and ors (eds) *Blockchain and Applications* (Cham, Springer, 2020) *Advances in Intelligent Systems and Computing* vol 1010, 93; H Mabrouk, 'Beyond Speculation: The Transformative Power of Blockchain Technology in Various Industries' (2023) *European Journal of Law Reform* 3, 5–9, describing TradeLens, a blockchain-based supply chain management platform. Eventually TradeLens was liquidated due to lack of commercial viability.

[159] See, however, T Krebs, 'Electronic Bills of Lading, Transnational and English law: Blocking the Blockchain?' (2023) 28 *Uniform Law Review* 323, arguing that the shipping industry is 'notoriously conservative' and that it may be more expedient to start digitalisation of bills of lading by using central

The providers operate as a link between the infrastructure layer where the blockchain lies and the application layer that contains the interface with the service subscribers and other users. Often, the services are cloud-based. Some providers have embraced tokenisation (see next section), including by using non-fungible tokens.

Because of the (then) novelty of this technology, some comments aimed at facilitating its use were inserted in the Explanatory Note. Those comments relate to the possible identification of the person in control by reference to a pseudonym, provided that the pseudonym could be traced back to an entity;[160] and to the expression of consent of any concerned parties to accept electronic transferable records by using the record in public permissionless blockchains that have no consent mechanism for access.[161] Moreover, the definition of 'electronic record' in the MLETR, art 2 was modified to accommodate the composite nature of information stored on a distributed ledger.[162]

A general advantage in the use of blockchain is that there is no need for a third party to establish trust: the technology operates in such a manner that trust should be built in the system. Other benefits relate to fulfilling functional equivalence requirements. In particular, the use of blockchain may ensure guarantee of integrity given that information is stored in blocks whose unilateral modification should be unlikely. Moreover, as noted, the use of non-fungible tokens may provide assurance of singularity.[163] Finally, the use of wallets for managing tokenised records may satisfy the control requirement.[164]

However, the use of blockchain faces certain challenges.[165] One issue that is getting increasing attention is the lack of interoperability, which may mean that documents issued on one blockchain cannot be moved to another blockchain. This may be because distributed ledgers are designed to be self-contained. Technical solutions are being tested. More generally, there is a mismatch between expectations of blockchain enthusiasts on the ability to migrate the entire ecosystem on the distributed ledger and the complexity of real-world transactions: at best, migration can be incremental.[166]

The guarantee of integrity (or 'immutability') is proportional to the size of the blockchain and may be more reliable in public blockchains. However, public

registries rather than distributed ones, which have limitations and whose technical standards are still underdeveloped.

[160] Explanatory Note, para 66.

[161] Explanatory Note, paras 78 and 117.

[162] Explanatory Note, para 35.

[163] DS Bloch, 'Non-Fungible Tokens: A Solution to the Challenges of Using Blockchain Bills of Lading in the International Sale of Goods' (2022) 1 *Journal of Law, Market & Innovation* n 1, 49.

[164] For an example of implementation of control with cryptography and tokenisation, UN/CEFACT, *Transfer of MLETR-Compliant Titles*, 11–12.

[165] LSE Trade Policy Hub, 'Benefits of the Digitalisation' (2023), 26: 'Impediments to implementation'.

[166] For trade finance, see J Winn, 'Will Blockchain Transform Trade Finance?' in C Hare and D Neo (eds), *Trade Finance: Technology, Innovation and Documentary Credits* (Oxford, Oxford University Press, 2021) 230.

blockchains may not fully guarantee data privacy and business confidentiality, especially when information may become publicly available.

Moreover, public blockchains have governance structures (called 'distributed autonomous organisations') whose functioning may make identification of the entities liable for blockchain malfunctioning difficult.

Immutability may also be used to ensure the automated performance of certain functions ('smart contracts'), as halting performance would require consensus of a very high number of participants. However, the law may require the possibility to stop performance ('killer switch'), which may be difficult to satisfy when designing systems based on distributed ledger technology.

Last, but not least, blockchain may be costly both financially and environmentally.

3.3.6. Tokenisation

Tokenisation is the digital representation of assets in a token that is typically issued on a distributed ledger. Digital trade ecosystems may deal with all forms of tokenised assets.[167] Tokenisation is being tested for issuing electronic transferable records that represent real-world assets such as money or goods, among other use cases. Electronic transferable records issued as tokens may be classified as exogenous tokens, which are defined as tokens representing rights that exist outside the ledger such as property rights or obligations to pay. The MLETR provides a legal framework for such operations.[168]

Trade financing may benefit from the distributed and decentralised nature of tokenisation. By issuing tokenised trade documents, cost for access to credit, especially of medium- and small-sized enterprises, could be lower, and related procedures could be simplified.[169] Moreover, an adequate ecosystem for trading tokenised electronic transferable records may innovate on existing practices as more information on the client and on the loan could be shared more effectively, and settlements could take place faster.[170]

Tokenisation may also facilitate securitisation of electronic transferable records and broaden the lending pool to non-bank entities, when allowed. Thus,

[167] This is the case of Project Ensemble of the Hong Kong Monetary Authority, which aims to establish a wholesale central bank digital currency (hence, tokenised money) sandbox that can be used for settlement of asset tokens, including electronic bills of lading.

[168] JM Garrido, 'Digital Tokens: A Legal Perspective' (2023) IMF Doc WP/23/151, 26 notes that 'The work of UNCITRAL on electronic transferable records provides a blueprint for the use of tokens in the area of negotiable instruments and documents of title'.

[169] For the impact of tokenisation of electronic transferable records on small- and medium-sized enterprises, Bank for International Settlements Innovation Hub, 'Project Dynamo: Catalysing Innovation for SME Growth' (2023).

[170] B Chen, 'Tokenization in Shipping and the Securitization of Trade Flows' *Forbes* (Jersey City, NJ, 17 January 2024).

tokenisation may help in mobilising illiquid assets and in reaching out to new investors interested in diversifying their portfolio.

Tokens representing electronic transferable records may be considered asset tokens, which are a subtype of utility tokens. However, the fact that the MLETR deals with pre-existing commercial documents and that it relies on the principle of functional equivalence means that those legal gaps that may affect tokenised digital assets are not relevant for tokenised electronic transferable records.

The legal nature of the token representing an electronic transferable record is that of a commercial document in electronic form,[171] and its transmission may take place by transfer of control, or transfer of control and endorsement. The link between the electronic transferable record and the real-world asset is provided in substantive law and is the same as that between the transferable document or instrument and the asset.

The technical design of tokenisation and, more generally, the use of distributed ledger technology may require dedicated solutions with respect to remedies for loss, illegal transfer or fraud involving the token. These technological features should be carefully evaluated when choosing the appropriate technical solution.

In conclusion, the legal nature of a commercial document usually prevails over the classification as a token.

3.3.7. Electronic Transferable Records and Digital Assets

One discussion that has emerged after the adoption of the MLETR is the relationship between electronic transferable records and digital assets. An electronic transferable record is defined in the Model Law as an electronic record that is functionally equivalent to a transferable document or instrument, ie a document that incorporates the right to delivery of goods or payment of money. In short, an electronic transferable record is a commercial document in electronic form.

The definition of digital assets is less straightforward. If a broad approach is taken, all electronic things of value are digital assets, and electronic transferable records are a subset of them.[172] However, the vast majority of electronic things of

[171] For the same conclusion see J Lai, 'Tokenisation of Documentary Intangibles' (2023) *Lloyd's Maritime and Commercial Law Quarterly* 92, stating that 'crypto-tokens that tokenise paper documents are functionally equivalent to paper documents because they can evidence and transfer rights in the same way as their paper counterparts'. Documentary intangibles include transferable documents and instruments.

[172] Law Commission, *Digital Assets: Final Report* (Law Com No 412, 2023) 2: 'The term digital asset is extremely broad. It captures a huge variety of things including digital files, digital records, email accounts, domain names, in-game digital assets, digital carbon credits, crypto-tokens and non-fungible tokens. The technology used to create or manifest those digital assets is not the same for each. Nor are the characteristics or features of those digital assets. We use "digital assets" as a general term, but

value, including electronic transferable records, already find adequate legal treatment: the discussion of digital assets should therefore focus on those assets that have not yet an adequate legal treatment, such as crypto assets, ie certain specific types of value (or asserted value) stored on digital medium that is often based on distributed ledger technology.

The adoption by the US Uniform Law Commission of UCC Article 12 in 2022 aims to provide a legal framework for digital assets.[173] UCC Article 12 applies to controllable electronic records, which is a novel legal notion referring to 'a record stored in an electronic medium that can be subjected to control under Section 12-105'. The definition of controllable electronic record does not include several digital assets defined elsewhere in the UCC, such as 'a controllable account, a controllable payment intangible, a deposit account, an electronic copy of a record evidencing chattel paper, an electronic document of title, electronic money, investment property, or a transferable record' (UCC § 12-102). This means that bills of lading and warehouse receipts in electronic form are not controllable electronic records. 'Transferable record' is defined in the Electronic Signatures in Global and National Commerce Act (ESIGN), s 201(a)(1) and in the Uniform Electronic Transactions Act (UETA), s 16(a) and may encompass promissory notes. The definitions of the other legal notions relevant for UCC § 12-102 are contained in UCC Article 9. In general, it may be said that UCC Article 12 has residual application, covering those documents and instruments that do not fall under UCC Article 7; UCC Article 9; UETA; and ESIGN. However, UCC Article 12 may apply to commercially significant transferable instruments, such as promissory notes.

To be a controllable electronic record, an electronic record needs to be subjected to control as defined in UCC § 12-105. That notion of 'control' is different from that of the MLETR. 'Control' in the MLETR is a factual situation equivalent to possession. 'Control' in UCC § 12-105(a) is a legal notion that applies 'if the electronic record, a record attached to or logically associated with the electronic record, or a system in which the electronic record is recorded' gives the person in its control: (a) power to avail itself of substantially all the benefit from the electronic record; (b) exclusive power to prevent others from availing themselves of substantially all the benefit from the electronic record; and (c) the ability to transfer control of the electronic record to another person. The record or system should also enable the person in control to readily identify itself as such.[174]

most of our report and recommendations are concerned with a subset of digital assets with particular characteristics'.

[173] However, certain pre-existing provisions in other UCC Articles were also amended: for UCC Article 9, see H Gabriel, 'The 2022 Amendments to Article 9 of the American Uniform Commercial Code' (2025) 18 *Law and Financial Markets Review* 6.

[174] In general, see Gabriel, 'The Concept and Necessity of "Control"' (n 85).

While control and identification of the person in control are elements in common with the MLETR, the reference to the 'power to avail itself of substantially all the benefit from the electronic record' touches upon substantive law matters and is not contained in the MLETR. In fact, UCC Article 12 applies to records that have no paper-based equivalent, and therefore substantive law notions are needed. For that reason, it is important to keep the notions of 'control' applicable to controllable electronic records and to electronic transferable records well distinct. At the same time, as noted, UCC Article 12 may also apply to records that have a paper-based equivalent, which may lead to unintended consequences.[175]

Building on UCC Article 12, UNIDROIT decided to prepare the Principles on Digital Assets and Private Law (DAPL).[176] In the DAPL Principles, the definition of 'digital asset' is broad and may encompass electronic transferable records within the meaning of the MLETR. More precisely, the DAPL Principles apply to digital assets, which are defined as electronic records capable of being subject to control.[177] In turn, electronic records consist of information stored in an electronic medium and capable of being retrieved,[178] and the notion of control is similar to that of UCC Article 12, ie it refers to substantive law attributes.[179] Also similar to UCC Article 12, the DAPL Principles include substantive law rules, some of which, such as duties of custodians of digital assets and innocent acquisition, cannot easily be applied to electronic transferable records, and may conflict with the substantive law of the electronic transferable records. However, unlike UCC Article 12, the DAPL Principles do not contain a disconnection clause ensuring that the DAPL Principles will not apply to electronic transferable records that have a paper-based equivalent. Challenges may arise when the desire to provide comprehensive legislation for digital assets interferes with well-settled law of transferable documents or instruments.

UNCITRAL Working Group IV discussed the relationship between the MLETR and the DAPL Principles at its 65th session.[180] The core concern regarded the possibility that the application of the DAPL Principles could introduce substantive law provisions, thus leading to a dual legal regime for transferable documents

[175] However, the UCC does not digitalise any commercial documents on the basis of the functional equivalence approach.

[176] For more information, see the Digital Assets and Private Law project's webpage at unidroit.org. The Principles were adopted at the 102nd session of the Governing Council of UNIDROIT, held in Rome on 10–12 May 2023, on the basis of the draft contained in document CD (102) 6. For general information on the work of UNIDROIT in this area, T Rodríguez De Las Heras Ballell, 'Tracing the path of the role of technology in UNIDROIT instruments', in B Köhler, R Gulati and T John (eds), *The Elgar Companion to UNIDROIT* (Cheltenham, Edward Elgar Publishing, 2024) 80.

[177] Principle 2(2).

[178] Principle 2(1).

[179] Principle 6.

[180] UNCITRAL, 'Report of Working Group IV (Electronic Commerce) on the Work of its Sixty-fifth Session' (25 April 2023) UN Doc A/CN.9/1132, paras 86–91.

and instruments, on the one hand, and electronic transferable records, on the other hand. This result is inconsistent with the principle of functional equivalence underpinning the MLETR, and may create significant barriers to trade. The outcome is also not in line with the intended goal of the DAPL Principles, ie filling the legislative vacuum on digital assets.

To prevent such challenges, different solutions may ensure the seamless interaction of the MLETR and the DAPL Principles. One suggestion is to exclude electronic transferable records, as defined in the MLETR, from the definition of 'digital asset' in the DAPL Principles. That suggestion was not taken up by UNIDROIT as it was felt that the DAPL Principles should have a broad scope. Another possibility operates at the interpretation and application stage, and relies on considering the MLETR as lex specialis and, as such, prevailing over the DAPL Principles, as lex generalis, in case of inconsistency between the two texts.

The challenges arising from commingling the notions of digital assets and electronic transferable records are evident in the recent Digital Assets Law of the Dubai International Financial Centre (DIFC).[181] The Digital Assets Law defines 'digital asset' in a rather technical manner,[182] and specifies that 'A Digital Asset is intangible property and is neither a thing in possession nor a thing in action'.[183] From these elements, it seems clear that an electronic transferable record is not a digital asset.

The Digital Assets Law also legally enables the use of electronic transferable records – namely, bills of exchange and promissory notes – by inserting provisions in the Law of Obligations.[184] These provisions are generally inspired by the ETDA 2023, and thus, indirectly, by the MLETR. However, there are two significant variations.

Firstly, the definition of control in art 153C of the Law of Obligations refers to: '(ii) the ability to obtain substantially all the benefit from the Electronic Trade Document' together with the ability of excluding others from obtaining the benefits, and of transferring these abilities to another person, which is considered the transfer of control. However, control in the MLETR and in the ETDA 2023 fulfils the functions of possession, and possession is a factual condition that has legal consequences but does not give the ability to obtain all benefits from a commercial document: the substantive law of the commercial document gives that ability and defines its limits. Hence, the definition of control in art 153C may interfere with substantive law.

[181] DIFC Law No 2 of 2024, further discussed with respect to digital assets in ch 4, section 4.1.
[182] See DIFC Law No 2 of 2024: 'Article 8. Definition. A thing is a Digital Asset if: (a) it exists as a notional quantity unit manifested by the combination of the active operation of software by a network of participants and network-instantiated data; (b) it exists independently of any particular person and legal system; and (c) the thing is not capable of duplication and use or consumption of the thing by one person or specific group of persons necessarily prejudices the use or consumption of that thing by one or more other persons.'
[183] See DIFC Law No 2 of 2024: Article 9 – Characterisation.
[184] DIFC Law No 5 of 2005.

Secondly, art 153C of the Law of Obligations explicitly foresees the possibility that an electronic trade document may be a digital asset. This means that the Digital Assets Law may apply to electronic transferable records, which opens the door to uncertainty around which provisions should prevail. It is also not easy to imagine how a commercial document in electronic form may meet the definition of digital asset. Finally, the definition of 'address' in the Digital Assets Law refers to the exclusive use of distributed ledgers for digital assets, which could hinder technology-neutral management of electronic transferable records.

4

Enacting the UNCITRAL Model Law on Electronic Transferable Records

4.1. National Laws on Electronic Transferable Records

The enactment of a model law may take place with variations or additions to the original text. Some of these new elements may provide useful clarifications and could be taken up in other jurisdictions. For this reason, it is useful to illustrate the main features of selected enactments of the UNCITRAL Model Law on Electronic Transferable Records (MLETR). In other cases, the enacting law is based on the general principles of the MLETR but does not reproduce its provisions. It is important to identify those principles in order to achieve cross-border legal recognition of electronic transferable records and technical interoperability. Certain laws that are not MLETR enactments but that deal with electronic transferable records may provide interesting examples of alternative approaches.

The process of enactment of a model law requires adaptation to the features of the receiving legal system. Among those features, the existence of electronic transactions laws based on the texts of the United Nations Commission on International Trade Law (UNCITRAL) is particularly relevant as it minimises the need to amend existing law or adjust the MLETR original text to it.

4.1.1. Bahrain

The Kingdom of Bahrain has been the first jurisdiction to enact the MLETR. Having enacted the UNCITRAL Model Law on Electronic Commerce (MLEC) in 2002,[1] Bahrain made a policy decision to review and update that law to better support the digital economy, including by enabling cloud computer services providers and fintech operators. The law reform exercise led to the adoption of the Electronic Communications and Transactions Law,[2] replacing the Electronic Transactions Law, of the Electronic Transferable Records Law[3] and of the Law

[1] Legislative Decree No 28 of 2002 in respect of the Electronic Transactions Law.

[2] Legislative Decree No 54 of 2018 Promulgating the Electronic Communications and Transactions Law.

[3] Law No 55 of 2018 with respect to Electronic Transferable Records.

on Providing Cloud Computing Services to Foreign Parties.[4] It also led to Bahrain's accession to the United Nations Convention on the Use of Electronic Communications in International Contracts (ECC). As the UNCITRAL Secretariat was involved in the law reform process, this was a useful early occasion to compile information on MLETR enactment.

The Electronic Transferable Records Law contains a few variations on the text of the MLETR. A significant one relates to scope of application. Bahrain did not adopt the definition of 'transferable document or instrument' contained in the MLETR, art 2 as the search for those documents and instruments under national law could create uncertainty. Instead, the Electronic Transferable Records Law, art 1(e) lists as documents that fall under the scope of the law bills of lading, letters of credit and warehouse receipts; and art 1(j) of the Electronic Transferable Records Law lists as instruments falling under the scope of the law cheques, bills of exchange and promissory notes. The Governor of the Central Bank of Bahrain may, by regulation, add documents (entitling delivery of goods) or instruments (entitling payment of money) to the list.

Article 1(h) of the Electronic Transferable Records Law defines an electronic transferable records management system as 'an information system for the issuance, transfer, control, presentation and storage of electronic transferable records in accordance with the rules set out in this law'. The notion of 'information system' is defined in technology neutral terms in the Electronic Communications and Transactions Law, art 1.

As noted, the MLETR makes frequent reference to the use of reliable methods in electronic transferable records management systems. However, mindful of the different approaches to the oversight of electronic signatures, UNCITRAL decided not to provide any guidance on the oversight of the management system, whose design was entirely left to enacting states.[5] Bahrain decided to adopt the 'two-tier' approach. Akin to what the Electronic Communications and Transactions Law foresees for trust service providers, art 15 of the Electronic Transferable Records Law contemplates the possibility for electronic transferable records management system operators to get accredited by a designated government agency. The effect of the accreditation is a presumption of reliability of the method used in the management system (Electronic Transferable Records Law, art 8, para 2).

The Electronic Transferable Records Law also foresees the accreditation of foreign operators (art 16). This provision complements art 14 of the Law, which reproduces the MLETR, art 19, on non-discrimination against foreign electronic transferable records. Foreign operators shall utilise standards at least equivalent to those required for Bahraini national operators and shall be accredited in a foreign jurisdiction. If these two conditions are satisfied, foreign operators do not have to further comply with requirements for accredited national operators. The foreign

[4] Legislative Decree No 56 of 2018 in respect of Providing Cloud Computing Services to Foreign Parties.

[5] Explanatory Note, para 197.

accrediting jurisdiction does not have to be the one where the foreign operator has its place of business. This is done to accommodate cases when the operator wishes to get accreditation, but no accreditation is available in its original jurisdiction.

Article 17 of the Electronic Communications and Transactions Law deals with the liability of electronic transferable records management system operators, which is a matter not dealt with in the MLETR. An operator shall be liable for damage due to its use of a method that is not reliable provided that the damage was the result of the operator's intention or negligence. Intention or negligence of the operator are presumed if the operator is accredited. The operator may avail itself of contractual limitations of liability if customers are duly informed in advance of those limitations and third parties may recognise them.

The Electronic Transferable Records Law does not contain rules on functional equivalence of the paper-based notions of writing and signature because those rules are contained respectively in the Electronic Communications and Transactions Law, art 5(c) and art 6. Article 2 of the Electronic Communications and Transactions Law indicates that the Law shall apply to all types of electronic transactions, including electronic transferable records, unless derogated by other law.

The Bahraini legislator did not enact the MLETR, art 3, on the uniform origin and the duty of uniform interpretation; however, the Electronic Transferable Records Law, art 3 indicates that in the interpretation of the law regard shall be had to the Electronic Communications and Transactions Law and to the jurisprudence issued by UNCITRAL on the MLETR. The reference to the UNCITRAL jurisprudence includes cases published in the Case Law on UNCITRAL Texts (CLOUT) database maintained by the UNCITRAL Secretariat.

Finally, the Bahraini legislator did not enact the MLETR, art 4, on party autonomy and privity of contract, which was considered unnecessary.

4.1.2. Costa Rica

Costa Rica adopted a law enabling the use of promissory notes and bills of exchange[6] that is not based on the MLETR. The law foresees the use of central registries for the management of electronic documents. The information stored in the registry is considered equivalent to that written on paper. It is possible only to change medium from paper to electronic. The principles and provisions of the law on electronic signatures and documents are applicable also to electronic promissory notes and bills of exchange.[7]

[6] Ley N° 10069, Ley sobre letra de cambio y pagaré electrónicos, de 9 de noviembre de 2021.

[7] Ley 8454, Ley de certificados, firmas digitales y documentos electrónicos, de 30 de agosto de 2005. It is considered that this law was influenced by the UNCITRAL Model Law on Electronic Signatures (MLES) and the principles on which the MLES is based.

The registry operators need to be licensed by the Superintendencia General de Valores (Sugeval), which is the financial markets authority of Costa Rica, and must guarantee interoperability between national licensed registries.[8]

From the MLETR perspective, the element of interest in this law is art 4, on fundamental principles. Among those principles it is possible to find those that underpin the MLETR, namely: technology neutrality (despite the identification of central registries as the only possible model to implement the law); functional equivalence; and non-interference with substantive law.[9] Article 4 refers also to functional equivalence of electronic signatures and, more generally, to functional equivalence of written form as set out in the law on electronic signatures and documents. However, the adoption of UNCITRAL general principles did not translate in the adoption of the MLETR.

4.1.3. Dubai International Financial Centre

The Dubai International Financial Centre (DIFC) is a free trade zone with law-making authority in commercial matters. The DIFC has adopted a Digital Assets Law[10] that amends existing DIFC legislation based on UNCITRAL texts on electronic commerce, insolvency and security interests to accommodate the features of digital assets. The DIFC Digital Assets Law contains provisions on electronic transferable records that amend the Law of Obligations.[11]

The Digital Assets Law refers to electronic transferable records as 'electronic trade documents', and singles out promissory notes and bills of exchange as examples of such documents. Transport documents are mentioned in article 153A, which defines paper trade documents.

Article 153B of the Law of Obligations, as amended by the Digital Assets Law, sets out the requirements for an electronic trade document, which are like those of the United Kingdom (UK) Electronic Trade Documents Act 2023 (ETDA) and of the MLETR: identification of the document, integrity, control, use of reliable methods, and fulfilment of the information requirements of the corresponding paper-based document. Importantly, the non-exhaustive list of circumstances relevant to determine reliability contained in the Digital Assets Law, art 153B, para 3 is akin to that contained in the ETDA, s 2(5) and to the MLETR, art 12.

However, the Digital Assets Law contains at least two elements that significantly diverge from the MLETR.

[8] Article 15 of Law No 10069.

[9] LM Argüello Rojas, 'Los principios de los títulos valores electrónicos en Costa Rica: a propósito de la entrada en vigor de la Ley n° 10069, "Ley sobre letra de cambio y pagaré electrónico"' (2023) 16 *Revista IUS Doctrina* 1, 17–21, confirms that these principles are inspired by the MLETR.

[10] DIFC Law No 2 of 2024.

[11] DIFC Law No 5 of 2005.

The first one relates to the definition of 'control', which is a factual notion in the MLETR. Article 153C, para 1 of the DIFC Law of Obligations (as amended by the Digital Assets Law) defines 'control' along the lines of Uniform Commercial Code (UCC) § 12-105 and of Principle 6(1) of the UNIDROIT Digital Assets and Private Law Principles (DAPL).[12] However, that notion of 'control' in UCC § 12-105 was developed for digital assets that do not fall under an existing substantive law. Accordingly, that notion refers to the ability to obtain substantially all the benefit from the Electronic Trade Document, to exclude others from obtaining that benefit, and to transfer the ability to obtain all the benefit as requirements to establish control:

Article 153C. (Control defined)

(1) For the purpose of Article 153B, a person has control of the document if:

(a) subject to Articles 153C(2) and 153(3), the Electronic Trade Document, or the relevant protocol or system, confers on that person:

(i) the exclusive ability to prevent others from obtaining substantially all the benefit from the Electronic Trade Document;

(ii) the ability to obtain substantially all the benefit from the Electronic Trade Document; and

(iii) the exclusive ability to transfer the abilities in Articles 153C(1)(a)(i) and 153C(1)(a)(ii) to another person (a 'change of control'); and,

(b) the Electronic Trade Document, or the relevant protocols or system, allows that person to identify itself as having the abilities set out in Article 153C(1)(a).

Such abilities belong to substantive law, hence, while such notion of 'control' is suitable for digital assets that have no substantive law, it may interfere with substantive law when applied to electronic trade documents.

The second one is the possibility that an electronic trade document may also be a digital asset, which is explicitly foreseen in art 153C, paras 2 and 3 of the Digital Assets Law. However, the definition of 'digital asset' in the Digital Assets Law does not seem to be compatible with the notion of a trade document, including because it may not be technology neutral:[13]

Article 8. Definition

A thing is a Digital Asset if:

(a) it exists as a notional quantity unit manifested by the combination of the active operation of software by a network of participants and network-instantiated data;

(b) it exists independently of any particular person and legal system; and

(c) the thing is not capable of duplication and use or consumption of the thing by one person or specific group of persons necessarily prejudices the use or consumption of that thing by one or more other persons.

[12] See ch 3, section 3.3.7.

[13] Article 8 of the DIFC law (definition of digital asset).

To sum up, it seems preferable to keep the notions of digital assets and of electronic trade documents separate despite the understandable desire to promote innovation in fintech and to create fully interoperable systems for digital trade financing.

4.1.4. France

In furtherance of the G7 endorsement of the MLETR,[14] the French Government requested a study of the possible reform of French law to enable the use of electronic transferable records based on the MLETR. This exercise, carried out by Paris Europlace and supported by International Chamber of Commerce (ICC) France and other entities, led to the preparation of a comprehensive report discussing the business, technical and legal aspects of trade financing digitisation.[15] The report recommends adopting the MLETR in France and promoting its broader adoption worldwide in light of the advantages of legal uniformity; developing innovative technical solutions to manage effectively the logistics supply chain, including by leveraging on qualified trust service providers; strengthening cooperation between private and public sector; and disseminating broad awareness, with a view to reinforcing human capacity in trade financing.

Based on a text contained in the report, a bill was drafted, introduced in the French Parliament, and eventually adopted.[16] The Law n 2024-537 reproduces the core elements of the MLETR while leaving to an implementing regulation the definition of the circumstances relevant for assessing the reliability of the methods used. It dovetails not only with existing national legislation, namely various codes, but also with relevant EU legal texts such as the eIDAS Regulation.

Article 14, paragraph 1 of the Law n 2024-537 contains a definition of 'titre transférable' corresponding to that of transferable document or instrument in the MLETR, art 2.[17] It then lists specific documents, including: promissory notes; bills of exchange; warehouse receipts; bills of lading, including those issued for inland waterway carriage of goods;[18] and certificates of insurance. The list is open-ended.

[14] See ch 9, section 9.3.

[15] B Collot, P Henry and S Teper, 'Accélérer la digitalisation des activités de financement du commerce international' (2023) available in English and French at www.diplomatie.gouv.fr.

[16] Loi n° 2024-537 du 13 juin 2024 visant à accroître le financement des entreprises et l'attractivité de la France, JORF n°0138 du 14 juin 2024. The enactment of the MLETR is contained in Title II of the law, entitled 'Faciliter la croissance à l'international des entreprises françaises par la dématérialisation des titres transférables'. For a comment on this law, see É Caprioli, C Combarieu and D Doise, 'La dématérialisation des titres transférables par la loi n° 2024-537 du 13 juin 2024 : l'avènement du connaissement électronique en droit français' in T Cremers (ed), *40 ans de dématérialisation des titres en France* (Paris, IRJS Éditions, 2024) Bibliothèque de l'Institut de Recherche Juridique de la Sorbonne – André Tunc, Tome 133, 143.

[17] Article 6.I. – Constitue un titre transférable l'écrit qui représente un bien ou un droit et qui donne à son porteur le droit de demander l'exécution de l'obligation qui y est spécifiée ainsi que celui de transférer ce droit.

[18] Article 13 of the Budapest Convention on the Contract for the Carriage of Goods by Inland Waterway (adopted 22 June 2001, entered into force 1 April 2005) (CMNI).

Paragraph 2 of the same article explicitly excludes a few documents from the scope of application of the Law although they may fall under the definition of 'titre transférable'. These exclusions take into account the special nature of these documents and the fact that they are sometimes already available in electronic form according to dedicated rules.

Article 15, para 1 of the Law n 2024-537 indicates that the 'titre transférable' may be issued and may circulate in electronic form under the conditions set in arts 1366 and 1367 of the French Civil Code, dealing respectively with functional equivalence requirements for the notions of 'writing' and of 'signature',[19] and according to a reliable method. Paragraph 2 indicates that the holder of the electronic transferable record is the person who has its exclusive control, which gives the ability to benefit from the rights incorporated in the record, to modify them and to transfer them. Paragraph 3 confirms that any annotation that could be made to a transferable document or instrument may be made also to an electronic transferable record provided its terms clarify nature and scope. According to para 4, the presentation of the electronic transferable record may be made by delivering it to the electronic address indicated by the recipient, or by allowing access to the record. The presentation is effective if the recipient acknowledges delivery or if it is otherwise possible to assume that the presentation has taken place. The use of an electronic registered delivery service may be useful to that end. Paragraph 5 indicates that transfer of exclusive control of the electronic transferable record will transfer or pledge the rights incorporated in that record in a manner akin to delivery and endorsement of a document of title. It also clarifies that endorsement in blank, ie to bearer, is possible provided the holder is identified as the person in exclusive control. Finally, para 6 indicates that the apposition of a seal or similar sign in conjunction with a signature may be effected in the electronic environment by inserting a timestamped reproduction of the seal or other sign in the electronic transferable record.

Article 16 of the Law n 2024-537 contains the requirements for establishing functional equivalence between a document of title and an electronic transferable record. According to its para 1, the electronic transferable records has the same legal effects of the paper-based document of title if it contains all the information required for the document of title and if a reliable method is used to: ensure singularity of the record; identify the holder as the person in control; establish the exclusive control of the holder on the record; identify the issuer and subsequent holders of the record during its lifecycle; maintain integrity and document any amendment occurring during the record's lifecycle. The notion of integrity refers to art 1366 of the Civil Code to clarify that the information should be preserved

[19] Article 1366 of the Civil Code requires identification of the originator of the document and assurance of its integrity. While the integrity requirement is not present in UNCITRAL provisions on the functional equivalence of 'writing', this difference is irrelevant with respect to the MLETR, which also requires integrity. Article 1367 of the Civil Code requires the use of a reliable identification method providing assurance of the link with the signed record. Moreover, the eIDAS Regulation applies in France.

with any subsequent amendment, similar to the notion of dynamic integrity contained in the MLETR, art 10, para 2.

Paragraph 2 of art 16 deals with change of medium, which has to satisfy the conditions agreed by creditor and debtor. It is possible to issue a paper-based document of title that cannot be converted to the electronic form if the document contains such a clause at the time of issuance. Importantly, para 2 also clarifies that change of medium neither affects the rights and obligations of the parties, nor constitutes novation, so that the resulting document incorporates the previous one.

Article 17 of the Law n 2024-537 modifies certain provisions contained in the Code de commerce, Code des transports, Code des assurances and Code monétaire et financier.

To sum up, the French Law provides a significant example of civil law enactment of the MLETR and contains valuable provisions complementing the MLETR. Based on this experience, ICC France decided to prepare a guide to the enactment of MLETR in civil law jurisdictions. The French Law also offers a blueprint for coordinating provisions between the MLETR and eIDAS. It is desirable that the implementing regulations will maintain alignment with MLETR general principles, especially technology neutrality.

4.1.5. Germany

German law allows the issuance of electronic transferable records since a major reform of German maritime law, effected by way of amendments to the German Commercial Code (Handelsgesetzbuch – HGB) entered into force in 2013. One consequence was the introduction of the possibility of issuing electronic bills of lading and sea waybills based on legislative provisions inspired by the Rotterdam Rules. Section 516 of the HGB requires that a bill of lading be signed; that an electronic record having the same functions as a bill of lading be deemed equivalent to a bill of lading, provided that the authenticity and integrity of the record are assured; and that details on the management of the electronic bill of lading be determined by a regulation. The HGB, s 443 contains similar provisions for the inland waterway bill of lading, and the HGB, s 475 does the same for warehouse receipts. The adoption of the implementing regulation has been delayed due to the desire to let the market develop adequate solutions.

Subsequently, these provisions were extended to cargo insurance certificates, thus completing the digitalisation of negotiable documents under German law.[20] These HGB provisions refer to a functional equivalence approach but identify only two elements, authenticity (ie origin) and integrity of the record, which are

[20] Bills of exchange are currently not used in German business practice, although there have been calls for their renewed use in electronic form.

typically linked with the use of electronic signatures based on public-key infrastructure. However, those two elements alone do not seem sufficient to define the legal requirements for the use of electronic transferable records, and there may be scope for introducing the notions of singularity and control of the MLETR in German law through the adoption of the HGB implementing regulation. This solution has been advocated by a broad coalition of commercial operators in order to, on the one hand, provide desirable additional guidance and, on the other hand, align German law with global trends and fully meet the G7 vision for electronic transferable records.[21]

4.1.6. Mexico

Mexico adopted a law ('the Mexican Law') aimed at enabling the use of documents of title in electronic form that is generally based on UNCITRAL principles – especially those of the MLEC – but not on the MLETR.[22] It was explained that the decision not to base the law on the MLETR was due to the urgency of adopting legislation in this field, although the MLETR was already available when the bill was introduced in Parliament.

The Mexican Law amends the law on documents of title[23] recognising the possibility of issuing those documents in electronic form. While the law on documents of title applies to all documents that meet certain requirements, it has specific provisions on the use of cheques, bills of exchange and promissory notes, but not on bills of lading.[24]

The Mexican Law indicates that documents of title in electronic form are considered data messages under the law on electronic transactions[25] and therefore their legal recognition and effect cannot be denied only because of their electronic form (art 5(3)).

The Mexican Law sets forth several requirements for the use of documents of title in electronic form. Written form requirements are met if the electronic document of title maintains its integrity and accessibility (art 5 bis (1)). The notion of integrity is similar to that contained in the MLEC. Moreover, the Mexican Law requires that the circulation of the electronic transferable records

[21] ICC Deutschland, 'Elektronische Transport- und Warenwertpapiere in Deutschland: Reformen und Verordnung als Katalysator des Papierlosen Handels' (2022) www.iccgermany.de.

[22] Decreto por el que se reforman, adicionan y derogan diversas disposiciones de la Ley General de Títulos y Operaciones de Crédito y de la Ley General de Organizaciones y Actividades Auxiliares del Crédito, Diario Oficial de la Federación, 26 de marzo de 2024, 6. For a comment, see MDP Castelán Luna and M Aceves Mejía, 'El principio de equivalencia funcional en los títulos de crédito electrónicos' (2024) 2-2024 *Saberes Administrativos* v 5, 8.

[23] Ley general de títulos y operaciones de crédito, Diario Oficial de la Federación, 27 de agosto de 1932.

[24] Provisions on bills of lading may be found in the Ley de Navegación y Comercio Marítimos, Diario Oficial de la Federación, 1 de junio de 2006, 1. See, for instance, art 129 of that law.

[25] Article 89 bis Código de Comercio.

may be traceable in the electronic transferable records management system (art 5 bis (2)). The electronic transferable record benefits from a presumption of integrity and accessibility if it may be accessed in the electronic transferable records management system (art 5 bis (3)). Any electronic signature recognised under Mexican law[26] may be used in connection with an electronic transferable record. Delivery, endorsement and presentation are effected through the electronic transferable records management system (arts 29, 39 and 40). Likewise, control of the electronic transferable record is effected through that system (art 17 (2)).

Finally, the Mexican Law contains specific provisions on electronic warehouse receipts, which are supposed to be managed in cryptographic information systems (art 229(3)). Only advanced signatures may be used in connection with electronic warehouse receipts (art 231(2)).

In conclusion, the Mexican Law has adopted a peculiar approach to electronic transferable records. It seems also that in the view of the Mexican Law certain technological assumptions underlie the design of the electronic transferable records management system, especially in the case of electronic warehouse receipts. These assumptions may violate technology neutrality and create implementation challenges as operators need to modify existing systems and procedures.

4.1.7. Netherlands

In 2024, a bill has been introduced in the Dutch parliament to give legal recognition to the use of electronic bills of lading.[27] The bill does not apply to other documents of title, without prejudice to their consideration in the future. The bill aims to introduce new articles 400, 401 and 402 at the end of Book 8 of the Civil Code and at making several consequential changes. The requirements for issuance of an electronic bill of lading contained in draft art 400 are similar to those set out in the MLETR, although reference is made to 'authenticity' instead of 'singularity'. However, the explanatory memorandum to the bill explains that the reference to 'authenticity' is aimed at preventing unauthorised duplication and issuance of electronic transferable records, which is the same goal of 'singularity'. Draft art 401 contains the conditions for equivalence between control and possession. Draft art 402 deals with change of medium. The eIDAS Regulation applies with regard to electronic signatures. The explanatory memorandum clarifies that the regime for bills of lading will operate in conjunction with that of the Hague–Visby Rules, which are currently in force in the Netherlands.

Curiously, the new provisions are temporary, at least in theory. The Netherlands have passed legislation to become a party to the Rotterdam Rules, although

[26] Article 89 Código de Comercio.

[27] 'Wet tot wijziging van Boek 8 van het Burgerlijk Wetboek in verband met de invoering van het elektronisch cognossement', WGK012588, available at wetgevingskalender.overheid.nl.

the instrument of ratification has not yet been deposited.[28] The bill is therefore concerned about respecting the treaty provisions, and, if the Rotterdam Rules enter into force in the Netherlands, the suggested new articles will be repealed together with the other provisions relating to bills of lading contained in the Civil Code. This solution may presuppose a conflict between the provisions of the Rotterdam Rules and those of the MLETR although the explanatory memorandum indicates that the bill is based on both texts. In practice, as noted, there is little conflict, if any, between the Rotterdam Rules and the MLETR. Moreover, while it may formally be wise to give way to treaty provisions, in practice the use of electronic bills of lading will be based on uniform MLETR-compliant standards, and the legal regime change is unlikely to have operational consequences.

The explanatory memorandum also discusses private international law matters. Article 10:154 of the Dutch Civil Code applies the Rome I Regulation[29] to contractual matters not covered by that Regulation. In doing so, the Explanatory Memorandum acknowledges that the electronic bill of lading may contain a choice of law clause, including with regard to form requirements and to the interpretation and performance of the contract. Article 10:162 of the Dutch Civil Code contains additional private international law rules specific to bills of lading. Dutch law must be chosen or otherwise be applicable so that the intended Dutch legal regime for electronic bills of lading could apply.

4.1.8. Singapore

Having been one of the more active delegations in drafting the MLETR and being generally a country at the forefront of digitalisation, Singapore was the first jurisdiction that considered enacting the Model Law. Its preparatory activities provide significant insight on MLETR adoption and implementation.

The first pillar of these activities is represented by public consultations on MLETR enactment. A first consultation on the then draft MLETR was carried out in 2017 on the basis of a consultation paper[30] that identified issues relevant for MLETR enactment in light of the Singapore Electronic Transactions Act,[31] which is based on the MLEC and the ECC.

[28] The deposit is conditional to the adoption of the Rotterdam Rules by major shipping countries. Switzerland has taken a similar approach.

[29] Regulation (EC) 593/2008 on the law applicable to contractual obligations (Rome I) [2008] OJ L 177/6.

[30] Infocomm Media Development Authority (IMDA) and Attorney General's Chambers (AGC), 'Joint IMDA–AGC Review of the Electronic Transactions Act (Cap. 88) – Review of Draft UNCITRAL Model Law on Electronic Transferable Records (Public Consultation Paper)' (2017). The consultation paper and the replies from industry are available at www.imda.gov.sg.

[31] The MLEC was enacted in Singapore with the Electronic Transactions Act, Act 25 of 1998, which was repealed by the Singapore Electronic Transactions Act, Act 16 of 2010, incorporating also the substantive provisions of the ECC. The MLETR was enacted with the Singapore Electronic Transactions (Amendments) Act 2021, Act 5 of 2021.

One issue of particular importance is the impact on the Electronic Transactions Act of the enactment of the general reliability standard contained in the MLETR, art 12. The Singapore Electronic Transactions Act did not contain any such standard and the consultation paper suggested that the reliability standard should apply only to electronic transferable records. This is an important issue whose practical relevance may be mitigated by the fact that electronic transferable records management systems may manage both transferable and non-transferable records, and thus apply the same reliability standards regardless of the transferability of the record. Moreover, jurisdictions that have enacted the UNCITRAL Model Law on Electronic Signatures (MLES), art 10 on the trustworthiness of the means utilised by the certification service provider, need to decide whether both standards should coexist, or a single standard should be adopted and, in the latter case, if the MLETR, art 12 should be retained, and with which modifications, if any.

The first two questions of the consultation paper asked generally whether Singapore should enact the MLETR and, if so, whether there would be any disadvantage in being an early enactor. The third question related to whether the MLETR, art 4, on party autonomy and privity of contract, should be enacted. The paper suggested it should not. The fourth question queried whether a system of accreditation for electronic transferable records management system operators should be introduced. The fifth question asked whether the MLETR, art 13, on indication of time and place, should be expanded to indicate the time of despatch and receipt of electronic transferable records, which could amount to issuance and transfer of those records.[32]

The replies strongly supported an early enactment of the MLETR by Singapore. They also highlighted that such early enactment could face implementation challenges, and that, while cross-border trade could benefit most from the application of the MLETR, this required onboarding foreign trade partners. Interestingly, the respondents were mostly from the financial sector, which was less represented than transport and logistics operators at UNCITRAL during the MLETR preparation.

A second consultation was carried out in 2019.[33] The object of this consultation was to expand the scope of application of the Electronic Transactions Act to topics such as wills, powers of attorney and contracts for the sale or other disposal of real estate.[34] The adoption of the MLETR was presented as enabling the application of the Electronic Transactions Act to transferable documents and instruments.

[32] Explanatory Note, para 145.

[33] IMDA, 'Consultation Paper Issued by the INFOCOMM Media Development Authority on Review of the Electronic Transactions Act (ETA) (Cap. 88)' (2019). The consultation paper and the replies from industry are available at www.imda.gov.sg.

[34] The exclusion of certain documents from the scope of application of the Electronic Transactions Act does not prohibit the use of those documents in electronic form; however, the assessment of the fulfilment of the relevant requirements would be a matter of judicial interpretation under common law: *SM Integrated Transware Pte Ltd v Schenker Singapore (Pte) Ltd* [2005] SGHC 58, CLOUT Case 661.

The consultation paper generically asked whether the MLETR should be enacted in Singapore and, accordingly, whether transferable documents and instruments should be removed from the matters excluded from the scope of application of the Electronic Transactions Act.

The replies from industry supported the use of transferable documents and instruments in electronic form and the adoption of the MLETR. Among those replies, the submission of the Singapore Shipping Association conveyed strong support for the use of all commercial documents in electronic form through a national trade platform. It noted the need to coordinate the adoption of the MLETR with other relevant legislation, namely the Bills of Lading Act,[35] whose s 1(5) foresees the possibility of adopting regulations on the use of electronic bills of lading. It suggested that the adoption of such regulations would further the case for foreign recognition of bills of lading in electronic form issued in Singapore, including by addressing conflict of law issues. It further noted that Singapore is a party to the Hague-Visby Rules,[36] which did not explicitly foresee the use of electronic bills of lading. In order to avoid arguments aimed at invalidating their use under treaty rules, it was suggested to amend the Carriage of Goods by Sea Act[37] along the lines of the Australian Carriage of Goods by Sea Act, which allows for the use of electronic transport documents.[38] In that regard, it should be recalled that one suggestion made at the onset of the work of the Working Group on the MLETR was to prepare a protocol to the ECC that could extend the scope of application of that treaty to electronic transferable records. Such amended convention could operate in conjunction with other treaties including the Hague-Visby Rules.

Another issue of general interest raised in the replies to the consultation related to the impact of the adoption of the MLETR on the use of cheques, which are the only transferable instrument that may be commonly used by consumers. In that regard, it was noted that the use of cheques was being discouraged in Singapore, and that a range of other payment options existed.

The issue of the evidentiary value of electronic records and documents after their conversion into another medium was also raised. Those concerns had been addressed by UNCITRAL, which clarified that replaced documents and records cease to have effect and validity only with respect to their transferability.[39]

The second pillar of Singapore's preparatory activities is represented by the work on the implementing information technology ecosystem. Singapore has used two separate systems for managing trade-related information: TradeNet, a

The position is shared with other common law jurisdictions: for the Eastern Caribbean Supreme Court in the Court of Appeal, see *BB Inc v Lewis Hamilton* [2017] ECSC J0407-2, CLOUT Case 2052.

[35] Bills of Lading Act 1994, Cap 384, enacting the UK Carriage of Goods by Sea Act 1992.

[36] 1412 UNTS 127.

[37] Carriage of Goods by Sea Act, Cap 33, enacting the UK Carriage of Goods by Sea Act 1992.

[38] This was done with the Carriage of Goods by Sea Amendment Act 1997, Act No 123 of 1997. The amendments were incorporated in the Carriage of Goods by Sea Act 1991, Act No 160 of 1991.

[39] Explanatory Note, para 170.

single window for customs clearance; and TradeXchange, aimed at facilitating exchanges among the trade and logistics community. Those two systems, together with Singapore Customs' backend system called eCustoms, have been merged in a single ecosystem called Networked Trade Platform.[40] Further evolving this facility, the Government of Singapore promotes conducting trade-related electronic exchanges in TradeTrust, which is a digital trade ecosystem made of 'a set of governance and legal frameworks, [technical] standards and future-ready digital infrastructure' and aimed at facilitating exchange of commercial and trade-related documents based on the use of distributed ledgers.

One legal cornerstone of TradeTrust is the adoption of UNCITRAL texts, namely the MLETR, to enable legal recognition of B2B exchanges. Another legal cornerstone is the conclusion of intergovernmental agreements enabling G2G exchanges.[41] Treaties such as the Digital Economy Partnership Agreement negotiated between New Zealand, Chile and Singapore assist in implementing this vision. Article 2.3(2) of the Digital Economy Partnership Agreement requires the states parties to the Agreement to make endeavours to adopt the MLETR.[42]

4.1.9. Spain

The Rotterdam Rules have inspired maritime law reform in Spain, which has also ratified the Rules. Article 262 of the Maritime Law[43] allows the issuance and use of electronic maritime bills of lading if carrier and shipper agree in writing. Carrier and shipper should determine in their contract the details of the electronic bills of lading management system with respect to the assurance of security of the electronic medium and integrity of its content, and to the mechanism for circulation, including presentation and termination. Article 264 of the Maritime Law establishes full legal equivalence between paper-based and electronic bills of lading. Articles 263, 265 and 266 of the Maritime Law deal with the procedures for change of medium. Article 267 extends the application of the rules on maritime bills of lading to bills of lading issued for multimodal or combined transport. As in the case of Germany, the MLETR could provide useful guidance to implementing these provisions, whose use in commercial practice is not documented.

With regard to other transferable documents and instruments, a draft Spanish commercial code foresees the issuance of cheques, promissory notes, bills of exchange and accepted invoices on paper or electronically.[44] Article 631-6 of the draft commercial code foresees the adoption of regulations establishing the

[40] Accessible at www.ntp.gov.sg.

[41] In the Asia-Pacific region, this could be done under the umbrella of the Framework Agreement on Facilitation of Cross-border Paperless Trade in Asia and the Pacific (CPTA) (adopted 19 May 2016, opened for signature 1 October 2016, entered into force 20 February 2021).

[42] See ch 9, section 9.5.

[43] Ley 14/2014, de 24 de julio, de Navegación Marítima.

[44] Art 631-1. The draft commercial code was approved by the Spanish Cabinet in 2022 but has not yet been approved by Parliament and is therefore not in force. Its text is available at transparencia.gob.es.

requirements that electronic transferable records must meet to guarantee the security of the support as well as the authenticity, integrity and intangibility of their content; the mode of transmission and of entitlement of the holder; and the loss of their validity or effectiveness.

4.1.10. Sweden

An interesting case regarding the enforceability of an electronic promissory note arose in Sweden. A promissory note had been executed in electronic form only. The debtor did not honour the note. When the creditor proceeded to enforce the note, the bailiff refused to do so as chapter 2, section 2 of the Enforcement Code 1981 requires presenting the original paper copy of a negotiable promissory note for verification of authenticity before its enforcement. The Supreme Court decided the case noting that an electronic promissory note cannot be possessed according to the notion of possession envisaged in the Debt Securities Act 1936, and therefore may not be considered a negotiable instrument.[45]

In the Supreme Court's view, possession of the note is essential to protect the creditor but does not necessarily presuppose the use of the paper medium. In other words, the Supreme Court considered the Debt Securities Act as technology-neutral and was open to recognising the legal validity of an electronic promissory note as long as its management system provided the same guarantees as paper. In a concurring opinion, the Chief Justice contemplated the possibility of dealing with electronic promissory notes, cited as an example of a similar document the electronic transport documents contemplated under the Rotterdam Rules and invited the legislator to consider adopting technology-neutral law ensuring exclusive control of the electronic promissory note to avoid double-spending issues.

The adoption of the MLETR in Swedish law, or the use of MLETR-compliant electronic transferable records under other law, are likely to satisfy the conditions set by the Supreme Court.[46] ICC Sweden has started coordinating MLETR awareness-raising activities in the country with a view to preparing a preliminary report on possible MLETR adoption in Sweden.[47]

4.1.11. Timor-Leste

Timor-Leste has adopted Decree-Law no 12/2024 of 13 February 2024,[48] containing the 'General Legal Regime of Electronic Commerce and Electronic

[45] Decision Ö 5072-16 of 2 November 2017, available in Swedish at www.domstol.se.

[46] See ICC Sweden, 'Digitalisation of International Trade: The Legal Status of Electronic Transferable Records in Sweden' (2024) for additional information on Swedish case law on electronic transferable records.

[47] See also the position of the Swedish Government in 'Svar på fråga 2023/24:1120 Digitalisering för ökad trygghet och effektivitet i global handel' (18 September 2024) www.riksdagen.se.

[48] Jornal da República, Série I, N° 7, p 180.

Signatures', which enacts MLEC, MLES, ECC and MLETR. The latter is applied to letters of credit, bills of lading and promissory notes (article 4, letter (l) of the Decree-Law).[49]

Interestingly, the general reliability standard contained in the MLETR, art 12 is applicable to all electronic transactions and to electronic signatures (article 7 of the Decree-Law), thus implementing the approach advocating for benchmarking the reliability requirements for the whole digital trade ecosystem against the most demanding requirements, ie those set forth for electronic transferable records.

Another noteworthy variation to the text of the MLETR is contained in article 61 of the Decree-Law, on endorsement. Instead of referring to the functional equivalence notions of writing and signature, as in the MLETR, art 15, it refers to the functional equivalence requirements for the notion of transferable document or instrument contained in the MLETR, art 10, para 1 (and the corresponding article 58, paragraph 1 of the Decree-Law).

4.1.12. United Kingdom

English law plays a prominent role in international trade and is often chosen as the law applicable to documents of title. It is therefore not surprising that the Law Commission of England and Wales, in the framework of its efforts to ensure that English law may deal appropriately with technological developments and emerging business practices, and in light of the adoption of the MLETR by Singapore, decided to study an adequate legislative treatment for enabling the use of electronic transferable trade documents. The goals of this initiative included increasing ease of business in the United Kingdom and preserving English law as a preferred law of choice for transferable documents and instruments. Particular care was given to ensuring that the law would seamlessly interact with pre-existing English statutes, although this meant departing from the language of the MLETR.[50]

The Law Commission prepared a comprehensive report outlining options for reform.[51] The report provides information on the reasons for reform and identifies the concerned trade documents and a number of features needed to enable their use in electronic form.[52] Because the report deals with a national law (unlike the

[49] The Decree-Law No 14/2017, on the Customs Code, contains some provisions on electronic signatures and electronic transactions inspired by UNCITRAL texts, but its application is limited to exchanges with the national single window for customs operations. It is unclear whether the Decree-Law No 12/2024 has implicitly repealed the provisions of the Customs Code.

[50] It may be argued that a similar analysis should have been carried out for Scottish law: however, on the one hand, Scottish law is conceptually different from English law; on the other hand, it is seldom applied to transferable trade documents.

[51] Law Commission, *Electronic Trade Documents: Report and Bill* (Law Com No 405, 2022).

[52] These features, which are present also in the MLETR, are: substantive information requirements; use of reliable systems; integrity; control; divestibility (transfer of control); identification of the document (singularity); identification of the person in control.

MLETR, which deals generally with all national laws), it can delve into matters such as the difference between transferability and negotiability, and the possession of intangibles, which were precluded to the drafters of the MLETR.

Importantly, the report acknowledges that, under the principle of functional equivalence, the person in control of an electronic transferable record enjoys the same rights that possession of a paper-based transferable document or instruments gives to a holder; however, it indicates that

> In order to benefit from the existing law on possession and to ensure that there is no difference in legal treatment between documents in different forms, we think it is clearer and more direct to extend the application of the concept of possession itself.[53]

Accordingly, recommendation 20 of the report states that 'Legislation should provide expressly that an electronic document is capable of being possessed'.[54] It is important to ensure that this statement of principle, which in itself may have limited practical consequences, does not affect interoperability and mutual legal recognition of electronic transferable records issued under English law and under the law of the MLETR-enacting jurisdictions.

The work of the Law Commission eventually led to the adoption of the UK Electronic Trade Documents Act 2023 (ETDA 2023).[55] Following the suggestions of the report, the functional equivalence requirements of singularity, control, and integrity set forth in the MLETR may be found in the ETDA 2023 albeit arranged differently. The circumstances relevant for the determination of reliability of the method used in managing the electronic transferable record are also similar. The main difference between the two laws lies in the legal mechanism to link possession and transferable records (or 'intangibles'): while the MLETR applies the functional equivalence principle, the ETDA 2023 declares that intangibles may be possessed, which has consequences also on the notion of 'control'.[56] This is done to ensure the availability of possessory remedies, namely, based on the tort of conversion.[57] It may however be argued that those remedies would also be available under a functional equivalence approach.

Another consequence of this approach is that the ETDA 2023 applies to documents that are subject to possession but not transferable, such as straight bills of lading. This is confirmed by ETDA 2023, s 1, which defines trade documents as documents in paper form, used in trade or trade finance, and which under law or custom require possession of the document to claim performance of an obligation. The definition does not require the trade document to be transferable.

[53] Law Commission, *Electronic Trade Documents* (2022) para 2.74.

[54] ibid para 7.46.

[55] Electronic Trade Documents Act 2023. An official Explanatory Note to the ETDA 2023 is available.

[56] On 'control' in the ETDA 2023 and in the MLETR, see C Pejovic and U Lee, 'Towards Global Legal Recognition of Electronic Trade Documents: Control or Possession?' (2024) 59 *Texas International Law Journal* 101, 112–114.

[57] J Lai, 'Conversion of cryptoassets' (2024) 55 *Computer Law & Security Review*, art 106060.

Moreover, the ETDA 2023 does not contain a 'safe harbour' provision such as the one contained in the MLETR, art 12(b).[58] Despite these and other minor differences, the ETDA 2023 may be considered aligned with the MLETR for legal and practical purposes.[59]

4.2. Legal Texts Influenced by the MLETR

International trade law is in constant evolution and the demand for uniform texts enabling digital trade is surging. It is therefore not surprising that the MLETR has already been used as a model for other uniform laws.

UNCITRAL has continued working on electronic transferable records with two legislative projects closely related to the MLETR, respectively on warehouse receipts, and on negotiable multimodal cargo documents.

Other organisations are also carrying out legal work based on the MLETR, namely, to align existing uniform contractual texts to the MLETR so as to ensure seamless interaction between statutes enacting the MLETR and contractual agreements.

Yet another line of work refers to the inclusion of the MLETR or of its core provisions in regional model laws. The Commonwealth Secretariat is preparing a draft model law on digital trade based on UNCITRAL model laws, including the MLETR. The model law, once adopted, aims to replace the Commonwealth Model Law on Electronic Transactions, 2002, which has been successful in promoting the adoption of UNCITRAL texts among Commonwealth members.

4.2.1. The UNCITRAL-UNIDROIT Model Law on Warehouse Receipts

Warehouse receipts are commercial documents released by a warehouse operator against the deposit of commodities. Warehouse receipts may be negotiable or

[58] The omission seems to be based on a misunderstanding as it was felt that the safety clause could impose an onerous burden on system operators by promoting the need for accreditation schemes: Law Commission (n 51) para 6.47. However, as evidenced also in case law (see comment to the MLETR, art 12 in ch 3), the safety clause operates absent any accreditation or similar scheme.

[59] The correlation between provisions of the ETDA 2023 and of the MLETR may be established as follows: ETDA 2023, s 1(1)(a) and MLETR, art 2, on the definition of transferable document and instrument; ETDA 2023, s 2(2)(a) and MLETR, art 10(1)(b)(i), on singularity; ETDA 2023, s 2(2)(b) and MLETR, art 10(1)(b)(iii), on integrity; ETDA 2023, s 2(2)(c) and MLETR, arts 10(1)(b)(ii) and 11(1)(a), on control, ETDA 2023, s 2(2)(d) and MLETR, art 11(1)(b), on identification of the person in control; ETDA 2023, s 2(2)(e) and MLETR, art 11(2), on transfer of control; ETDA 2023, s 2(5) and MLETR, art 12(a), on the circumstances relevant to determine the reliability of the methods used; ETDA 2023, s 4 and MLETR, arts 17 and 18, on change of medium. Moreover, ETDA 2023, s 3(3) achieves the same legal effect with regards to possession as functional equivalence under the MLETR. For details, see the comparison between the MLETR and ETDA 2023 in Stephenson Harwood LLP in collaboration with IMDA, 'TradeTrust-enabled Electronic Bills of Lading: A Legal and Practical Analysis of Their Use in Global Trade' (2023), section 6.

non-negotiable. If they are negotiable, they may be used to transfer the property or the right to delivery of the deposited goods and as collateral for trade financing. Hence, negotiable warehouse receipts are a transferable document and, when in electronic form, an electronic transferable record.

The legislator may include warehouse receipts in the scope of application of the law when enacting the MLETR, or may decide not to do so in light of their special status. Warehouse receipts for agriculture commodities may be used predominantly at the domestic level to promote access to credit for small farmers. Warehouse operators are subject to a regulatory regime. The law may already foresee the use of electronic warehouse receipts, typically with the use of a centralised registry. Although this solution may create data silos, it has the benefit of being tested and widespread. On the other hand, alignment of the legal regime of electronic warehouse receipts with MLETR has the advantage of enabling data exchanges across the supply chain, so that the warehouse receipt may incorporate information on the source of the commodity and on its transport, including certifications of compliance with applicable regulations on sustainability, etc. The adoption of an open ecosystem for electronic warehouse receipts may also facilitate interaction with the electronic security registry, if existing, when security interests are taken in the warehouse receipt.

UNCITRAL and the International Institute for the Unification of Private Law (UNIDROIT) carried out a joint project on the codification of the law of warehouse receipts. The outcome of that joint project is the UNCITRAL – UNIDROIT Model Law on Warehouse Receipts (MLWR), which contains a full set of provisions that allow using warehouse receipts for trade financing under both the single document and the dual document (ie warehouse receipt and pledge bond) approach.[60]

During the consideration of the MLWR, UNCITRAL Working Group I decided that the provisions dealing with electronic warehouse receipts needed to be closely aligned with the MLETR framework not only for legal consistency, but also to ensure that the warehouse receipt could be integrated in the broader digital trade ecosystem. Other commercial documents in electronic form and the internet of things may provide information on the goods covered by the receipt such as date and place of origin, compliance with regulatory and other standards, conditions of carriage, etc. This information may not only provide assurance on the quality of the goods, but also on their existence, thus preventing documentary credit fraud.

[60] On the MLWR see P Wehling, 'A Roadmap for Legal Reform: the Future UNCITRAL/UNIDROIT Model Law on Warehouse Receipts' (2023) 38 *Butterworths Journal of International Banking & Financial Law* 553; D Neo, 'Drafting a Model Law on Warehouse Receipts', in B Köhler, R Gulati and T John (eds), *The Elgar Companion to UNIDROIT* (Cheltenham, Edward Elgar Publishing, 2023) 442. On the preparatory work, M Dubovec and A Elias, 'A Proposal for UNCITRAL to Develop a Model Law on Warehouse Receipts' (2017) 22 *Uniform Law Review* 716.

The Working Group also decided to adopt a medium-neutral approach to electronic warehouse receipts.[61] That policy decision was taken not to give prominence to paper-based warehouse receipts – as would have been the case under the functional equivalence approach – when the use of electronic warehouse receipts was actively promoted. The medium-neutral approach of the MLWR does not go as far as referring to information as an abstract notion but is implemented in a concrete manner by drafting provisions that, as a rule, are equally applicable to both media.

In practice, the adoption of the medium-neutral approach means that the requirements for electronic transferable records that are formulated as functional equivalence rules in the MLETR are instead formulated as conditions for legal recognition and effect of the electronic warehouse receipt in the MLWR. Thus, the MLWR, art 6 corresponds to the MLETR, arts 10 and 11, and the MLWR, art 7 corresponds to the MLETR, art 12.

The MLWR does not refer to the notion of endorsement because warehouse receipts are not endorsed for the purpose of an action in regress according to the chain of endorsements. For this reason, the MLWR recognises control as the sole manner of transferring an electronic warehouse receipt.[62] This is reflected in the definition of holder of an electronic negotiable warehouse receipt contained in the MLWR, art 3(b).

The MLWR contains a provision on the loss or destruction of the electronic warehouse receipt that was necessary because of a similar provision regarding the paper-based document. Thus, the MLWR, art 13, para 2 indicates that loss or destruction of an electronic warehouse receipt occurs when any of the conditions for an electronic warehouse receipt set out in art 6, paras 1 and 3, ceases to be met; hence, loss of singularity, integrity or control, and non-reliability of the methods used. It also clarifies that the issuance of a replacement warehouse receipt may include reinstatement of control over the electronic warehouse receipt. These considerations apply to any electronic transferable record.

Similarly, the MLWR provides an insight on how security interests in electronic transferable records may be taken. The comment for art 19 of the Guide to Enactment of the MLWR explains that three methods are available to use a warehouse receipt as a collateral. These three methods are: (i) registration in a registry established pursuant to an applicable secured transactions law; (ii) taking control of an electronic warehouse receipt; and (iii) taking possession of a paper-based warehouse receipt. The notion of control is used in the MLWR as an autonomous method to establish third-party effectiveness, and must be complemented by a rule that would provide that a secured creditor in control of an electronic warehouse receipt would have priority over another security right made effective against third parties by registration. In the MLETR, the notion of control is used to achieve

[61] UNCITRAL, 'Report of Working Group I (Warehouse Receipts) on the Work of its Forty-first Session' (16 February 2024) UN Doc A/CN.9/1165, paras 12–13.

[62] Ibid, para 60.

functional equivalence with that of possession, and the priority rule would be found in general secured transactions law.

The MLWR addresses in full matters relating to the use of warehouse receipts. However, this presupposes the desire to amend the substantive law of those receipts. Jurisdictions that do not wish to do so may enact the MLETR as enabler (among other commercial documents) of electronic warehouse receipts without amending existing law.

Jurisdictions that have already enacted the MLETR and wish to adopt the MLWR may either adopt the MLWR in full and exclude warehouse receipts from the scope of application of the MLETR enactment, or adopt the MLWR without provisions on the use of electronic warehouse receipts (for example, MLWR, arts 6, 7, 13, para 2, and the definition of 'holder of a negotiable electronic warehouse receipt').

4.2.2. The UNCITRAL Draft Instrument on a Negotiable Cargo Document

Because of historical reasons linked to the duration of sea journeys, negotiable transport documents usually require a maritime leg. However, the increasing use of rail cargo for long-distance carriage of goods, such as between China and Europe, has created a business demand for negotiable transport documents to be used as collateral for trade financing also with regard to cargo that is not seaborne. To address that need, in 2019 the Government of the People's Republic of China submitted a proposal to UNCITRAL suggesting legislative work on negotiable railway consignment notes.[63] The topic was eventually retained on the Commission's work programme and assigned in 2022 to UNCITRAL Working Group VI for drafting a new legislative text, possibly in the form of a treaty.

Earlier drafts of the instrument took an eclectic approach based on several provisions inspired by the MLETR and other elements inspired by the eCMR and the Rotterdam Rules.[64] Discussions at Working Group VI progressively further aligned the text with that of the MLETR, mindful of the growing importance of the MLETR enactments in facilitating the use of electronic means for trade and transport and of the requests of UNCITRAL in that sense.[65] As the instrument on negotiable cargo documents is based on a medium-neutral approach, the MLWR is also a relevant blueprint for this drafting exercise.

[63] UNCITRAL, 'Work Programme – Possible Future Work Regarding Railway Consignment Notes – Proposal by the Government of the People's Republic of China' (14 June 2019) UN Doc A/CN.9/998.

[64] UNCITRAL, 'Negotiable Cargo Documents' (8 February 2024) UN Doc A/CN.9/WG.VI/WP.103.

[65] UNCITRAL, 'Report of Working Group VI (Negotiable Cargo Documents) on the Work of its Forty-fifth Session' (20 December 2024) UN Doc A/CN.9/1199.

The Government of Singapore submitted a proposal to the 44th session of Working Group VI[66] suggesting that all the provisions on negotiable electronic cargo records contained in the draft instrument should be replaced with a single general provision requiring states to adopt an appropriate legal framework enabling and governing the use of electronic equivalents of negotiable cargo documents, such as that contained in MLETR. The reasons for this alternative approach are: avoiding unnecessary duplication of effort; providing flexibility to cater for developments in technology and business practice, especially if the final form of the instrument is a treaty, which is not as easily amendable as national law; reducing obstacles to adoption of the draft instrument in light of the existing variety of laws dealing with electronic transferable records; promoting the adoption of UNCITRAL instruments; and promoting legal standardisation and harmonisation.[67] However, the proposal of Singapore was not adopted.

4.2.3. Alignment of Contractual Texts with the MLETR

The adoption of the MLETR requires adjusting the contractual framework of business operators. Thus, electronic transferable records management systems operators need to revise their standard terms and conditions and their rulebooks to refer to the appropriate national law enacting the MLETR, and to reflect the fact that the MLETR is enacted as a statute (as opposed to contract-based documents). Changes in applicable law also require aligning dispute resolution clauses on choice of forum and jurisdiction, or arbitration clauses. Parties issuing the electronic transferable records (for example, carriers issuing bills of lading) need to revise their standard terms and conditions.

Another set of contractual rules that needs revision and alignment with the MLETR are the uniform rules prepared by the ICC for incorporation into a contract by reference. Likewise, other international non-governmental organisations are preparing texts that may facilitate the application of the MLETR or pave the way to the adoption of the MLETR.

ICC Uniform Rules for Digital Trade Transactions

In 2019, the ICC prepared a dedicated set of rules for the use of electronic communications called the Uniform Rules for Digital Trade Transactions (URDTT).[68]

[66] UNCITRAL, 'Preliminary Draft Provisions for a New Instrument on Negotiable Cargo Documents. Submission from the Government of Singapore' (25 January 2024) UN Doc A/CN.9/WG.VI/WP.104.

[67] ibid, para 4.

[68] D Meynell (ed), *Implementing URDTT Version 1.0* (Paris, ICC, 2022); A Mugasha, 'Technological Innovation in Trade Finance and the Law: From the Bank Payment Obligation and Blockchain to the Uniform Rules on Digital Trade Transactions' (2022) 38 *Banking & Finance Law Review* 217.

The URDTT are compatible with UNCITRAL texts on electronic commerce, including the MLETR.[69]

The URDTT aim to facilitate end-to-end commercial exchanges taking place in electronic form only. These exchanges are referred to as digital trade transactions and are defined as 'a process, as agreed between the Principal Parties, whereby Electronic Records are used to evidence the underlying sale and purchase of goods or services, and the incurring of a Payment Obligation' (URDTT, art 1). More precisely, the URDTT cover the contract of sale of goods or services in electronic form, the payment obligation and the trade finance undertaking of a third party called the 'financial service provider'. Like other contractual texts, the URDTT apply only when parties to the transaction agree, and to the extent that they are not expressly modified or excluded.

The URDTT, art 8 deals with non-compliance of an electronic record with the terms and conditions of the digital trade transaction. In that case, the recipient of the electronic record must inform the originator of each reason for non-compliance in a single notice within two business days (calculated until 23.59.59 universal time coordinated of the second day) from the day of receipt of the electronic record. Once the notice of non-compliance is sent, the digital trade transaction cannot proceed unless the originator submits a compliant electronic record; or the terms of the digital trade transaction are amended so that the electronic record is compliant; or all the parties accept the non-compliant document. If no notice of non-compliance is sent, the electronic record will be presumed to be accepted by the recipient. These rules may be used to supplement the MLETR with respect to digital trade transactions. For instance, they could be incorporated in the rulebook of the electronic transferable records management system provider.

A payment obligation must contain, among other data elements, a unique reference linking the payment obligation and the digital trade transaction (URDTT, art 12(c)(i)). While a payment obligation may not be included in a document of title, this unique reference may help to establish a link between an electronic transferable record and the sales contract that it relates to.

eUCP and eURC

Other sets of uniform rules aim to supplement already widely used uniform rules with regard to electronic means.

The Uniform Customs and Practice for Documentary Credits (UCP 600) is a set of contractual rules that facilitates the use of letters of credit. The UCP 600 are complemented by the eUCP, which were first adopted in 2007. In 2019 the eUCP was revised to include, among other things, a revised definition of 'electronic

[69] See D Meynell, *From a Bill to an Act. The Electronic Trade Documents Act* (London, ICC UK, 2023) for a comparison between MLETR, ETDA and URDTT.

record' that included 'logically associated information' (eUCP, art e3).[70] In 2023 another revision of the eUCP was adopted that contained a reference to electronic transferable records in the definition of electronic record (eUCP, art e3) as well as a new definition of 'electronic transferable record' (eUCP, art e3).

The ICC has undertaken similar work to supplement its Uniform Rules for Collections (URC 522), which facilitate the collection of owned money or assets, to accommodate presentation of electronic records alone or together with paper documents. The URC 522 are used by banks in trade financing, for instance to ensure that documents representing the goods, such as bills of lading, are presented timely and according to the contractual agreement (for example, against payment). The resulting eURC, first adopted in 2019, were aligned with the MLETR in 2023 (eURC Version 1.1). Amendments are similar to those made in 2023 to the eUCP (see eUCP, art 4e).

Negotiable FIATA Multimodal Transport Bill of Lading

Another MLETR-related initiative is the Negotiable FIATA Multimodal Transport Bill of Lading (eFBL).[71] The eFBL is a contract-based document that may be used by freight forwarders that comply with certain requirements, including liability insurance coverage. The benefits expected from the use of eFBL are similar to those generally associated with the use of electronic transferable records. FIATA supports the efforts to promote MLETR as well as ongoing UNCITRAL work on a negotiable multimodal transport document.[72]

[70] ICC, *Users Guide to the eUCP* (Paris, ICC, 2021) provides insight on the eUCP Version 2.0.
[71] FIATA is the International Federation of Freight Forwarders Associations: see www.efbl.fiata.org.
[72] See section 4.2.2 of this chapter.

5

The UNCITRAL Model Law on the Use and Cross-border Recognition of Identity Management and Trust Services

5.1. Legal Recognition of Electronic Documents and Data

Documents may need to contain certain information and meet certain form requirements to have legal effect. For instance, a cheque may be required to contain the word 'cheque' to be legally valid, and a contract for the transfer of interests in real estate usually needs to be drafted in writing, often with the assistance of a notary public. In case of dispute on the legal effect of a document, a third party, such as a judge or an arbitrator, may formally declare its validity.

To ensure that documents have the same legal effect regardless of the jurisdiction where recognition is sought, it is necessary to refer to the notion of cross-border legal recognition of documents.[1] Cross-border legal recognition is not an end in itself, but a means to an end, ie facilitating commercial transactions across borders. There is no single solution to legal recognition, but a variety of mechanisms are used. These mechanisms often build on practical needs, rather than on legal theory, and reflect different approaches and priorities.

First, the adoption of uniform or harmonised commercial law texts (respectively, treaties and model laws) may contribute to reducing legal diversity. For instance, a bill of lading may be issued under English law and the Hague-Visby Rules. Its recognition may have different effects depending on whether the recognising jurisdiction is a party to the Hague-Visby Rules as treaty adoption may limit or offset the application of mandatory rules (or 'ordre public').

Second, the jurisdiction where recognition is sought may, under its principles of private international law, allow the parties to choose the law applicable to the

[1] In the field of electronic transactions law, legal recognition has also a specific meaning as a principle underpinning the texts of the United Nations Commission on International Trade Law (UNCITRAL): see ch 3, commentary on the Model Law on Electronic Transferable Records (MLETR), art 3.

document (principle of party autonomy in the choice of law).[2] This solution gives great flexibility to commercial parties. The chosen law may also determine the form requirements: this is explicitly recognised in the Model Law on Electronic Signatures (MLES), art 12, para 5 with regard to electronic signatures.

However, mandatory provisions may hinder legal recognition: for instance, certain countries require that commercial documents be drafted in the local language.[3] If the local language version of the document is not available, recognition cannot be granted. Moreover, some jurisdictions may not allow a choice of applicable law in some cases, and many – especially in developing countries – are silent on private international law matters.

Another approach to cross-border legal recognition relies on third parties performing certain functions aimed at providing assurance of certain document qualities (for example, apostille and legalisation of paper documents). In this case, an institutional mechanism, possibly based on a dedicated international agreement, may be set up. This is a mechanism favoured by public authorities, which typically rely on national laws and may feel uncomfortable dealing with a foreign document that has not been validated domestically. However, this solution requires participation of each state, which may be time-consuming and difficult to complete, and the use of an institutional mechanism, which may be costly.[4]

Cross-border recognition of paper-based documents and of electronic records is not a fully settled matter. However, while some mechanisms for paper-based documents are already in place, those for electronic documents are still in development. Existing solutions are often document- and jurisdiction-specific. This approach may work for paper-based documents, which are handled individually. It is possible to give legal recognition to a foreign electronic document, ie a document that has been issued abroad, or under a foreign law, or that has any other significant foreign element that triggers legal consequences. For instance, the Additional Protocol to the Convention on the Contract for the International Carriage of Goods by Road concerning the Electronic Consignment Note[5] gives legal recognition to electronic consignment notes issued under the Convention on the Contract for the International Carriage of Goods by Road and ensures their legal recognition among state parties to the Protocol. The advantage of focusing on individual documents is easier implementation in a well-defined environment, which brings a higher level of legal predictability, especially when a treaty is applicable. The disadvantage is the possible creation of data silos by adopting industry-specific standards and solutions. For this reason, mechanisms for the recognition of electronic records should ideally apply to all types of commercial

[2] For a classic discussion of party autonomy, see HE Yntema, '"Autonomy" in Choice of Law' (1952) 1 *American Journal of Comparative Law* 341.

[3] See ch 3, commentary on the MLETR, art 6.

[4] See, eg, the Convention Abolishing the Requirement of Legalisation for Foreign Public Documents (adopted 5 October 1961, entered into force 24 January 1965) (Apostille Convention) 527 UNTS 189.

[5] See ch 2, section 2.3.

documents and to all jurisdictions and be technology neutral to avoid creating technology-specific requirements that cause workflow fragmentation.

Recognition of electronic documents and recognition of data are complementary: it is not sufficient to give legal recognition to a foreign electronic document, but it is also necessary to give assurance of the quality of the data constituting that document. When the focus shifts from documents to data, the recognition mechanism should rely on the application across borders of trust services, which are services for the assurance of data quality. A general mechanism for cross-border recognition of trust services is a fundamental component of the digital trade ecosystem. This is one of the main goals pursued by the UNCITRAL Model Law on the Use and Cross-border Recognition of Identity Management and Trust Services (MLIT), especially its provisions on trust services. By recognising the effect of the application of the foreign trust service, the content of the foreign electronic document may also be validated (for example, as complete and authentic). The set of provisions on identity management complement those on trust services by providing assurance of the correct identification of the physical and legal persons involved in trade. From that perspective, identification may be considered an element of data quality assurance.

Reciprocity is a possible requirement of legal recognition. Referred also to as 'mutual recognition', reciprocity means that the parties to a cross-border legal recognition arrangement reciprocally grant legal recognition, often coupled with technical interoperability. The arrangement itself may be bilateral or plurilateral. The eIDAS Regulation is an example of plurilateral mechanism for the legal recognition of foreign data.

Alternatively, the recognising jurisdiction may do so unilaterally, ie the legal recognition of foreign data and documents is granted regardless of whether the jurisdiction of origin does the same. This approach is followed in UNCITRAL texts. For example, MLES, art 12 places on the same level national and foreign electronic signatures and certificates when assessing their reliability. The treatment of foreign electronic signatures and certificates as national ones effectively gives them legal recognition regardless of reciprocity in the jurisdiction of origin.

Another important distinction pertains to whether the mechanism to grant legal recognition operates before (ex ante) or after (ex post) the relevant electronic exchange. A mechanism ex ante will recognise all data and documents that meet certain conditions and may be managed by a single central entity or may be decentralised. The cross-certification of electronic signature certificates issued using a public key infrastructure (PKI), which may be carried out by individual certification service providers, constitutes an example of ex ante decentralised recognition mechanism.[6] On the other hand, an ex post recognition mechanism relies on the

[6] UNCITRAL, *Promoting Confidence in Electronic Commerce: Legal Issues on International Use of Electronic Authentication and Signature Methods* (Vienna, United Nations, 2009), paras 169–172. For an introduction to technical and policy aspects of PKI, see C Tullis and D Black, 'Public Key

decision of a court or of other adjudicating body to confirm that the requirements for legal recognition are met. Ex ante and ex post recognition mechanisms may operate jointly under the so-called 'two-tier' approach.[7]

The legal basis for recognition of foreign data and documents is usually found in a statute (law or regulation). The statute may simply recognise party autonomy or set up a more complex mechanism. Details of legal recognition mechanisms are often found in secondary legislation such as regulations, especially when they apply to specific documents and are limited to exchanges between pre-identified entities (for example, customs authorities).

Finally, the legal effect of the recognition may vary and should be specified in the law. The law of the recognising jurisdiction may grant foreign data and documents the same legal status as national data and documents. Alternatively, legal recognition mechanisms may recognise the legal effect attributed to the jurisdiction of origin. In the case of the application of party autonomy, the effect will be determined by the law chosen. In any case, it seems desirable to apply the same law to form requirements and to substantive matters.[8]

5.2. The Fundamentals of the MLIT

Shortly after the finalisation of the MLETR, the need for faster and more pervasive digital trade transformation to counter the effects of the COVID-19 pandemic and build more resilient supply chains became evident. Awareness of the need to build a digital trade ecosystem effective not only domestically but also across borders increased. Supply chains massively rely on data generated by people and by objects, and it became imperative to provide assurance of data qualities such as origin and integrity to buttress the digital trade ecosystem.

Hence, digital trade is witnessing two major shifts in focus: (a) from documents to data; and (b) from national to international exchanges. However, such trends are not unchallenged. In particular, two matters could hinder it. The first is the transition from offline to online identification. Offline identification is far from perfect, and malicious acts based on identity misrepresentation occur regularly. However, online transactions may occur at a much higher rate than offline ones, and therefore the risk may be higher online. Second, it is necessary to get data quality assurance, for example, of the integrity of the data message and of the time when it was generated, sent and received. Identification of the party and

Infrastructure: Implementing High-Trust Electronic Signatures' (2025) World Bank Digital Public Infrastructure Policy Note Series.

[7] See ch 7, section 7.3.

[8] This conclusion assumes that the applicable private international law rules consider the form requirement as a substantive requirement, and therefore governed by the chosen law. This may not apply if the form requirement is considered a procedural requirement, ie subject to the lex fori, or a mandatory requirement of the law of the jurisdiction where recognition is sought.

information on data quality are key to developing the digital economy. These two goals need to be achieved with appropriate legal and technical means. For that reason, specific notions have been developed: respectively, identity management and trust services. Identity management allows the unique identification of a subject in a context, and trust services provide data quality assurance.

The complementarity of identity management and trust services is at times obfuscated by the seemingly different focus of the two notions. In some jurisdictions, identity management – especially of physical persons – is often seen as a matter related to law and order, and therefore ultimately relevant for public entities such as civil registries and police. Trade considerations may not be prevalent, especially outside the common law tradition. On the other hand, jurisdictions that do not have a tradition of central management of civil records and vital statistics may instead consider identity management as a mostly commercial matter. In both cases, data is the lifeblood of modern commerce, and despite significant limitations to data exchanges, such as data privacy and data protection regulations, trade considerations are prominent when dealing with data.

Another challenge to digital transformation may arise from excessive reliance on technical standards, regional or national, which may violate the principle of technology neutrality and hinder interoperability. Reliance on technical rather than legal standards may indicate limited appreciation for the principle of proportionality as it may impose requirements that are not needed to conclude the relevant transactions. Legislative provisions reflecting preference for a technical approach may also be difficult to reconcile with contractual agreements.

The MLIT addresses these issues by providing a comprehensive framework for the legal recognition and effect of electronic identity and data, for assessing reliability of identity management and trust services, and for establishing obligations and liability of service providers. It addresses three basic questions: (a) the legal status of identity management and trust services generally; (b) the level of assurance of identity management services and the level of reliability of trust services;[9] and (c) the obligations of service providers.[10] The MLIT clearly establishes legal recognition of the result of the application of identity management and of trust services. Moreover, and for the first time at the global level, it deals extensively with cross-border aspects.

[9] The notions of 'level of assurance' and 'level of reliability' refer to the compliance of the service with a pre-set description of the features to be complied with for the service to offer a certain degree of confidence in the result of its application. For instance, an identity management scheme that relies on self-asserted identities may offer no level of assurance on the veracity of the purported identity as that identity was not validated by any external source. See also the definition of 'level of assurance' in UNCITRAL, 'Legal Issues Related to Identity Management and Trust Services. Terms and Concepts Relevant to Identity Management and Trust Services' (6 February 2018) UN Doc A/CN.9/WG.IV/WP.150, para 42.

[10] T Smedinghoff, 'Is It Legal? Will It Be Trusted? What Are the Rules? – Enabling Electronic Identity Management Under the New UNCITRAL Model Law' (2024) at ssrn.com, 4–5, with regard to identity management (but the same considerations apply to trust services).

The MLIT builds on the general principles of uniform commercial and e-transactions law, on relevant pre-existing UNCITRAL provisions, and on other laws of a more prescriptive nature, namely the eIDAS Regulation.[11] In line with the mandate of UNCITRAL, it does not deal with regulatory matters, and explicitly excludes any impact on data privacy and data protection law. While fundamental principles underlying UNCITRAL texts[12] find application in the MLIT, some details may vary, especially with regard to the application of the principle of functional equivalence.

The MLIT is technology neutral with respect to technologies, methods and products, and is compatible with both centralised and decentralised trust architectures. Being technology neutral, the MLIT is open to standards that are commonly recognised.[13] Such standards may be global (such as those prepared by the International Telecommunication Union – ITU – and by the International Organization for Standardization – ISO), regional (such as those prepared by the European Telecommunications Standards Institute – ETSI) or national but widely known and used internationally (such as those prepared by the US National Institute of Standards and Technology – NIST). In certain cases, private institutions may create de facto standards. However, there is currently no global consensus on applicable standards.

The application of the principle of functional equivalence in the MLIT is qualified. The provisions on electronic identification (MLIT, art 9) and on trust services, except for website authentication, (MLIT, articles 16–20), are drafted as functional equivalence rules. However, they apply also when a legal requirement for paper-based transactions does not exist. Finally, the MLIT recognises party autonomy, but sets limits to it, namely by preventing parties from opting out of liability for non-compliance with the obligations set out in the MLIT, arts 6 and 14, and in imposing conditions to allow limitation of liability of the service provider.

5.3. The Drafting of the MLIT

Identity management and trust services were first discussed at the UNCITRAL Colloquium held in New York from 14 to 16 February 2011, which provided an overview of then ongoing technical and policy efforts. There was broad consensus

[11] On the eIDAS Regulation, H Jacquemin (dir), *L'identification électronique et les services de confiance depuis le règlement eIDAS* (Bruxelles, Larcier, 2016); G Finocchiaro, 'Una prima lettura del reg. UE n. 910/2014 (c.d. eIDAS): identificazione on line, firme elettroniche e servizi fiduciari' (2015) XXXVIII *Le Nuove Leggi Civili Commentate* 419.

[12] See ch 3, commentary on the MLETR, art 3.

[13] For a broad panorama of standards, including historical information, see I Alamillo and ors, *Digital Identity Standards: Analysis of Standardisation Requirements in Support of Cybersecurity Policy* (2023, Athens, European Union Agency for Cybersecurity – ENISA). The publication also covers standards for trust services with an identity component and for credentials.

on the importance of the topic for compliance and the possible gains in efficiency and effectiveness of online services using common identity management concepts and rules.[14] Among the different topics discussed at the colloquium, priority was given to work on electronic transferable records, whose scope and terms were considered more defined than those of the work on identity management and trust services, which was therefore to be carried out later.

During the preparation of the MLETR, some European delegations stressed the importance of working on identity management and trust services and its complementarity with the work on electronic transferable records. Eventually, Austria, Belgium, France, Italy, and Poland (with the involvement of the American Bar Association) presented a proposal to UNCITRAL illustrating recent developments, namely the adoption of the eIDAS Regulation.[15] That proposal identified as relevant issues related to the cross-border use of identity management and trust services removing legal barriers, granting uniform legal effect, assessing trustworthiness and allocating liability. These issues would become core features of the MLIT.

An additional reason to put forward the proposal was the desire to overcome the limits set by eIDAS, art 14, which required concluding a formal international agreement (as defined under the Treaty on the Functioning of the European Union, art 218)[16] for cross-border recognition of qualified trust services.[17] Requiring the conclusion of a treaty may be justified with regard to granting access to certain core governmental services; however, it sets the bar too high for some commercial and non-commercial services requiring lower levels of assurance and reliability. On the other hand, mechanisms relying on assessments carried out by specific bodies such as those foreseen in the eIDAS Regulation may not be acceptable to those who are not involved in managing those bodies. Hence, the need to build a digital bridge between business established in and outside the European Union, including with states associated with the European Union or involved in a process of approximation to European Union law.

[14] UNCITRAL, 'Present and Possible Future Work on Electronic Commerce' (21 March 2011) UN Doc A/CN.9/728. On the relationship between MLIT and eIDAS, see E Caprioli, M Fernandez Gonzalez and D Gobert, 'Vers une internationalisation des principes du Règlement eIDAS', in H Jacquemin (dir), *L'identification électronique*, 275.

[15] UNCITRAL, 'Possible Future Work in the Area of Electronic Commerce – Legal Issues Related to Identity Management and Trust Services. Proposal by Austria, Belgium, France, Italy and Poland' (5 May 2015) UN Doc A/CN.9/854.

[16] Consolidated Versions of the Treaty on European Union and the Treaty on the Functioning of the European Union (adopted 13 December 2007, entered into force 1 December 2009) OJ C 202/1.

[17] The mechanism has been modified by the Regulation (EU) 2024/1183 of the European Parliament and of the Council of 11 April 2024 amending Regulation (EU) No 910/2014 as regards establishing the European Digital Identity Framework [2024] OJ L2024/1183 (eIDAS 2 Regulation), which also foresees the possibility of recognising equivalence between non-European Union trust services and qualified European Union services by way of implementing acts adopted in accordance with the examination procedure referred to in art 48, para 2 of the same Regulation. It may be suggested that foreign non-qualified trust services could be recognised under the general non-discrimination rule.

In response to a request of UNCITRAL, and building on the outcome of a colloquium held on 21 and 22 April 2016, the UNCITRAL Secretariat prepared a paper outlining certain core features of the project.[18] Besides preliminary considerations on the form of the work product – which was clearly of a legislative nature – and the relevance of UNCITRAL fundamental principles, the paper identified as fundamental issues to be discussed with regard to identity management: rights and obligations of the parties; reliability in the various steps of the identity management cycle; consequences of reliability on liability; system rules and other contractual agreements such as service level agreements; mutual legal recognition and other matters related to legal interoperability.[19] Those issues remained relevant throughout the project and were applicable also to trust services. The paper also identified the possible mechanisms for assessment of reliability: ex ante, ex post and based on party autonomy.

The discussions of the Working Group reflected two different positions: a more regulatory approach, based on the ex ante mechanism and typical of the eIDAS Regulation, and a more flexible approach, relying more broadly on freedom of contract and party autonomy in defining the rights, obligations and liabilities associated with the use of identity management and trust services. The views of the United States of America, representing the latter approach, were illustrated in a paper submitted for the consideration of UNCITRAL Working Group IV at its 60th session, which took place from 19 to 23 October 2020.[20] In addition, there was support for preserving the UNCITRAL legacy by applying to the extent possible general principles underpinning UNCITRAL texts on electronic commerce and taking into account those UNCITRAL provisions directly relevant for trust services.

UNCITRAL tasked Working Group IV with the consideration of the matter, which was done during ten sessions, albeit not exclusively spent on that topic. Besides sharing some of the first sessions with the consideration of contractual aspects of cloud computing,[21] some sessions took place in abridged form due to the restrictions related to the containment of the COVID-19 pandemic, and informal intersessional work was carried out to compensate for those limitations.

The draft text of the MLIT, together with a guide to enactment, was submitted to UNCITRAL at its 55th session for consideration and adoption, after circulation to states and international organisations for comment. At that session, UNCITRAL

[18] UNCITRAL, 'Legal Issues Related to Identity Management and Trust Services' (3 May 2016) UN Doc A/CN.9/891.

[19] ibid para 52.

[20] UNCITRAL, 'Reconsideration of Approach to Identity Management and Trust Services – Submission by the United States of America' (30 September 2020) UN Doc A/CN.9/WG.IV/WP.165.

[21] UNGA, 'Report of the United Nations Commission on International Trade Law. Forty-ninth Session' (2016) UN Doc A/71/17, paras 235–236.

adopted the text and the guide to enactment, the latter subject to those amendments needed to reflect UNCITRAL decisions. Working Group IV finalised the guide to enactment at its 64th session.[22]

Inspired by the structure of the eIDAS Regulation, the MLIT contains two core chapters respectively on identity management and on trust services. Identity management is dealt with first, and the provisions in the identity management chapter are used as a template for the trust services chapter, although the provisions on identity management are sometimes more detailed. The other two chapters, which are the first and the last ones, are common to identity management and trust services and deal respectively with general provisions and with cross-border recognition.

Identity management and trust services are dealt with in the MLIT with a similar enabling approach. However, they significantly differ when it comes to regulation, which does not fall under the mandate of UNCITRAL. Identity management – especially foundational identity – raises strong privacy and similar concerns that call for detailed regulation: information relating to identification of physical persons belongs to the most sensitive category of information. For instance, one significant issue is over-sharing personal information, ie providing attributes that are not required for the intended identification purpose. This can be done because of poor design or because of the desire to collect additional information, for instance, for marketing analysis purposes. On the other hand, trust services – including those with an identity component – aim to facilitate and support data exchanges and therefore pertain to an enabling environment rather than a regulatory one. While care is needed to comply with applicable regulation, including on data protection and data privacy, the main goal of the application of trust services is to ensure consistent reliability of data (in the case of trade, across the supply chain).

Moreover, while keeping with its enabling nature, the MLIT has a more prescriptive nature than its closer UNCITRAL predecessor, the MLES. This feature shows the influence of eIDAS and, more generally, of civil law and European law models on the MLIT. In particular, the MLIT lists detailed obligations of service providers and sets conditions on their ability to limit liability. It also stresses the necessity to preserve the applicable regulatory regime, especially on data privacy and data protection.

[22] In accordance with United Nations rules and practice, the text of the MLIT and its Guide to Enactment are available at no cost on the UNCITRAL website in the six official languages of the United Nations. Likewise, the pre-session documents and reports of the meetings of the Working Group and of the Commission are available on the UNCITRAL website. Few articles discuss the MLIT, besides: Smedinghoff, 'Is it legal?' (2024), see A Madrid Parra, 'Identidad y autenticación electrónicas: la atalaya de UNCITRAL' in R Perea Ortega (ed), *Estudios sobre derecho digital* (Cizur Menor, Editorial Aranzadi, 2021), pt 2, 199.

5.4. The General Provisions of the MLIT

As noted, the MLIT is comprised of four chapters on: 'General Provisions'; 'Identity Management'; 'Trust Services'; and 'Cross-border Recognition'. In this section, commentary is provided on the general provisions of the MLIT, while the remaining chapters of the MLIT are discussed in the following chapters of this book.

Article 1. Definitions

For the purposes of this Law:

(a) *[...];*
(b) *'Data message' means information generated, sent, received or stored by electronic, magnetic, optical or similar means;*
(c)–(i) *[...];*
(j) *'Relying party' means a person who acts on the basis of the result of identity management services or trust services;*
(k) *'Subscriber' means a person who enters into an arrangement for the provision of identity management services or trust services with an identity management service provider or a trust service provider;*
(l)–(m) *[...].*

Article 1 on definitions sets out the fundamental notions for both identity and trust services. The definitions may be divided in three groups: relevant for both identity management and trust services; relevant only for identity management; relevant only for trust services. The definitions in art 1 are complemented by a list of 'Terms and concepts relevant to identity management and trust services' compiled by the UNCITRAL Secretariat during the preparation of the MLIT.[23]

The notions of 'data message', 'relying party' and 'subscriber' are common to identity management and trust services. The notion of 'data message' is the building block of UNCITRAL texts on electronic commerce, having been first introduced in the MLEC, art 2(a). The definition contained in the MLIT, art 1(b) does not modify the original notion though it omits the references to technologies that are not broadly used anymore.

The notion of 'relying party' is inspired by that contained in the MLES, art 2(f). It refers to the person who relies – actively or passively – on the identification or on the assurance of data quality. It is however important to note that the relying party may bear the consequences of the failure to carry out the intended action: for instance, a mistaken identification under know-your-customer regulation.

The notion of 'subscriber' identifies the client of a service. The subscriber must have a contractual or other arrangement (for example, use of state-issued identity cards mandated by law) with the identity management or trust service provider. The relying party often will not have any arrangement with the identity

[23] UNCITRAL, 'Legal Issues Related to Identity Management and Trust Services. Terms and Concepts Relevant to Identity Management and Trust Services'.

management or trust service provider, but in certain circumstances may have such an arrangement.[24]

Article 2. Scope of application

1. *This Law applies to the use and cross-border recognition of identity management and trust services in the context of commercial activities and trade-related services.*
2. *Nothing in this Law requires the identification of a person.*
3. *Nothing in this Law affects a legal requirement that a person be identified or that a trust service be used in accordance with a procedure defined or prescribed by law.*
4. *Other than as provided for in this Law, nothing in this Law affects the application to identity management services or trust services of any law applicable to data privacy and protection.*

The MLIT builds on shared principles and terminology to provide a uniform legal treatment for identity management and for trust services. It has a broad and ambitious scope as it applies to both private and public IdM systems and to all trust services, not just listed ones. This is in line with modern identity management legislation that foresees the existence of both public and private identity services providers, thus significantly innovating on the notion that only public entities may manage identity, for example, by providing a national electronic identity card. However, public entities may be able to limit their liability for identity management services by statute, and this limitation may be broader than the one available to private entities. This may give a possibly unfair competitive advantage to public identity management service providers.

In principle, the application of the MLIT is limited to commercial activities and trade-related services to respect the mandate of UNCITRAL, which is limited to trade: trade-related services are those that facilitate trade, such as electronic single windows for customs operations. However, it is expected that the MLIT will also be applied to non-commercial transactions, as the notions of identity and of trust service are universal and not limited to the commercial nature of the transaction. This expansion of the scope of application of the MLIT is similar to that seen in the MLEC, whose application to both commercial and non-commercial transactions is common and recommended to maintain legal uniformity and facilitate electronic exchanges.

According to the eIDAS Regulation, art 2, para 2, that Regulation does not apply 'to the provision of trust services that are used exclusively within closed systems resulting from national law or from agreements between a defined set of participants'. Such a limitation to the scope of application of the MLIT has not been discussed during its preparation. It is doubtful that parties could opt out entirely from the application of the MLIT, as this may, for instance, bypass the application of functional equivalence standards. Party autonomy may operate in other manners, such as by letting the parties agree on the reliability of the methods used.

[24] Smedinghoff (n 10), 11–12.

The MLIT, like other UNCITRAL texts on electronic commerce, has an enabling nature: this means that it aims to remove existing legal obstacles to the use of identity management and trust services but does not change the regulatory landscape. This is reflected in the MLIT, art 2, para 2, which clarifies that no new duty to identify arises from the Model Law. Similarly, the MLIT introduces no new obligation to use any specific trust service (MLIT, art 3, para 1).

The MLIT, art 2, para 3 reminds that existing obligations to identify are not affected by the Model Law. The same principles apply to obligations to use a certain trust service. In practice, the obligations to identify may arise from statute or from contract. Statutory obligations are often regulatory in nature, but may also be contained in commercial law (for example, the obligation contained in the Uniform Customs and Practice for Documentary Credits UCP 600, art 19 to identify the carrier in a transport document and to have certain named entities sign the document). Both statutory and contractual provisions requiring identification may prescribe the identity process to be used, the level of assurance that the identification should achieve or the type of identity credentials to be used. In that manner, it is possible that statute or contract require the use of specific identity management services. Similarly, the parties may agree on specific communication methods, which may also pursue an identification function (for instance, by using PKI-based signatures).

Likewise, the MLIT does not change any other law, including law on data privacy and protection, which is explicitly mentioned in the MLIT, art 2, para 4 given its prominence: data privacy and protection law is critical to avoid misuse of identity information, including by collecting and aggregating it.[25]

Article 3. Voluntary use of identity management and trust services

1. *Nothing in this Law requires a person to use an identity management service or trust service or to use a particular identity management service or trust service without the person's consent.*
2. *For the purposes of paragraph 1, consent may be inferred from the person's conduct.*

Article 3 clarifies that the MLIT, as such, does not impose any requirement to use identity management or trust services. Such obligation may however arise from other laws.

Moreover, according to the MLIT, art 3 the use of identity management and of trust services, or of any specific identity management or trust service, is voluntary, which is in line with the principle of the voluntary use of electronic communications. However, other laws may introduce this obligation. In that case, to preserve

[25] The eIDAS 2 Regulation provides an illustration of the interaction between data privacy and identity management, namely European Digital Identity Wallets. Wallets should have, among other features, a dashboard to ensure the user's control, use privacy-preserving technologies, such as zero knowledge proof, and ensure unobservability by not collecting data and not having insight into the transactions of the users. See also A Ortalda and S Leucci 'Identità digitale e protezione dei dati personali: punti di incontro e rischi nelle discipline eIDAS e RGPD' (2022) 4 *Rivista italiana di informatica e diritto* 145.

technology neutrality it is preferable to refer to services generally described (for example, identity credentials satisfying a certain level of assurance) than to a specific service (for example, national electronic identity card).

One principle that may be inferred from the MLIT, art 3 is that the parties to an electronic transaction are able to determine the identity management or trust service appropriate for their transactions, and to prove the legality of that determination in court.

Article 4. Interpretation

1. *In the interpretation of this Law, regard is to be had to its international origin and to the need to promote uniformity in its application and the observance of good faith in international trade.*
2. *Questions concerning matters governed by this Law which are not expressly settled in it are to be settled in conformity with the general principles on which it is based.*

The MLIT, art 4 contains the principle of uniform interpretation of UNCITRAL texts that has already been illustrated with regard to the MLETR, art 3.[26] The MLIT, art 4 also contains the reference to the observance of good faith in international trade that is common in UNCITRAL texts but was omitted in the MLETR.[27] The corresponding provision of the CISG has found significant judicial application.[28]

[26] See ch 3, section 3.2, commentary on the MLETR, art 3.
[27] Ibid.
[28] UNCITRAL, *Digest of Case Law on the United Nations Convention on Contracts for the International Sale of Goods* (United Nations, Vienna, 2016) commentary on CISG, art 7.

6

Identity Management

6.1. What is Identity Management?

Identity is a set of attributes distinguishing a person in a particular context.[1] The attributes may include information such as name, address, age, gender, civil status, nationality as well as additional information on family composition, educational and professional qualifications, etc.

Because of the lack of personal interaction and knowledge online, reliable identification of a remote person is fundamental to build trust in the digital economy and, more generally, in electronic transactions. To be reliable, the identification process must be adequate to determine with sufficient assurance the relevant identity attributes of the person to be identified.

Identification is the process of verifying that a certain person possesses the relevant attributes, often in response to an identity claim. Identity management is comprised of three steps: (a) the attribution of identity (also called 'foundational identity') to a person; (b) the onboarding of that person in an identity management scheme, with release of credentials against adequate assurance of identity; and (c) the use of those credentials, including their successful verification.

The UNCITRAL Model Law on the Use and Cross-border Recognition of Identity Management and Trust Services (MLIT) deals with the second and third step, which are respectively called 'identity proofing' and 'electronic identification',[2] and presupposes the existence of the first step.[3] The wrongful attribution of foundational identity would undermine the following steps. There is therefore an assumption underlying the MLIT that foundational identity is reliably attributed.

The collection of attributes during identity proofing may include basic attributes that are first recorded in civil registries for natural persons and in business

[1] For an introduction to identity management, see Guide to Enactment, paras 51–56. See also T Smedinghoff, 'The Legal Framework for Digital Identity' in G Finocchiaro, L Balestra and M Timoteo (eds) *Major Legal Trends in the Digital Economy: The Approach of the EU, the US and China* (Bologna, Il Mulino, 2022) 245.

[2] In other laws, the third step is called 'authentication'.

[3] For an overview and technical description of the second and third steps and of related standards, see OECD, *G7 Mapping Exercise of Digital Identity Approaches* (Paris, OECD Publishing, 2024).

and similar registries for legal persons. Those basic attributes constitute the foundational identity of a person.[4]

Identity management systems are used to manage identity proofing and electronic identification and may be carried out by a single entity performing all processes (directly or with the help of contractors) or by multiple entities. The identity management service provider may have a public or private nature. Moreover, an identity management service provider may offer different identity management services.

As noted, identity management under the MLIT and the eIDAS Regulation applies to physical and legal persons. For trade purposes, identification of legal persons (and of objects) may be more relevant than identification of physical persons, especially when consumer transactions are excluded. On the other hand, identification of physical persons poses more challenges due to sensitive aspects involved such as data privacy and data protection.

In general, it is important to bear in mind that physical persons may have multiple identities, that those identities are made of several attributes, which need to be validated separately in light of the identification purpose, and that identification of any entity is the outcome of a process and not a status.

6.2. The Evolution of Identity Management

Identification is a basic social function that permits associating human beings with a status and enables exchanges based on trust. In a general sense, 'trust' is the reasonable expectation of future behaviour based on past events. In the context of identity management, 'trust' is the belief in the accuracy of a statement related to an attribute. Moreover, reliable identification may link past events to an individual, thus significantly increasing the predictability of the future behaviour of that individual (for example, a person with a very good and well-documented credit history is likely to pay the outstanding balance of a credit card on time).

Historically, individuals have first been identified by reference to their extended family or kinship.[5] Birth in a social group attributed status vis-à-vis other groups and inside the group. Distinctive marks such as clothes, tattoos and jewellery confirmed that status. The need for further evidence of identity was limited as long as individuals operated in a restricted area where personal connections were well-established.

The appearance of more complex forms of social aggregation gave rise to centrally managed systems for identifying human beings and recording major events in their lives, typically for paying taxes, serving military duties and

[4] See section 6.3 of this chapter.
[5] R Sacco, *Antropologia giuridica* (Bologna, Il Mulino, 2007) 248–249.

discharging similar obligations. Registries were kept by religious and secular authorities, which could operate at the local level or on a bigger scale under a central coordinating authority.

As long-distance individual mobility grew, the need arose to issue identification documents for specific purposes such as guaranteeing protection to travellers. In the commercial field, a merchant was often trusted based on past interactions, common dealings and extended family connections rather than formal identification based on presentation of credentials. Trust was – and still is – one of the main benefits of being recognised as a member in good standing of the communitas mercatorum.

Eventually, improved forms of central government took responsibility for identifying individuals by maintaining civil registration and vital statistics records and providing readily available evidence of that information in passports, identity cards and similar documents.[6] For instance, in France this happened around 1792;[7] in the United Kingdom, possibly, in 1794.[8] With those developments, the state started taking responsibility for identity attribution, which was linked to the condition of a citizen and not to that of a member of a religious or ethnic group, or to kinship or extended family. Features were added: notably, around 1920, passports started being signed by their holder,[9] which meant adding a biometric security feature to the document.

Because of the trust placed in them, such documents started being used for purposes other than the originally intended ones. For instance, a driving licence may be used as proof of age for selling controlled substances.[10] This solution, although common, is far from being satisfactory. One of the concerns is that the issuing public authority usually does not accept liability for misuse or abuse of its documents, regardless of whether they are used for the intended use or not. Moreover, while some legal systems require carrying identity proof at any time, others – especially in common law jurisdictions – do not. However, there are limited methods to prove the identity of a person without documents.

[6] É Millard, 'Le rôle de l'état civil dans la construction de l'Etat', Mélanges en l'honneur du Doyen F.-P. Blanc (Perpignan – Toulouse, Presses Universitaires de Perpignan et Presses Universitaires de Toulouse 1 Capitole, 2011) 721; M Lloyd, *The Passport: The History of Man's Most Travelled Document* (Stroud, Sutton Publishing, 2003); J Torpey, *The Invention of the Passport: Surveillance, Citizenship and the State* (Cambridge, Cambridge University Press, 1999); G Noiriel, 'L'identification des citoyens : Naissance de l'état civil républicain' (1993) 13 *Genèses. Sciences sociales et histoire* 3. For an overview of the public law and human rights implications with regard to Spain, see AI Blasco, 'Digital Identity in a European User-Centric Ecosystem and Its Similarities with the Digital Euro Proposal' in C Pastor Sempere (ed) *Governance and Control of Data and Digital Economy in the European Single Market* (Cham, Springer, 2025) Law, Governance and Technology Series, vol 71, 453, 454–455.

[7] P Granville Edge, 'Vital Registration in Europe. The Development of Official Statistics and Some Differences in Practice' (1928) 91 *Journal of the Royal Statistical Society* 346.

[8] See the timeline provided in Home Office, 'A History of the UK Passport' at homeofficemedia.blog.gov.uk.

[9] C Robertson, *The Passport in America: The History of a Document* (New York, Oxford Academic, 2012) 54 (ch 3 'Signature').

[10] This happens even though the assumption of those substances before driving is strongly discouraged or forbidden.

Another historical development regarded the involvement of professional third-party identity service providers, such as public notaries. The introduction of legal personality for companies and other entities added another layer of identification needs that were first satisfied with dedicated registries. All these forms of identity management presupposed direct interaction and in-person identification.

The broader use of electronic communications led to the proliferation of online identification. This was first done by setting up application-specific systems and requirements. Furthermore, the identity management notion of 'signing in' to an information system was developed. This identity management procedure involves three steps. The first step (referred to as 'identification') foresees the release of electronic credentials against paper-based identifiers (for which the issuer accepts no liability). The second step (known as 'authentication') consists of the verification of the credentials. The third step (known as 'authorisation') provides access to the information system in case of successful verification.

However, it was soon realised that such a fragmented approach was repetitive, redundant, and inefficient. The need for greater efficiency, standardisation, and interoperability in online identification became evident and a variety of technical solutions have been proposed. The next step in linking identity management and electronic signatures was the introduction of the notion of a single sign-on as a measure to contain the multiplication of information systems, which led to an exponential increment of costs and of credentials needed to access them.

Single sign-on may be seen as an early example of identity management federation, which is an arrangement under which all concerned parties decide to use identity credentials across systems based on an agreed common set of policies, practices and protocols.[11] The rules containing the common set may be called a 'trust framework'. Identity management federation aims to improve usability, privacy and security of existing applications and is popular in the United States of America, among other jurisdictions.[12] It may be considered an example of a bottom-up approach (as opposed to the regulatory top-down approach). The legal issues posed by identity management federation are, in several ways, similar to those posed by identity management (for example, liability, privacy and security, and relationship with existing identification duties), the main difference being that federated identity management relies on a contractual framework rather than having explicit statutory recognition.

Identity management schemes, which may be operated by commercial, public or other entities, serve a variety of functions and purposes and offer different levels of assurance of an asserted identity. A survey has identified 25 use cases for identity management, the main applications being customer onboarding, fraud prevention, and compliance with know your customer (KYC) and anti-money

[11] Guide to Enactment, para 56.

[12] OpenID Connect, which is promoted by the OpenID Foundation is an example of identity federation protocol. See openid.net for additional information.

laundering (AML) regulation.[13] Signature of electronic documents is ranked at sixth place in this use cases list. Just like offline identity finds application in specific contexts, online identity is applied to actual electronic transactions and not in abstract. Such application can be carried out with the use of trust services, ie online services that provide assurance of data quality, namely of its origin.

The usefulness of identity management systems is proportional to their acceptance, ie the number of users and the variety of applications that use such systems. Early practice has sometimes seen the emergence of identity management systems and services that are not interoperable and therefore hinder cross-border legal recognition due to excessive reliance on technical details, which may undermine technology neutrality and interoperability. Moreover, complexity of identity management schemes, especially public ones, may discourage their adoption by the private sector.

Absent universal models, the diversity of legal and contractual provisions may pose challenges to the mutual recognition of identity management schemes and ultimately affect broader participation in identity management. The availability of legislative texts that establish uniform rules based on technology neutrality and other shared principles is therefore desirable.

6.3. Foundational and Transactional Identity

A fundamental distinction in identity management pertains to foundational identity versus transactional identity.

Foundational identity reflects the unique attributes of the entity and is attributed only once to physical and legal persons. It is data about an immutable quality that may not be changed if compromised. Therefore, it is advisable to share foundational identity data sparingly and selectively.

Physical persons are given their foundational identity in civil records and vital statistics (CRVS),[14] where they are identified with information relating to parents,

[13] Office for Digital Identities & Attributes, Department for Science, Innovation & Technology, 'Digital Identity Sectoral Analysis 2024: Interim Findings' (2024).

[14] CRVS systems contain information about births and deaths of physical persons. They may also contain additional information such as marriages, divorces, and cause of death. A well-functioning CRVS system is considered critical for the functioning of a modern state. For instance, it allows it to measure progress towards social and economic development goals: see, eg, S Mills, JK Lee and BM Rassekh, 'Benefits of Linking Civil Registration and Vital Statistics with Identity Management Systems for Measuring and Achieving Sustainable Development Goal 3 Indicators' (2019) 38 *Journal of Health, Population and Nutrition* (supp 1) art 18. However, many countries, especially developing ones, do not have yet in place comprehensive CRVS systems. On the relationship between CRVS and identity, see M Bruggeman, 'Etat civil et identité : quel(s) rapport(s) ?' in J Eynard (ed), *L'identité numérique : Quelle définition pour quelle protection ?* (Bruxelles, Larcier, 2020) 59.

date of birth, biometrics, etc. The foundational identity of legal persons is found in commercial registers.[15]

With regard to physical persons, identity management has a strong national security component, for instance, with respect to distribution and verification of electronic identity cards and similar documents. Those documents may also be used for identification for commercial purposes. However, the security requirements for the issuance and management of such documents may not be fully compatible with their use in commercial procedures. Moreover, as mentioned, concerns about compromising foundational identity recommend caution in its use. For these reasons, foundational identity is seldom used as such: that use may be compared to when a physical person must exhibit its paper-based birth certificate. More often, credentials used in transactions are derived from foundational identity and contain only some of its attributes. The use of foundational identity may be restricted to avoid sharing sensitive information abroad. These limitations have been acknowledged in discussions around identity management by promoting self-sovereign identities, ie identities that are managed by the person to be identified in a decentralised manner with a view to sharing attributes selectively, and other measures to curb abuses in the use of foundational identity and digital identity more generally.

Foundational identity of physical persons is relevant for human rights. Several aspects of its management pertain to the right to data privacy. Additional issues relate to the right of human beings to have a digital identity, which is an expression of the right to the registration of birth and other identity attributes.[16] The implementation of this right is pursued by target 16.9 of the United Nations' 'Sustainable Development Goals', which demands an increase in the percentage of children under age five that have their birth registered, including in electronic form, with a civil authority.[17]

On the other hand, transactional (or functional) identity uses information associated with an entity that is relative to a certain context. Each entity may have multiple transactional identities. The entity may therefore be identified with regard to certain proxies or aliases that can provide different levels of assurance, ranging from a stronger one, such as the national identity or registration number, to weaker ones, such as a cell phone number or an email address. The reliability of the transactional identities may be built over time as it is proportional to the number of transactions successfully validated. Transactional identity providing a higher level of assurance may link to foundational identity by using credentials

[15] UNCITRAL has adopted in 2018 a Legislative Guide on Key Principles of a Business Registry aimed at facilitating registration of micro, small and medium-sized enterprises (MSMEs) through simplified registration.

[16] See, eg, art 24, para 2 of the International Covenant on Civil and Political Rights (adopted 16 December 1966, entered into force 23 March 1976) 999 UNTS 171 regarding the right to birth registration and the name.

[17] The World Bank ID4D programme provides an illustration of how this right may be pursued in developing countries.

directly or indirectly derived from it.[18] For instance, creditworthiness based on the use of credit and debit cards may be considered as an attribute of transactional identity when it comes to online shopping, but the cards are issued based on a higher-level credential that relies on foundational identity verification in the onboarding process.

In other cases, such as a profile in a social media, there may be no verification based directly or indirectly on foundational identity. In such cases, identity is self-asserted. For instance, a small business may open a social media page to advertise and accept orders. Self-asserted transactional identity information provided may be sufficient for the intended purposes, especially if validated over time with relevant information and with coherent interaction offline and online (for example, shipment of goods, processing of payments). Also, transactional identity derived from commercial operations may focus on specific features of the identity subject rather than its abstract identification. The identity verification process based on various data sources relating to previous transactions is known as data-centric identity affirmation and may be the only one available when CRVS management is weak or absent. However, the level of assurance provided by data-centric identity affirmation may be lower than that provided using stronger credentials.

One main benefit of using transactional identity is that it can be easily replaced in the event of compromise. This explains its widespread and common use for low value transactions. Moreover, transactional identity may be the only identity possible if CRVS are not available. For instance, electronic cards may be given to provide and record medical care to displaced persons based on self-asserted identification. On the other hand, transactional identity information is aggregated over time and from various sources, and, unlike foundational identity, does not originate from a single authoritative source. This may impede satisfying higher identification requirements with transactional identity alone.

The distinction between foundational and transactional identity may be clearer in theory than in practice. Generally, applications requiring higher levels of assurance may use foundational identity or closely derived credentials. Also, most identification processes may require credentials related to foundational identity (for example, name, surname, date of birth) and other credentials (for example, professional qualification). Moreover, public identity management schemes may prefer to use identity-related information originating from public sources – ie foundational identity – on the assumption that identity information originating from other sources may not provide sufficient guarantee of its quality.

[18] World Trade Organization and International Chamber of Commerce Digital Standards Initiative, *Standards Toolkit for Cross-border Paperless Trade* (Paris, International Chamber of Commerce, 2022), 10, lists the following identifier standards for subjects: Legal Entity Identifier, ISO 17442; W3C Decentralised Identifier; Business Identifier Code, ISO 9362; Trader Identification Number.

At the operational level, one view suggests that the emerging use of digital identity wallets[19] will facilitate bridging the differences between types of identity and promoting their use by providing the adequate level of assurance for each intended use. Thus, the identity wallet may become the 'killer app' to achieve the widespread use of identity management. In that regard, it should be noted that digital identity wallets may be managed by private sector operators but contain public sector credentials. If digital wallets use open standards, they may also favour interoperability and the creation of open ecosystems in which third parties may develop wallet-based applications.

To sum up, the distinction between foundational and transactional identity is useful for illustrative purposes. Paying attention to the relationship between those types of identity may help avoid conceptual and practical misunderstandings.

6.4. The Current Identity Management Framework

Identity management has significant relevance for attaining a number of social and economic goals. For instance, it is the object of a specific target of the United Nations Sustainable Development Goals,[20] and is relevant for other targets.[21] The World Bank ID4D initiative aims to provide a significant contribution to addressing these issues.[22]

A comprehensive identity management policy framework may be found in the Recommendation on the Governance of Digital Identity of the Organisation for Economic Co-operation and Development (OECD).[23] The Recommendation is built around three pillars. The first pillar, entitled 'Developing User-Centred and Inclusive Digital Identity', provides guidance on how to design and implement user-friendly identity management systems and to encourage their uptake by physical and legal persons. The second pillar, on 'Strengthening the Governance of Digital Identity', assists in defining roles and responsibilities in identity management, emphasises the importance of protecting data privacy and security, and encourages legal and regulatory uniformity as well as technical interoperability. The third pillar, on 'Enabling Cross-Border Use of Digital Identity', recommends

[19] See ch 7, section 7.3, comment to the MLIT, art 16.

[20] Target 16.9: providing legal identity for all.

[21] For example, Target 1.4: ensuring access of the poor to economic resources; Target 10c: reducing remittances costs; and Target 16.5: reducing corruption.

[22] See the website of ID4D at id4d.worldbank.org.

[23] OECD, 'Recommendation of the Council on the Governance of Digital Identity' (8 June 2023) OECD Doc OECD/LEGAL/0491.

considering cross-border scenarios when developing identity management systems, and encourages international cooperation.

The OECD Recommendation does not deal with technical and legal details. However, the recital acknowledges the work of several organisations relevant for technical and legal implementation.[24]

A significant step towards the conceptualisation of identity management was made with the adoption of the eIDAS Regulation in the European Union. With eIDAS, for the first time the law went beyond the notion of electronic signature to address more generally identity management and trust services, and to provide a legal framework for national and regional use. Concepts and provisions of eIDAS have been adopted elsewhere, for instance in Benin[25] and in Ukraine,[26] and have significantly inspired the MLIT.

Other legislative approaches to identity management are being explored. In the United States, the Virginia Electronic Identity Management Act[27] offers a complete set of provisions for federated identity management. Identity service providers are not liable if they comply with mandated standards and contractual agreements (§ 59.1-552). Interestingly, § 59.1-553 of the Act explicitly indicates that the use of a compliant identity credential or identity attribute satisfies the requirement for a commercially reasonable security or attribution procedure set in various United States and Virginia payments laws.[28] Payments services are one major area of application of identity services.

Another model is emerging in common law jurisdictions such as Australia, New Zealand and the United Kingdom. In the United Kingdom, the goal of digital identity under this approach is to provide 'solutions for creating, managing, and verifying digital representations of individuals. This enables secure, trusted, and effective proof of identity and attributes across online and in-person interactions, and a way to gain verified access to products and services'.[29] A taxonomy of digital identity identifies five main areas:[30] identity foundations; identity verification; attribute verification; trust services; and identity data and intermediaries. Identity is provided and verified in support of other services such as attribute verification or trust services. The identity data and intermediaries area relates to transferring, aggregating and analysing identity-related data, which is a matter excluded from the MLIT. The taxonomy may be useful to identify the various phases of identity

[24] These organisations are: the European Committee for Standardization (ETSI); the International Organization for Standardization (ISO); the International Electrotechnical Commission (IEC); the National Institute of Standards and Technology (NIST); the World Wide Web Consortium (W3C); the European Commission; the Financial Action Task Force; UNCITRAL; and the World Bank.

[25] Loi n° 2017–20 du 20 avril 2018 portant code du numérique en République du Bénin.

[26] Law No 2155-VIII of 05.10.2017 'On Electronic Identification and Electronic Trust Services' and implementing decisions available at czo.gov.ua.

[27] Code of Virginia, Title 59.1 Trade and Commerce, Chapter 50.

[28] The same notion is used in art 5, para 2(a) of the UNCITRAL Model Law on International Credit Transfers.

[29] Office for Digital Identities & Attributes, 'Digital Identity Sectoral Analysis 2024: Interim Findings'.

[30] ibid, appendix.

management in a comprehensive manner and how existing legislation, including the MLIT, relates to other laws.

Recently, the Data (Use and Access) Bill has been introduced in the UK Parliament.[31] The bill foresees the creation of a trust framework (named the Digital Identity and Attributes Trust Framework) for digital verification services, which are defined as 'verification services provided [...] by means of the internet' to ascertain or verify a fact about an individual from information originating from a source other than the concerned individual. Digital verification services are to be used in instances when verification of identity or of specific identity attributes is needed. The Bill establishes a public register of persons providing digital verification services, who may use a trust mark. The effect of this legislation is to give statutory recognition to the previous UK digital identity and attributes trust framework without the need to create a national digital identity card system. The implementation of the Digital Identity and Attributes Trust Framework, which is designed for private services, will need to be coordinated with that of the public GOV.UK One Login scheme, which is designed primarily for public services but whose application could be extended to the private sector.

In New Zealand, the Digital Identity Services Trust Framework Act 2023 establishes a trust framework for digital identity. A digital identity service is defined as 'a service or product that, either alone or together with 1 or more other digital identity services, enables a user to share personal or organisational information in digital form' (s 10(1)). The Act contains detailed rules on the functioning of the trust framework, including accreditation thereto. Trust framework providers may use accreditation marks to identify their accredited services (s 13(1)). However, they may also provide non-accredited services, which may be offered also by entities that are not participating in the trust framework. Interestingly, the Act foresees the immunity of the trust framework providers from liability for the actions of users of their services under certain conditions (s 104). The Act is complemented by the Digital Identity Services Trust Framework Rules 2024, which offer additional guidance on applicable standards and other operational aspects with regard to authorisation, privacy, security and data management. A similar mechanism was set up in Australia with the Digital ID Act 2024.[32]

6.5. The Identity Management Provisions of the MLIT

The first substantive part of the MLIT, contained in its chapter II, provides guidance on how to manage identity. This is based on three assumptions: (a) identity

[31] The Bill is available at bills.parliament.uk.
[32] For information on Australia's Digital ID System see digitalidsystem.gov.au.

is a relative, ie contextual, notion; (b) identity management is made of two stages (identity proofing and electronic identification); and (c) identity management normally involves three parties (provider, subscriber, relying party).[33] As noted, the MLIT does not deal with the attribution of foundational identity.

In the MLIT, identity management systems must manage both identity proofing and electronic identification. Identity proofing is 'the process of collecting, verifying, and validating sufficient attributes to define and confirm the identity of a person within a particular context', ie onboarding the subject in an identity management system. Electronic identification is 'a process used to achieve sufficient assurance in the binding between a person and an identity', ie 'authenticating' the subject to achieve sufficient assurance of reliable identification.

The MLIT contains no duty to identify but gives general legal recognition to identity management and establishes rules on the functional equivalence between the result of online and offline identification. Thus, the MLIT sits between the laws that require identification, but does not specify how to identify with electronic means, and the operational rules, including rulebooks, that apply to the specific identity management system.[34] In short, the MLIT is the legal interface between the duty to identify and the identification procedure.

The MLIT is compatible with different approaches, including the use of federated identity management.[35] Although the federation model has not been extensively discussed during the drafting of the MLIT,[36] it may be assumed that contractual agreements that comply with the MLIT could underpin the federation scheme.

The MLIT does not address the identity management market structure or the relationship between foundational identity and identity management services.

Article 1. Definitions

For the purposes of this Law:

(a) 'Attribute' means an item of information or data associated with a person;
(b) […];
(c) 'Electronic identification', in the context of identity management services, means a process used to achieve sufficient assurance in the binding between a person and an identity;
(d) 'Identity' means a set of attributes that allows a person to be uniquely distinguished within a particular context;
(e) 'Identity credentials' means the data, or the physical object upon which the data may reside, that a person may present for electronic identification;

[33] T Smedinghoff, 'Is It Legal? Will It Be Trusted? What Are the Rules? – Enabling Electronic Identity Management Under the New UNCITRAL Model Law' (2024), 9.

[34] Smedinghoff, 'Is It Legal?', 12.

[35] On the various approaches, with a focus on federated identity management, see World Bank, *Federated Ecosystems for Digital ID: Current Approaches and Lessons* (Washington, DC, World Bank, 2022).

[36] But see Guide to Enactment, para 56.

(f) *'Identity management services' means services consisting of managing identity proofing and electronic identification;*

(g) *'Identity management service provider' means a person who enters into an arrangement for the provision of identity management services with a subscriber;*

(h) *'Identity management system' means a set of functions and capabilities to manage identity proofing and electronic identification;*

(i) *'Identity proofing' means the process of collecting, verifying, and validating sufficient attributes to define and confirm the identity of a person within a particular context;*

(j)–(m) *[…].*

As noted,[37] the MLIT, art 1 on definitions sets out the fundamental notions for both identity and trust services.[38] With respect to the definitions relevant for identity management, it should be noted that, while 'identity management' itself is not defined, it is clear that the result of its application is reliable identification of legal and physical persons, ie the establishment of sufficient assurance of the link between a person and an identity. Identification is the result of a two-step process involving the issuance of the identity credentials and their verification. Accordingly, an identity management system is made of two necessary components, though not necessarily performed by the same service provider or in the same system: identity proofing; and electronic identification. The Working Group held extensive discussions on whether the term 'authentication' or 'electronic identification' should be used. Eventually, 'authentication' was discarded because of its multiple and not always consistent meanings, especially in the technical field.[39]

While trust services clearly apply only to data messages, ie data in electronic or similar form, identity management has an inherent electronic component but does not need to be exclusively electronic. For instance, credentials may be stored on physical media such as electronic identity cards. Moreover, the definition of identity management does not require its application to an online transaction. This may mean that identity management may be carried out with regard to offline transactions, for example, entering a controlled area. That conclusion however implies that providers of such services should be subject to all obligations of identity management services providers, which may be excessively onerous.

[37] See ch 5, section 5.4.

[38] On the different notions of identity and the contextual, conceptual, and functional dilemmas associated with it, see M Robles-Carrillo, 'Digital Identity: An Approach to its Nature, Concept, and Functionalities' (2024) 32 *International Journal of Law and Information Technology* 1, eaae019.

[39] Authentication is a way to verify the validity and claimed identity of a user, device, transaction, or another entity before granting access to a particular system: OECD, Recommendation of the Council on the Governance of Digital Identity [OECD/LEGAL/0491], 2023.

Object Identification

An important issue that is not dealt with in the MLIT (and in the eIDAS Regulation) relates to the need of assuring the quality of data generated by physical and digital objects on the Internet of Things. This would entail the application of the MLIT to objects. In previous drafts of the MLIT, the notion of 'identity' referred to that of an 'entity' comprising a physical or a legal person, or a digital or a physical object. Objects are significantly more numerous and generate a significant larger amount of data than persons, as they constitute the pattern of the Internet of Things. Objects may be identified, and may also be assigned a persistent foundational identity, for instance a Digital Object Identifier (DOI). A commercial transaction may also be persistently identified by associating all related documents to an identifier.

The Working Group discarded the suggestion to apply the MLIT to objects based on the argument that this could imply attributing legal personality. However, the purpose for identifying persons and objects is different: persons are identified to attribute the legal effect of their actions, while objects are identified as data sources. Any legal consequence arising from data generated by objects should be ascribed to a person. Identification does not confer legal personality, and digital and physical objects may be identified uniquely, but cannot have legal personality.

Currently, certificates are used to identify the objects and to validate the data they generate. It may be argued that trust services may also be used to link a data message with the object it originates from, although attribution of the data message will always be to a legal or physical person. However, this view goes against the traditional opinion that sees trust services applied directly to persons. In any case, general rules applicable to all smart devices and scripts seem preferable to a piecemeal approach for each type of device,[40] although technical specifications for each type of device may still be needed to finetune the general rules. Additional guidance would be welcome to ensure a thorough understanding of legal mechanisms and effects of identification of objects as well as to promote uniformity of technical standards in the currently fragmented market. Similar issues arise with regard to the related matter of machine identity management.

To sum up, identity management does not apply to objects, and its complex legal and regulatory machinery may be excessive for managing objects' identity. It is arguable whether objects may be the subject of trust services, for example, an object generating data may sign a data message in an automated manner on behalf of its owner.

[40] For an example of legislation dedicated to a single device, see Regulation (EU) 165/2014 of the European Parliament and of the Council of 4 February 2014 on tachographs in road transport [2014] OJ L 60/1, and subsequent modifications.

Article 5. Legal recognition of identity management

Subject to article 2, paragraph 3, the result of electronic identification shall not be denied legal effect, validity, enforceability or admissibility as evidence on the sole ground that:

(a) The identity proofing and electronic identification are in electronic form; or
(b) The identity management service is not designated pursuant to article 11.

The MLIT, art 5 applies the principle of legal recognition of (or non-discrimination against) the use of electronic means in the identity management context.

Article 5(a) refers to the use of electronic means in identity proofing and electronic identification. It is possible that identity proofing and electronic identification may not entirely take place online but may rely on offline procedures and physical credentials. The MLIT, art 5 also applies to such hybrid identification schemes.

Article 5(b) underlines that the absence of designation of the identity management service according to the MLIT, art 11 does not affect the legal effect of the application of the identity management service as long as the other requirements set out in the MLIT are met.

The MLIT, art 5 does not suffice alone to satisfy identification requirements that are set in other laws. For instance, the requirements for compliance with KYC regulations may be different from those for electronic identification.[41] It is for the legislator to decide if, and how, the result of electronic identification may satisfy regulatory requirements. The reference to the MLIT, art 2, para 3 aims to preserve the application of other law mandating the use of specific identity management services, including designated ones.

Although the MLIT, art 5 does not explicitly require the use of a reliable method, the use of a method that is not reliable may justify denying the legal effect to the result of electronic identification. Moreover, it may be impossible for an identity management service provider to discharge its obligations under the MLIT, art 6 by using unreliable methods.

Article 6. Obligations of identity management service providers

An identity management service provider shall, at a minimum:

(a) Have in place operational rules, policies and practices, as appropriate to the purpose and design of the identity management system, to address, at a minimum, requirements to:
  (i) Enrol persons, including by:
    a. Registering and collecting attributes;
    b. Carrying out identity proofing and verification; and
    c. Binding the identity credentials to the person;
  (ii) Update attributes;

[41] E Caprioli, 'Les points d'ombre dans l'application du règlement eIDAS', in Eynard J (ed), *L'identité numérique : Quelle définition pour quelle protection ?* (Bruxelles, Larcier, 2020) 123, 133–137.

(iii) Manage identity credentials, including by:

a. Issuing, delivering and activating credentials;

b. Suspending, revoking and reactivating credentials; and

c. Renewing and replacing credentials;

(iv) Manage the electronic identification of persons, including by:

a. Managing electronic identification factors; and

b. Managing electronic identification mechanisms;

(b) Act in accordance with its operational rules, policies and practices, and any representations that it makes with respect to them;

(c) Ensure the online availability and correct operation of the identity management system;

(d) Make its operational rules, policies and practices easily accessible to subscribers, relying parties and other third parties;

(e) Provide easily accessible means that enable a relying party to ascertain, where relevant:

(i) Any limitation on the purpose or value for which the identity management service may be used; and

(ii) Any limitation on the scope or extent of liability stipulated by the identity management service provider; and

(f) Provide and make publicly available means by which a subscriber may notify the identity management service provider of a security breach pursuant to article 8.

The MLIT, art 6 provides a list of obligations that apply to any identity management service provider regardless of whether the service is designated. As non-compliance with these obligations triggers liability, this approach may hinder market entrance of new providers wishing to offer simple services that do not benefit from designation. On the other hand, it may be difficult to separate designated and non-designated services offered by the same service provider. Moreover, there could be significant interaction between providers offering designated and non-designated services. The policy behind the MLIT, art 6 aims to promote predictability and reliability and offer a fair playing field to all.

The obligations of the identity management service provider relate to: operating the identity management system correctly (MLIT, art 6(c)); preparing, publishing and complying with operational rules, practices and policies (MLIT, art 6 (a), (b), (d) and (e)); and responding to data and security breaches[42] (MLIT, art 6 (f), and art 7).[43]

The violation of these obligations may entail liability under the MLIT, art 12. In adopting this approach, the MLIT favours imposing liability on service providers through statutory standards of care. This approach is different from the more liberal attitude that allows broad use of limitation of liability clauses, or even statutory

[42] While the MLIT, art 7 refers to data breaches as comprising breach of security or loss of integrity, the MLIT, art 8 refers only to compromised identity credentials, which are referred to as a security breach in the MLIT, art 6(f).

[43] Smedinghoff (n 33) 31.

limitations of liability, to promote technological innovation and strengthen market offerings.

The obligations described in the MLIT, art 6(a) are modelled on the identity management lifecycle: their description aims to cover all core functions performed during that lifecycle. The operational rules, policies and practices are system rules that describe roles of the participant in the actual identity management system[44] and that are often compiled in a contractual document. As such, the system rules may also bind the subscriber and, where a contractual link exists, the relying party. However, the obligation of the identity management service provider to abide by the operational rules, policies and practices finds a statutory basis in the MLIT, art 6(b).

Article 6(b) and (c) operationalises the obligations contained in system rules by requiring the service provider to act in accordance with them and, more generally, to ensure the availability and correct functioning of the identity management system. While the MLIT, art 6, unlike the MLIT, art 14, does not contain an explicit reference to the need to ensure continuity in case of a business termination, such matter should nevertheless be foreseen in the operational rules, policies and practices.

The obligations contained in the MLIT, art 6(d), (e) and (f) relate to information requirements.

Article 6(d) requires that operational rules, policies and practices – ie the technical description of how the identity management service functions – be made available to all interested parties: subscribers, relying parties, and other third parties with an interest (for example, potential third parties). This information is necessary to assess the reliability of the service and the level of assurance it provides.

Similarly, art 6(e) mandates disclosing any limit to the purpose or value for which the identity management service may be used, or to the liability of the service provider. The service provider must comply with the conditions set out in art 10, paras 3 and 4, in order to limit liability.

Finally, art 6(f) refers to the obligation of providing a mechanism for reporting security breaches according to the MLIT, art 8, and of making that mechanism known.

The obligations of the identity management service provider are absolute and may not be varied or derogated from as long as they are relevant to the design and functioning of the specific identity management system and service.[45] They offer the basis for the statutory liability of the identity management service provider according to the MLIT, art 12. This approach presupposes the existence of a tripartite service scheme comprising provider, subscriber and relying party. An issue may arise if the service provider is also the relying party, for example, a bank

[44] ibid 34.
[45] Guide to Enactment, para 91.

provides electronic signatures services to be used for online banking. In that case, the full application of the obligations under the MLIT, art 6 might be considered excessive.[46] On the other hand, requiring compliance with all obligations may protect the subscriber.

The service provider may fulfil its obligations directly or with the help of third parties, and remains in any case liable for their performance towards subscribers, relying parties and any other concerned party. Among specific roles that are not defined under the MLIT, the role of the personal identification data provider (which could be the operator of a civil registry) may be prominent.

The MLIT, art 6 does not exhaust the list of obligations of identity service providers. Especially for providers of qualified services, the law may set additional organisational and technical obligations.

Article 7. Obligations of identity management service providers in case of data breach

1. *If a breach of security or loss of integrity occurs that has a significant impact on the identity management system, including the attributes managed therein, the identity management service provider shall, in accordance with the law:*
   (a) *Take all reasonable steps to contain the breach or loss, including, where appropriate, suspending the affected service or revoking the affected identity credentials;*
   (b) *Remedy the breach or loss; and*
   (c) *Notify the breach or loss.*
2. *If a person notifies the identity management service provider of a breach of security or loss of integrity, the identity management service provider shall:*
   (a) *Investigate the potential breach or loss; and*
   (b) *Take any other appropriate action under paragraph 1.*

The MLIT, art 7 foresees a specific obligation for identity management service providers in case of security breach or integrity loss. This obligation is in addition to any other similar obligation arising under other law, namely data privacy and protection law.

The mechanism foreseen in the MLIT, art 7 is triggered by the occurrence of a security breach or integrity loss that has a significant impact on the identity management system, or by notification by any person of a potential security breach or integrity loss. The requirement that the breach or the loss should have a 'significant impact'[47] avoids requiring the service provider to take action on breaches or losses of minimal duration, or those which affect the identity management system or service marginally. This qualification aims to mitigate the burden imposed on the service provider.

Once the breach or loss occurs, or the identity service provider is aware that it may have occurred, the identity service provider must investigate it and, when

[46] Smedinghoff (n 33) 12.
[47] This notion is taken from the eIDAS Regulation, art 19, para 2.

confirmed, contain it, remedy it, and notify of the loss. Containing the loss may require suspending the service or revoking the credentials, but does not have to, depending on factual circumstances. This is why art 7, para 1(a) qualifies the steps to be taken as 'reasonable'.

The legislator may wish to clarify further details such as the persons to be notified of the breach or loss, or the content and timing of the notification. Such details may be similar to those set in other law for data breach notification.

Article 8. Obligations of subscribers

The subscriber shall notify the identity management service provider, by utilizing means made available by the identity management service provider pursuant to article 6 or by otherwise using reasonable means, if:

(a) The subscriber knows that the subscriber's identity credentials have been compromised; or

(b) The circumstances known to the subscriber give rise to a substantial risk that the subscriber's identity credentials may have been compromised.

The MLIT, art 8 contains the only obligation imposed on the subscriber. The subscriber must notify the service provider by using the means provided according to the MLIT, art 6 (f), or any other reasonable means, that the identity credentials have been compromised, or that the subscriber knows of a possible substantial risk that the identity credentials may have been compromised. The notification triggers the remedial mechanism contained in the MLIT, art 7. However, the subscriber's failure to notify does not per se relieve the service provider from liability arising from a breach of security or loss of integrity. A similar provision may be found in the UNCITRAL Model Law on Electronic Signatures (MLES), art 8, para 1(b).

Evidence of 'compromised credentials' may include cases of the unauthorised use of the credentials by a third party, or the inability of the subscriber to use the credentials.

The standard required in the MLIT, art 8 (b) for triggering the notification duty is intentionally high to avoid placing an excessive burden on the subscriber, who may not have technical knowledge or other relevant expertise. A similar approach is taken in the MLES, art 8, para 1(b)(ii).

The MLIT does not impose on the subscriber obligations like those contained in the MLES, art 8, paras 1(a) and (c), which require the signatory to exercise reasonable care in the use of its signature creation data, or in its material representations relevant for the use of a certificate. However, the contract between the service provider and the subscriber may contain such obligations.

The MLIT also does not impose any obligation on the relying parties, unlike the MLES, art 11. Given the absence of any contract between the service provider and the relying parties, any obligation of the relying party is to be found in other laws.

Article 9. Identification of a person using identity management

Subject to article 2, paragraph 3, where the law requires the identification of a person for a particular purpose, or provides consequences for the absence of identification, that requirement is met with respect to identity management services if a reliable method in accordance with article 10, paragraph 1 or article 10, paragraph 4, is used for the identity proofing and electronic identification of the person for that purpose.

The MLIT, art 9 establishes the requirements for functional equivalence between the result of offline and online identification. Offline identification is traditionally carried out using paper documents verified by a human. Online identification is typically carried out by automated machine verification of credentials. The outcome of the online verification may be considered equivalent to that of the offline process if reliable methods are used in all phases of identity proofing and electronic identification. The reliability of the method may be assessed ex ante or ex post. The application of the MLIT, art 9 does not affect specific duties to identify, as specified in the MLIT, art 2, para 3.

The MLIT, art 9 refers to identification for a 'particular purpose' to acknowledge that the law may require identification for a specific reason (for example, age verification; access to specific services), which may require verification of selected credentials of the subject.

The MLIT, art 9 operates if a duty to identify offline exists. It may also operate if such a duty does not exist, but identification is needed for a specific purpose, for instance, to access an online environment or to control a digital asset. Similarly, the general rule on the legal effect of identity management contained in the MLIT, art 5 operates regardless of the existence of a duty to identify offline.

Jurisdictions that wish to enact a general rule on the legal effect of identity management tied to the use of reliable methods for greater legal certainty may do so on the basis of the MLIT, art 9 by inserting a provision drafted along the following lines: 'Identity management services shall use a reliable method in accordance with article 10, paragraph 1 or article 10, paragraph 4, for the identity proofing and electronic identification of a person for a particular purpose.'

Article 10. Reliability requirements for identity management services

1. *For the purposes of article 9, the method shall be:*
   - *(a) As reliable as appropriate for the purpose for which the identity management service is being used; or*
   - *(b) Deemed to be as reliable as appropriate if proven in fact by or before a court or competent adjudicative body to have fulfilled the function described in article 9, by itself or together with further evidence.*
2. *In determining the reliability of the method, all relevant circumstances shall be taken into account, which may include:*
   - *(a) Compliance of the identity management service provider with the obligations listed in article 6;*

(b) Compliance of the operational rules, policies and practices of the identity management service provider with any applicable recognized international standards and procedures relevant for the provision of identity management services, including level of assurance frameworks, in particular rules on:

(i) Governance;
(ii) Published notices and user information;
(iii) Information security management;
(iv) Record-keeping;
(v) Facilities and staff;
(vi) Technical controls; and
(vii) Oversight and audit;

(c) Any supervision or certification provided with regard to the identity management service;
(d) Any relevant level of assurance of the method used;
(e) The purpose for which identification is being used; and
(f) Any relevant agreement between the parties, including any limitation on the purpose or value of the transactions for which the identity management service might be used.

3. *In determining the reliability of the method, no regard shall be had:*

(a) To the geographic location where the identity management service is provided; or
(b) To the geographic location of the place of business of the identity management service provider.

4. *A method used by an identity management service designated pursuant to article 11 is presumed to be reliable.*
5. *Paragraph 4 does not limit the ability of any person:*

(a) To establish in any other way the reliability of a method; or
(b) To adduce evidence of the non-reliability of a method used by an identity management service designated pursuant to article 11.

As noted,[48] the notion of reliability of the methods used is a cornerstone of the texts on electronic commerce of the United Nations Commission on International Trade Law (UNCITRAL). The reliability requirement aims at reconciling flexibility in the choice of technology and predictability of the legal effects of the technology chosen. As also noted, the two available approaches for assessing the reliability of the method are called 'ex ante' and 'ex post'. The legal effect of the ex ante and ex post approaches is the same: proving reliability of the method used. The difference lies in the allocation of the burden of proof.

The ex ante (ie 'before the use') approach consists of identifying reliable services before their actual use. The assessment is carried out by competent bodies, against

[48] See ch 3, commentary on art 12 of the UNCITRAL Model Law on Electronic Transferable Records (MLETR).

pre-determined technical requirements and at the request of the service provider. If the result of the assessment is positive, it is published in a public list.

One main advantage of this approach is that users and third parties may rely on the determination of reliability to utilise confidently the service assessed as reliable. Moreover, that service may benefit from a legal presumption of reliability, which is usually not absolute but has the effect of reversing the burden of proof.

On the other hand, the ex ante approach may introduce elements of discrimination against services that are in fact reliable but have not been assessed by the designating authority. It may also be misunderstood as requiring assessment as a condition for attributing legal effect to any service, which may result in market distortion and violation of the principle of technology neutrality.

From a policy perspective, this approach may encourage regulation. For this reason, it may be favoured by regulation-oriented jurisdictions such as civil law ones and those of economies in transition.

The ex post (ie 'after the use') approach postpones the assessment of reliability to the time when an actual dispute on the reliability of the method used arises. It provides a high degree of flexibility in accommodating the needs of the parties, but a lower degree of predictability when compared to the ex ante approach. It has also the advantage of being used only in case of need, thus minimising costs when there is no dispute.

From a policy perspective, the ex post approach is seen as business-friendly as the parties to a transaction enjoy broad freedom to choose method or product. In case an issue on reliability should arise, the ex post assessment may validate such agreement, although its effects would not usually apply to third parties.

However, the ex post approach may not provide the maximum level of guidance to business and users on the legal effects of the service. Moreover, depending on the selection of circumstances relevant to assess reliability, it may lead to different results in different jurisdictions and may be costly to administer in judicial proceedings.

Unlike the MLETR, art 12, which relies only on the ex post assessment though it is compatible with ex ante mechanisms, the MLIT, art 10 places equal reliance on ex ante and ex post reliability assessment mechanisms ('two tier' approach).[49] The different approaches of the MLETR and the MLIT reflect diversity in legislative models and legal traditions.[50]

The combination of ex ante and ex post approaches allows maximisation of the benefits of each approach. In carrying out the ex-ante assessment, it is possible to refer to technology neutral descriptions of levels of reliability for trust services

[49] A similar approach is followed in the European Union, but with three levels (simple, advanced, and qualified). The requirements for the advanced level have been specified in the eIDAS 2 Regulation (arts 32a and 40a).

[50] A similar difference exists between the UNCITRAL Model Law on Electronic Commerce and the MLES.

and of levels of assurance for identity management schemes. If those descriptions are widely accepted, they can be used to establish equivalence of services and schemes across borders.

The MLIT, art 10 is the core provision for the assessment of reliability of the methods used for identity management. It may also be a blueprint for instances when the use of a reliable method is required by an UNCITRAL text or other law.

Article 10, para 1(a) clarifies that the method used must be as reliable as appropriate under the circumstances, and for the specific purpose for which the method is used. The method should therefore be reliable for the specific purpose for which identity management is being used (for example, open a bank account; cash a cheque at the bank teller).

As usual in UNCITRAL texts, reliability should be assessed as a relative quality.[51] This approach allows taking into consideration factors other than technology when assessing the reliability of the signature method used. Moreover, the reference to 'method' includes the use of multiple processes, procedures and devices by multiple persons. For instance, where the 'purpose' for identifying an individual is to open a bank account, a method that requires the prospective customer to present to the bank an electronic identity card issued in compliance with KYC standards, and then the bank to use a KYC-compliant device to read the contents of the card, might be considered reliable. Conversely, where the purpose is to identify an individual seeking to establish an account for the purchase of small value goods at a consumer website, a method as simple as a user created username and password, coupled with a valid credit card number, might be considered reliable for that purpose.

Article 10, para 1(b), which is based on the United Nations Convention on the Use of Electronic Communications in International Contracts (ECC), art 9, para 3(b)(ii), is a safety clause that aims to avoid repudiation of methods that have in fact achieved their function, alone or (as it is often the case) together with further evidence. The function is the identification of a person for a particular purpose, as indicated in the MLIT, art 9. Without this safety clause, the reliability test could be abused so as to lead to invalidating an output on the sole grounds that the method in abstract was not as reliable as appropriate, thus possibly exempting one party from its legal obligations.[52]

Aptly, this test has been defined as 'reliability in practice' while the one in art 10, para 1(a) is referred to as 'reliability in theory'.[53] In short, there is no need to prove in abstract the reliability of the method used if that method has been proven

[51] See ch 3 at section 3.2.3, commentary on the MLETR, art 12.

[52] See the case law cited in ch 3, section 3.2.3, commentary on the MLETR, art 12, under 'Safety Clause'.

[53] KW Chong and JS Chao, 'United Nations Convention on the Use of Electronic Communications in International Contracts: A New Global Standard' (2006) 18 *Singapore Academy of Law Journal* 116, 130.

as reliable in fact. This provision is found also in the ECC, art 9, para 3(b)(ii) and in the MLETR, art 12, para (b). The wording contained in pre-existing UNCITRAL texts has been slightly modified in the MLIT, art 10 to explicitly encompass cases when adjudication is not carried out by a court.

The MLIT, art 10, para 2 contains an open-ended list of circumstances relevant for ex-post reliability assessment. Compared to similar lists in other UNCITRAL texts (see for example, the MLETR, art 12), the list has been adjusted to identity management. Moreover, this list features several objective elements that complement the traditional subjective approach that refers to circumstances such as business nature, frequency of transactions between the parties and established practices, equipment used, etc. Customs, including those specific to the relevant business sector and geographic region, and any practice established by the parties, may also be relevant.

The MLIT, art 10, para 2(a) contains a reference to the compliance of the identity management service provider with the obligations listed in the MLIT, art 6 whose effect is to signal that in case of non-compliance the method used is likely non-reliable. Article 10, para 2(b) indicates that identity management services that follow recognised standards may be considered reliable. The standards may be regional or international. Possibly, they may be also national standards widely used in several jurisdictions. Article 10, para 2(c) establishes a link between the reliability assessment and compliance with regulatory or industry requirements by referring to the existence of an oversight mechanism or of a certification.

Article 10, para 2 (b) and (d) both refer to the notion of 'level of assurance'. A level of assurance is a term of art not defined in the MLIT that is used to refer to a description of the requirements that an identity management scheme must meet to provide a certain degree of confidence in the identification. The Guide to Enactment of the MLIT illustrates the notion of 'level of assurance',[54] which is used in parallel with that of 'level of reliability' for trust services. Currently, levels of assurance may be defined in national or regional law or regulations, or by the private sector for use in certain applications, but there is no universally accepted definition of levels of assurance.[55] With the broader use of cross-border identity management, universally accepted levels of assurance may emerge.

The references to external standards and evaluations used in the assessment of reliability are complemented by references to the features of the relevant identity transaction contained in art 10, para 2(e), which refers to the actual purpose of the

[54] Guide to Enactment, paras 159–164. On the notion of 'level of assurance' see also C Tullis, N Constantine and A Cooper, 'Electronic Signatures: Enabling Trusted Digital Transformation' (2024) World Bank Digital Transformation Policy Note Series, 4.2.

[55] OECD, *G7 Mapping Exercise*, Annex B provides an overview of identity and authentication assurance levels in Canada, the European Union, Japan, the United Kingdom and the United States of America (the publication was prepared at the request of the G7 Presidency).

identification, and art 10, para 2(f), which refers to the parties' agreement, including limitations on value and purpose of the relevant transaction.

Article 10, para 3 clarifies that the assessment of reliability shall be carried out on geographic-neutral grounds, ie without regard to foreign elements such as the place of business of the identity service provider or the place where the identity service is provided. This is an important element of the mechanism for cross-border recognition of identity management.[56]

Article 10, para 4 critically links the MLIT, arts 10 and 11, respectively on ex post and ex ante reliability assessments, by stating that the designation of reliable services according to the MLIT, art 11 has the effect to presume the reliability of the methods used.

Article 10, para 5 clarifies the effects of that presumption, which is rebuttable, with the burden of proof allocated on the party alleging non-reliability. Moreover, the existence of designated identity management services under the MLIT, art 11 does not prevent ex post determination of reliability of any non-designated service under the MLIT, art 10. This conclusion is obvious from the MLIT, art 5(b); however, the matter is often raised, especially in jurisdictions where the existence of certified, qualified or otherwise designated services – typically, electronic signatures – is interpreted, namely at the technical level, as a denial of the legal effects of non-designated services.

Article 11. Designation of reliable identity management services

1. *[A person, organ or authority, whether public or private, specified by the enacting jurisdiction as competent] may designate identity management services that are presumed reliable.*
2. *The [person, organ or authority, whether public or private, specified by the enacting jurisdiction as competent] shall:*
   - *(a) Take into account all relevant circumstances, including the factors listed in article 10, in designating an identity management service; and*
   - *(b) Publish a list of designated identity management services, including details of the identity management service provider.*
3. *Any designation pursuant to paragraph 1 shall be consistent with recognized international standards and procedures relevant for performing the designation process, including level of assurance frameworks.*
4. *In designating an identity management service, no regard shall be had:*
   - *(a) To the geographic location where the identity management service is provided; or*
   - *(b) To the geographic location of the place of business of the identity management service provider.*

The MLIT, art 11 complements the MLIT, art 10 by providing the mechanism for ex ante designation of reliable identity management systems. A jurisdiction that does not wish to set up a mechanism for ex ante designation may decide not to

[56] See ch 8.

enact the MLIT, art 11. However, it may not be desirable to enact art 11 without enacting the MLIT, art 10 as this may restrict recognition of identity management schemes and services in actual use.

The law may indicate an entity tasked with carrying out the designation, or may give that power to an oversight authority, which may in turn identify one or more designating entities. The designating entity could be a public oversight body, or one or more private companies delegated by the competent public entity. Several states may appoint a single common designating authority to save costs, share expertise and facilitate mutual recognition.

The designation process, which must take place according to predetermined rules, may be divided into three phases: the submission by the identity management service provider of the request for designation of one or more specified services; the evaluation of the service; and, in the event of a positive outcome, the inclusion of the designated service in a trusted list.[57]

The designating entity must first set up a designation process consistent with international standards and procedures. These standards, which are referred to in the MLIT, art 11, para 3, are different from those referred to in the MLIT, art 10, para 2(b) as the former are specific to the designation of reliable identity services (for example, standards regarding conformity assessments, audits, and similar procedures used in certifying an entity) while the latter are specific to the provision of the identity services.

To ensure consistency between ex post determination and ex ante designation, art 11, para 2(a) requires that the designation process take into account the circumstances listed in the MLIT, art 10, para 2. However, certain circumstances such as parties' agreements may be less relevant for designation than for determination, or not relevant at all for designation.

The MLIT, art 11, para 4 reaffirms the application of the principle of non-geographic discrimination to the designation of reliable services. At a minimum, this means that the designating authority should take into account requests for designation of services originating from foreign providers under the same conditions applicable to domestic providers. Designation of a foreign service under the ex ante approach triggers automatic recognition of legal effects, including the presumption of reliability of the methods, in all the instances that the designated foreign service is used.

The MLIT, art 11 may be enacted to operate in a manner similar to the eIDAS regulation so that the designations made by the competent authority in a state will have automatically the same legal effect in other participating states. This provision may also operate in more complex scenarios: for instance, a designating authority that is recognised by several states may designate as reliable a service offered by a provider located in a state that is not among those recognising the designating authority. This may be useful in developing countries that do not have resources to

[57] Smedinghoff (n 33) 24–25.

maintain national designating authorities, and therefore may decide to appoint a supranational entity, and whose markets are too small to sustain local commercial identity management service providers.

Once one or more designating entities have been identified, and those entities have adopted adequate designating processes, an identity management service provider may apply for designation of one or more services. Implementing regulations will specify technical requirements, documentation to be submitted and costs, if any. Again, the identity management service provider shall not be required to have its place of business in the same state where designation is sought, although certain guarantees may be asked, for example, with regard to business continuity and preservation of archives.

Potential subscribers and relying parties need to know which services have been designated as this is an important consideration in the choice of the service provider. For this reason, according to art 11, para 2(b), the entity in charge of designation must maintain and publish a list of designated services (also known as 'trusted list'). The list may contain information such as any limit to the purpose or value of the transaction for which the service may be used. If there are multiple designating entities, a consolidated list may be kept.[58] Trusted lists should also permit automated consulting to validate the status of a service during its use.

Because of its enabling nature, the MLIT does not deal with the regulatory framework applicable to the designating entity. Such framework, which may be quite complex, is usually managed by a public oversight body. The framework includes procedure and requirements to become a designating entity, as well as sanctions for violations of the related obligations.

Article 12. Liability of identity management service providers

1. *The identity management service provider shall be liable for loss caused to the subscriber or to the relying party due to a failure to comply with its obligations under articles 6 and 7.*
2. *Paragraph 1 shall be applied in accordance with rules on liability under the law and is without prejudice to:*
   - *(a) any other basis of liability under the law, including liability for failure to comply with contractual obligations; or*
   - *(b) any other legal consequences of a failure of the identity management service provider to comply with its obligations under this Law.*
3. *Notwithstanding paragraph 1, the identity management service provider shall not be liable to a subscriber for loss arising from the use of an identity management service to the extent that:*
   - *(a) That use exceeds the limitations on the purpose or value of the transaction for which the identity management service is used; and*
   - *(b) Those limitations are contained in the arrangement between the identity management service provider and the subscriber.*

[58] National law may allow or require the inclusion also of non-qualified services in a public list.

> 4. *Notwithstanding paragraph 1, the identity management service provider shall not be liable to a relying party for loss arising from the use of an identity management service to the extent that:*
>   (a) *That use exceeds the limitations on the purpose or value of the transaction for which the identity management service is used; and*
>   (b) *The identity management service provider has complied with its obligations under article 6, subparagraph (e) with respect to that transaction.*

The MLIT, art 12 provides a legal framework for the liability of identity service providers regardless of whether they provide services designated reliable or not. Some European delegations were particularly supportive of inserting a provision on liability in the MLIT, as the eIDAS Regulation also deals with liability matters, albeit not necessarily in the same manner.[59] The MLIT liability regime is different from that of the MLES because the MLIT provides liability only for the service provider, unlike the MLES, art 8, para 2 that allocates liability to the signatory, and the MLES, art 9, para 2 that does the same to the certification service provider. Moreover, the MLIT introduces a new source of liability while the MLES, art 8, para 2 and art 9, para 2 refer to other law under which liability may arise.

The MLIT, art 12, para 1 provides a statutory basis for the liability of the identity service provider towards the user and the relying party for breach of its obligations under the MLIT, arts 6 and 7, regarding respectively obligations during the identity management lifecycle and in case of data breach.

Article 12, para 1 operates regardless of whether the same obligations are also contained in contractual agreements. However, the statutory liability is not strict or 'no-fault': the identity service provider may be able to prove that it is not liable for the breach.[60] Although the MLIT is not explicit on this point, placing the burden of proof on the identity service provider is consistent with the rationale that underpins the MLIT, art 12, which is to provide an incentive for the identity service provider to comply with the obligations set out in the MLIT, arts 6 and 7 and to encourage obtaining adequate insurance coverage.

The identity service provider is liable for the delivery of the service regardless of the involvement of subcontractors. This means that the identity service provider is held responsible for the delivery of the service throughout the identity management lifecycle. Moreover, the MLIT, art 12 does not apply to subcontractors. The service provider will usually have contractual and other actions against them. Other concerned parties may also have actions against subcontractors arising under law other than the MLIT.

[59] The eIDAS Regulation, arts 11 and 13 set common liability rules, respectively, for identity management and trust services. The details for the operationalisation of these rules are left to national legislation, similar to the MLIT. On the eIDAS liability regime see M Tescaro, 'Le regole di responsabilità del regolamento «eIDAS»' (2017) XL *Le Nuove Leggi Civili Commentate* 542.

[60] For a similar solution under eIDAS, see Tescaro, 'Le regole di responsabilità' (2017), 547.

The MLIT, art 12, para 2(a) clarifies that art 12 operates alongside other sources of liability, ie contractual and extra-contractual,[61] and does not modify them. The MLIT, art 12 however provides a more comprehensive and more rigorous basis for liability than the other ones. Similarly, the MLIT, art 12, para 2(b) is a reminder that art 12 does not exhaust the consequences for non-compliance with the obligations set in the MLIT, arts 6 and 7 that may arise under another law. National law may provide guidance on matters such as the amount of recoverable damages, required degree of fault, etc. It may also establish different liability regimes depending on the public or private nature of the service provider. The different regimes may be explicit, or implicit due to the application of, respectively, the liability regime under administrative law and under private law.[62]

If the provider and the relying party are the same entity, the joint operation of the MLIT, arts 6, 7 and 12 ensures that the subscriber is not affected by the failure of the service provider to meet its core obligations.

Article 12, para 3 specifies the conditions that the identity service provider must meet to limit its liability towards subscribers. The insertion of a provision explicitly recognising limitation of liability was advocated by non-European delegations due to the concern that unlimited exposure to liability would make insurance impossible, and ultimately hinder the offer of identity management services. The first condition is that limitations exist on the purpose or the value of the transaction for which the identity service is used. These limitations may also change with the concerned party (for example, the value may be higher for the subscriber and lower for the relying parties, which may be numerous). The second condition is that the limitation is reflected in the arrangement, ie in the contract with the subscriber or any other relevant document (for example, if the identity service is provided by a public entity, the relationship may have an administrative nature). The possibility of inserting limitation clauses in the contract between provider and subscriber is also acknowledged in the MLIT, art 10, para 2(f).

Article 12, para 4 similarly specifies the conditions that the identity service provider must meet to be able to limit liability towards relying parties. Since there is no contractual relationship, under the MLIT, art 6(e) the identity service provider must provide the relying party with easy access to information on any limitation on the purpose or value for which the identity management service may be used, and on the scope or extent of the liability undertaken by the provider.

[61] Similarly, ibid 554–555.
[62] Caprioli, 'Les points d'ombre dans l'application du règlement eIDAS' (2020), 131–132.

7

Trust Services

7.1. Trust Services in General

One defining feature of digital transformation is the prevailing use, analysis and sharing of data. However, raw data is of little use: data quality must be assured. A trust service is an electronic service that provides a certain level of assurance on the qualities of a data message such as origin, integrity, timeliness, etc. Reliable trust services are critical to build trust in exchanges of electronic data, including electronic documents. Quality assurance is necessary both for national and international use.

Virtually all states have national laws that deal with electronic signatures, which provide assurance of origin of the signed message and, sometimes, of its integrity and of the occurrence of certain events in time. However, the law often considers electronic signatures an equivalent of handwritten signatures, and rarely a trust service. Other trust services receive piecemeal legal treatment, and in few jurisdictions only. The Regulation (EU) No 910/2014 of the European Parliament and of the Council of 23 July 2014 on electronic identification and trust services for electronic transactions in the internal market and repealing Directive 1999/93/EC (eIDAS Regulation) represents an early effort to provide a comprehensive legislative framework for trust services,[1] which is however limited in geographical scope. The UNCITRAL Model Law on the Use and Cross-border Recognition of Identity Management and Trust Services (MLIT) is the first uniform global legislative text on trust services.

The MLIT specifically lists certain trust services. Most of them correspond to those existing in the original eIDAS Regulation: electronic signatures; electronic seals; electronic time stamps; website authentication; and electronic registered delivery services. It also identifies the trust service of electronic archiving, which has been added later to the eIDAS Regulation.

At the same time, the MLIT adopts an open-ended approach to trust services: the definition of 'trust service' is open to recognising any trust service, unlike the eIDAS Regulation that recognises only named trust services. States may at the time of the MLIT enactment add any trust service they wish to recognise or exclude those that they do not consider necessary; importantly, they may give an

[1] On the origin of the eIDAS Regulation and its implementation with regard to qualified trust services, see Institut luxembourgeois de la normalisation, de l'accréditation, de la sécurité et qualité des produits et services (ILNAS), 'Trust Services under the eIDAS Regulation' V1.0 (2018).

oversight authority the ability to add or delete recognised trust services according to need. In the MLIT, any change in the number and type of trust services does not affect the framework for their legal treatment. In this manner, for instance, the additional trust services identified in the revision of the eIDAS Regulation may be included in enactments of the MLIT.[2] The modifications to the original eIDAS Regulation introduced with the eIDAS 2 Regulation are generally compatible with the MLIT.

During the preparation of the MLIT, an even broader approach to dealing with trust services was suggested, based on a more general description of what trust services aim to provide (the 'who, what, where, when and why' of data). That approach, which did not gather support in the Working Group, may nevertheless be useful to appreciate the purpose and function of trust services.

7.2. General Provisions on Trust Services in the MLIT

Chapter III of the MLIT, on trust services, follows closely the structure and content of chapter II, with a few adjustments and simplifications. It features a provision on legal recognition of the effect of the application of trust services.

Each trust service (except website authentication, which cannot have an offline equivalent because websites by definition are only in electronic form) has a dedicated provision drafted as a functional equivalence rule referring to the paper-based function. This approach can be appreciated in light of the historical importance of the principle of functional equivalence. A different approach, not anchored to form requirements of paper documents, could have been taken to highlight the importance of trust services as dataflows enablers.

The assessment of reliability of the methods used to provide trust services uses the same 'two tier' approach that combines ex post determination and ex ante designation.

The chapter also contains a list of the obligations of trust service providers and a closely related provision on liability.

Article 1. Definitions

For the purposes of this Law:

(a) – (k) [...];

(l) 'Trust service' means an electronic service that provides assurance of certain qualities of a data message and includes the methods for creating and managing electronic signatures, electronic seals, electronic time stamps, website authentication, electronic archiving and electronic registered delivery services;

[2] Regulation (EU) 2024/1183 of the European Parliament and of the Council of 11 April 2024 amending Regulation (EU) No 910/2014 as regards establishing the European Digital Identity Framework [2024] OJ L2024/1183 (eIDAS 2).

(m) 'Trust service provider' means a person who enters into an arrangement for the provision of one or more trust services with a subscriber.

The MLIT, art 1 sets out the fundamental notions for both identity and trust services. The notions of 'data message', 'relying party' and 'subscriber' are common to identity management and trust services.[3] The notions of 'trust service' and 'trust service provider' are relevant only for trust services. A trust service provides assurance of data quality. The notion of 'trust service' being open-ended, the list of named trust services is merely illustrative and reflects those trust services identified in eIDAS. While attempts to expand that list (for example, with the inclusion of escrow services)[4] were not successful, the fact that the list is open-ended facilitates the inclusion of new types of trust services.

The MLIT does not require that the trust service be provided for remuneration. Hence, its provisions also apply to trust services provided for free.

Article 13. Legal recognition of trust services

The result deriving from the use of a trust service shall not be denied legal effect, validity, enforceability or admissibility as evidence on the sole ground that:

(a) It is in electronic form; or
(b) The trust service is not designated pursuant to article 23.

The MLIT, art 13 contains the formulation of the principle of legal recognition of the result of the application of a trust service. It is formulated, as usual, in negative terms, ie prohibiting discrimination against the legal effect of the use of trust services, and applies to both named and unnamed trust services.

While the article might at a first glance seem superfluous, given that trust services are by definition in electronic form, it brings useful clarity in highlighting that the object of the legal recognition is the result of the application of the trust service, ie a statement about data quality.

Article 1(b) indicates, for the avoidance of doubt, that the principle also applies to trust services that have not been designated according to the MLIT, art 23. The effect of this provision is similar to that of the UNCITRAL Model Law on Electronic Signatures (MLES), art 3, on the equal treatment of signature technologies, which clarifies that the MLES does not 'exclude, restrict or deprive of legal effect any method of creating an electronic signature' that satisfies functional equivalence requirements.

Article 14. Obligations of trust service providers

1. A trust service provider shall, at a minimum:

(a) Have in place operational rules, policies and practices, including a plan to ensure continuity in case of termination of activity, as appropriate to the purpose and design of the trust service;

[3] See ch 5, section 5.4, commentary on the MLIT, art 1.

[4] For a description of escrow services, see M Ryan and T Sweet, 'Software Escrow – Its Evolution, Use in Legal Frameworks and The Influence of AI' (*Society for Computers & Law*, 12 December 2024) www.scl.org.

(b) Act in accordance with its operational rules, policies and practices, and any representations that it makes with respect to them;
(c) Make its operational rules, policies and practices easily accessible to subscribers, relying parties and other third parties;
(d) Provide and make publicly available means by which a subscriber may notify the trust service provider of a security breach pursuant to article 15; and
(e) Provide easily accessible means that enable a relying party to ascertain, where relevant:
(i) Any limitation on the purpose or value for which the trust service may be used; and
(ii) Any limitation on the scope or extent of liability stipulated by the trust service provider.

2. If a breach of security or loss of integrity occurs that has a significant impact on a trust service, the trust service provider shall in accordance with the law:
(a) Take all reasonable steps to contain the breach or loss, including, where appropriate, suspending or revoking the affected service;
(b) Remedy the breach or loss; and
(c) Notify the breach or loss.

The MLIT, art 14 outlines the obligations of trust service providers similarly to how the MLIT, arts 6 and 7 outline the obligations of identity management service providers. These obligations need to be complied with throughout the lifecycle of the trust service, ie creation, verification and validation (including, if applicable, preservation and management of remote electronic signature creation devices) and apply to providers of any trust service.[5]

The obligations contained in the MLIT, art 14 may not be derogated from and provide a basis of statutory liability under the MLIT, art 24. This has practical importance, including when the trust service is provided according to a bilateral scheme (and not the trilateral scheme envisaging provider, subscriber and relying party as discrete entities). For example, a bank may provide at no cost to its clients in-house electronic signatures to carry out e-banking: even in that case, the bank may not derogate from its core obligations as trust service provider.

The obligations contained in the MLIT, art 14 may be grouped in three categories.

The first category relates to operational rules, policies and practices (art 14, para 1 (a), (b) and (c)). The trust service provider must have in place operational rules, policies and practices that are specific to the given trust service, including its intended use. The rules, policies and practices must include measures to ensure continuity in case of termination of activity (for example, for insolvency). The trust service provider has an obligation to comply with the operational rules, policies and practices, and an obligation to make them known to all interested parties.

[5] The eIDAS 2 Regulation, art 19(a) has introduced requirements for non-qualified service providers. However, if requirements are differentiated, they should be attached to the service and not to the provider, as the same provider may offer designated and non-designated services (or qualified and non-qualified services, in eIDAS terminology).

As for identity management, the obligation of the trust service provider to comply with the operational rules, policies and practices has a statutory basis and may not be derogated from. Those operational rules, policies and practices may also contain contractual obligations for the subscribers. It is arguable whether reliance on the results of the application of the trust service could imply a relationship with the relying parties besides the obligation towards them that the service provider has under the MLIT, art 14.

The second category regards breach of security and loss of integrity (art 14, para 1(d), and para 2). The trust service provider has a duty to contain any significant breach or loss, to remedy it and to inform affected entities of it. The considerations made under the MLIT, art 7 apply also to the MLIT, art 14, para 2, and this obligation operates alongside any other similar obligation arising under other law, namely data privacy and protection law.[6]

Upon notification of a potential security breach or integrity loss by any person, or its discovery by the trust service provider, the service provider should investigate it and, when confirmed, contain it, remedy it and notify of the loss. The breach or the loss should have a 'significant impact' to lessen the burden imposed on the provider.

The trust service provider must also offer the means to be used by the subscriber to inform the provider in case the trust service is or may be compromised. The expected reaction to that notification is similar to that described in the MLIT, art 7, para 2 although that provision is not reproduced in the MLIT, art 14.

The third category relates to the ability of the trust service provider to limit its liability towards relying parties (art 14, para 1(e)). Since the limitation may not be contained in a contract, the relying parties should have easy access to information on any limitation of the purpose or value for which the trust service may be used, and on the scope or extent of liability of the trust service provider. This provision is complemented by the MLIT, art 24, para 4.

Article 15. Obligations of subscribers

The subscriber shall notify the trust service provider, by utilizing means made available by the trust service provider pursuant to article 14, paragraph 1 or by otherwise using reasonable means, if:

(a) The subscriber knows that data or means used by the subscriber for access and usage of the trust service has been compromised; or

(b) The circumstances known to the subscriber give rise to a substantial risk that the trust service may have been compromised.

The MLIT, art 15 contains the only obligation of the subscriber of a trust service, ie the duty to notify an actual or possible deficiency of the trust service.

[6] The European Union Agency for Cybersecurity (ENISA) publishes an annual report on trust services security incidents based on the notifications received from European Union (EU) national supervisory bodies. The report provides guidance on the incident reporting process and on the types of incidents.

More precisely, and similar to the MLIT, art 8, the MLIT, art 15 recognises that the subscriber may not be in a position to ascertain whether the trust service has actually been compromised. Hence, the MLIT, art 15 makes a distinction between the 'data or means used by the subscriber for access and usage of the trust service', which are under control of the subscriber, and the general possibility that the trust service has been compromised: in the former case, the duty of notification arises in case of actual breach, while in the latter case the circumstances known to the subscriber must suggest a substantial risk of breach, ie an assessment that breach is likely to occur, to trigger that duty.

The subscriber has a duty to notify a security breach through the means made available by the trust service provider (MLIT, art 14, para 1(d)) or through any other reasonable means. The consequences for failure of the subscriber to notify are to be assessed under general law.

The MLIT does not contain any obligation for parties relying on the result of the application of a trust service. For reference, the MLES, art 11 establishes an obligation for the party relying on an electronic signature to take reasonable steps to verify the reliability of an electronic signature or of a certificate, and to observe any limitation on the value and use of the certificate.

[For the commentary on the MLIT, arts 16 to 21, on named trust services, see below.]

Article 22. Reliability requirements for trust services

1. *For the purposes of articles 16 to 21, the method shall be:*
   - *(a) As reliable as appropriate for the purpose for which the trust service is being used; or*
   - *(b) Deemed to be as reliable as appropriate if proven in fact by or before a court or competent adjudicative body to have fulfilled the functions described in the article, by itself or together with further evidence.*
2. *In determining the reliability of the method, all relevant circumstances shall be taken into account, which may include:*
   - *(a) Compliance of the trust service provider with the obligations listed in article 14;*
   - *(b) Compliance of the operational rules, policies and practices of the trust service provider with any applicable recognized international standards and procedures relevant for the provision of trust services;*
   - *(c) Any relevant level of reliability of the method used;*
   - *(d) Any applicable industry standard;*
   - *(e) The security of hardware and software;*
   - *(f) Financial and human resources, including existence of assets;*
   - *(g) The regularity and extent of audit by an independent body;*
   - *(h) The existence of a declaration by a supervisory body, an accreditation body or a voluntary scheme regarding the reliability of the method;*
   - *(i) The purpose for which the trust service is being used; and*
   - *(j) Any relevant agreement between the parties, including any limitation on the purpose or value of the transactions for which the trust service might be used.*

3. *In determining the reliability of the method, no regard shall be had:*
   (a) *To the geographic location where the trust service is provided; or*
   (b) *To the geographic location of the place of business of the trust service provider.*
4. *A method used by a trust service designated pursuant to article 23 is presumed to be reliable.*
5. *Paragraph 4 does not limit the ability of any person:*
   (a) *To establish in any other way the reliability of a method; or*
   (b) *To adduce evidence of the non-reliability of a method used by a trust service designated pursuant to article 23.*

The MLIT, art 22 provides guidance on the factors relevant to assess the reliability of the methods used for delivering trust services. Each method is specific not only to the relevant trust service but also to the specific function pursued. The structure of the MLIT, art 22 is similar to that of the MLIT, art 10, and therefore the same considerations apply. The two articles differ significantly in the list of relevant circumstances contained in para 2, which is, however, in both cases open-ended.

The circumstances contained in the MLIT, art 22, para 2 are based on those contained in the MLES, art 10 and in the UNCITRAL Model Law on Electronic Transferable Records (MLETR), art 12. Maintaining uniformity between reliability requirements is critical to promote the design, deployment and use of comprehensive digital trade ecosystems that deal with all types of documents, transactions, and data.

The MLIT, art 22, para 2(a) refers to the compliance of the trust service provider with the obligations listed in the MLIT, art 14, which relate to the provision of the service, including mitigation of data breach, and to information duties. It is completed by art 22, para 2(b), on compliance of the provider's operational rules, policies and practices with any relevant recognised international standards and procedures. The MLIT, art 14, para 1(b) requires the compliance of the service provider with these rules, policies and practices and any related representation.

Article 22, para 2(c) refers to the level of reliability of the method used and, consequently, of the trust service.

The references to the conformity with any applicable industry standard (art 22, para 2(d))[7] and to the security of hardware and software (art 22, para 2(e)) relate to technical features of the system, while the reference to financial and human resources, including existence of assets (art 22, para 2(f)) regards the qualification of the provider.

The circumstances in art 22, para 2(g) and (h), relating to the existence of audit procedures and of declarations regarding the reliability of the method, may be

[7] For a discussion of a technical standard for electronic signatures, see Z Lu, 'Optimization of Security Algorithms for Digital Authentication and Electronic Signatures in International Electronic Commerce Regulations' (2024) 12 *International Journal of Intelligent Systems and Applications in Engineering* 21s, 152 at ijisae.org.

particularly relevant in ex post determinations, and may be part of the ex ante designation process.

Finally, the circumstances in art 22, para 2(i) and (j) regard the specific purpose of the use of the trust service and any agreement of the parties. Contractual agreements may be relevant between service providers and subscribers, but not for third parties. In its essence, the agreement relates to the freedom of the parties to choose the technology and method, and therefore the security level, appropriate for their transactions. This means that the agreement of the parties could prevail over the assessment of reliability made by a third party, including designation pursuant to the MLIT, art 23. However, the MLIT does not contain a general rule similar to the MLES, art 5, which allows the parties to derogate from or vary the effect of any provision of the MLES, unless the agreement would not be valid or effective under applicable law.

The MLIT, art 22, para 5 may find judicial application given the practical relevance of trust services and their frequent use. For instance, there could be procedures that need to be followed by the user (such as exclusive control of trust service creation data and devices) to comply with the designation requirements, which the user may not have followed in practice. This could provide an argument in support of rebutting the presumption of reliability of a designated trust service.[8]

Article 23. Designation of reliable trust services

1. *[A person, organ or authority, whether public or private, specified by the enacting jurisdiction as competent] may designate trust services that are presumed reliable.*
2. *The [person, organ or authority, whether public or private, specified by the enacting jurisdiction as competent] shall:*
   - *(a) Take into account all relevant circumstances, including the factors listed in article 22, in designating a trust service; and*
   - *(b) Publish a list of designated trust services, including details of the trust service provider.*
3. *Any designation pursuant to paragraph 1 shall be consistent with recognized international standards and procedures relevant for performing the designation process.*
4. *In designating a trust service, no regard shall be had:*
   - *(a) To the geographic location where the trust service is provided; or*
   - *(b) To the geographic location of the place of business of the trust service provider.*

The MLIT, art 23 provides for designation of trust services presumed reliable according to mechanisms like those envisaged in the MLIT, art 11 for identity

[8] Judgment of the European Court of Justice of 20 October 2022, *'EKOFRUKT' EOOD v Bulgaria* 2022/C 472/18, in OJ C 472/16, 12.12.2022, reminds, among others, that the judge must ascertain that the qualified signature meets the relevant standards in case of challenge. See also the case note by T Douville, 'La présomption de fiabilité des signatures électroniques : un modèle pour le droit de l'Union ?', *Recueil Dalloz*, 20 avril 2023, n 15, 740.

management services. Hence, mutatis mutandis, the same considerations apply. The main difference lies in the relevant factors listed in the MLIT, arts 10 and 22.

Trust service providers often offer a range of trust services, some of which may qualify for designation, while others may not. A trust service must be validly designated at the time of its use to benefit from the presumption of reliability. The fact that a trust service has been designated as presumed reliable, but has lost that designation, does not prevent the possibility of otherwise proving its reliability at the time of use according to MLIT, art 22.

The enacting jurisdiction may decide whether the same or a different entity should be tasked with designating both reliable identity management services and reliable trust services. This may depend on the governance of civil records and vital statistics, among other considerations.

The list of designated trust services may include foreign trust services that are deemed equivalent to designated national trust services and foreign trust services that have been designated reliable as such.

Article 24. Liability of trust service providers

1. *The trust service provider shall be liable for loss caused to the subscriber or to the relying party due to a failure to comply with its obligations under article 14.*
2. *Paragraph 1 shall be applied in accordance with rules on liability under the law and is without prejudice to:*
   - *(a) any other basis of liability under the law, including liability for failure to comply with contractual obligations; or*
   - *(b) any other legal consequences of a failure of the trust service provider to comply with its obligations under this Law.*
3. *Notwithstanding paragraph 1, the trust service provider shall not be liable to a subscriber for loss arising from the use of a trust service to the extent that:*
   - *(a) That use exceeds the limitations on the purpose or value of the transaction for which the trust service is used; and*
   - *(b) Those limitations are contained in the arrangement between the trust service provider and the subscriber.*
4. *Notwithstanding paragraph 1, the trust service provider shall not be liable to a relying party for loss arising from the use of a trust service to the extent that:*
   - *(a) That use exceeds the limitations on the purpose or value of the transaction for which the trust service is used; and*
   - *(b) The trust service provider has complied with its obligations under article 14, subparagraph 1(e) with respect to that transaction.*

The MLIT, art 24 provides for liability of trust service providers akin to that provided in the MLIT, art 12 for identity service providers. The regime applies to all types of trust services, not just designated ones, and to public and private trust service providers alike, subject to any possible exception found in the law enacting the MLIT or in other law.[9]

[9] For a discussion of instances of liability arising from the use of electronic signatures, see S Mason, *Electronic Signatures in Law* (London, University of London Press, 2016) ch 15.

The nature of the liability arising from the MLIT, art 24 is statutory. The MLIT, art 24 does not displace any contractual or extra-contractual source of liability.

The MLIT does not contain any provision about the liability regime of other parties such as the subscriber and the relying party. Jurisdictions wishing to add such provisions may find inspiration in the MLES, art 8, on the conduct of the signatory (who is a subscriber),[10] and in the MLES, art 11, on the conduct of the relying party. Otherwise, the terms and conditions of use of the trust service may provide the basis for liability of such parties. The violation of the obligation of the subscriber to notify compromised data or trust services set in the MLIT, art 15 may also give rise to liability, albeit under general liability rules.

The behaviour of the subscriber and of the relying party may also concur to limit the liability of the service provider under other applicable law.

7.3. Electronic Signatures

7.3.1. From Handwritten to Electronic Signatures

The need to build trust by accurately identifying the parties to a transaction is a basic commercial necessity. For that reason, since the early days of trade different identification methods were established, which relied on the presence of witnesses or on the use of documents that could be validated by the affixation of signatures and seals.[11]

Over time, it became possible to identify the basic functions of handwritten signatures based on use cases. These functions include: attribution of a writing; association of a person with the content of a document, including its approval, or intent to be bound (for example, by a contract); or proof of the signatory's presence at a given place and time. These functions presuppose the correct identification of the signatory, but this is not an intrinsic quality of the paper document: identification derives from external processes.

Because of the link between identification and signature, it is possible to refer to the notion of 'authenticity' as a quality relating to origin: a document or a painting are authentic if they originate from the purported author. 'Signature' becomes then a method to validate attribution, though within certain limits: a signed document may be typed, and a signed painting may be produced with the contribution of the artist's studio assistants. Different notions exist of how the identification

[10] In case of fraud, the signatory, also called holder of the signature creation device, may be found liable under civil law but not under criminal law rules: MA Hjort, P Kalamees and L Kask, 'Misuse of Electronic Signatures and eID Owner Liability: A Comparative Analysis of Estonian and Norwegian Legislative Frameworks and Practice' (2025) 36 *European Business Law Review* 287. This outcome is due to the different standards applied to assess negligence for civil liability and criminal conduct.

[11] For an introduction (not focusing on UNCITRAL texts), see S Mason, *The Signature in Law. From the Thirteenth Century to the Facsimile*, OBserving Law (London, University of London Press, 2022).

process in conjunction with a signature takes place: civil law jurisdictions tend to require the direct participation of the signatory, while common law jurisdictions are more flexible as long as the link between individual and signatory may be established, even a posteriori.

Similar needs arose at an early stage of the use of electronic transactions and were exacerbated by lack of personal interaction and prior acquaintance.[12] Reproducing online the functions of handwritten signatures seemed obvious but was not sufficient. From a legal and functional perspective, the creation of a comprehensive legal framework for identity management and trust services is an evolution of the notion of electronic signature, which plays a crucial role in modern digital trade.

Historically, electronic signatures have been used as a method to link signatory and signed message. Their ability of doing so in a trustworthy manner depends on the methods used, including choice of technology.[13] Electronic signatures with more advanced features, such as those based on cryptography, play a fundamental role in ensuring the authenticity and integrity of electronic communications.

The basic requirements for legal recognition of a signature, regardless of its medium, are to identify the signatory and clarify its intent with respect to the signed message. The identification of the signatory requires the use of a method to identify the signatory but not necessarily identification itself: for instance, a seal may identify a monarch and establish its will with respect to the parchment upon which the seal was affixed; a website may attribute an order to the person who has signed into it with username and password, and who is paying with a pre-stored credit card. However, functions fulfilled by electronic signatures could go beyond by validating additional qualities such as assurance of the integrity of the signed data message and that an event took place at a certain point in time (timestamping).

The need for reliable online identification increased with the shift from closed to open networks.[14] Participants in closed networks are usually identified before

[12] A Fitzgerald and A Moens, 'Regulating electronic commerce – emerging principles for the regulation of Internet transactions' in International Academy of Comparative Law, *Convergence of Legal Systems in the 21st Century. General Reports delivered at the XVIth International Congress of Comparative Law* (Bruxelles, Bruylant, 2006) 1565.

[13] One of the first reported cases on the legal validity of electronic signatures used to identify the sender of an electronic communication was decided by the New Hampshire Supreme Court more than 150 years ago: *Howley v Whipple* (48 NH 487 (1869)). For a detailed discussion of authentication methods see UNCITRAL, *Promoting Confidence in Electronic Commerce: Legal Issues on International use of Electronic Authentication and Signature Methods* (Vienna, United Nations, 2009). For an introduction to the law of electronic signatures (not discussing in detail UNCITRAL texts), see S Mason and D Seng (eds), *Electronic Evidence and Electronic Signatures*, 5th edn, OBserving Law (London, University of London Press, 2021); for a recent overview of the matter, see C Tullis, N Constantine and A Cooper, 'Electronic Signatures: Enabling Trusted Digital Transformation' (2024) World Bank Digital Transformation Policy Note Series.

[14] D Gobert and E Montero, 'La signature dans les contrats et les paiements électroniques : l'approche fonctionnelle' in S Cavanillas Mugica and ors (eds), *Commerce électronique : le temps des certitudes* (Bruxelles, Bruylant, 2000) 53.

gaining access to the network; however, prior identification is not always possible in open networks. Hence, the need arose for a dedicated legal framework to promote confidence in the identities of the parties operating in open networks. In response, states adopted legislative provisions on electronic signatures, often based on texts prepared by the United Nations Commission on International Trade Law (UNCITRAL).

As the use of electronic signatures increased, so did the variety of their applications as well as differences in the understanding of the notion of electronic signature. That notion, originally understood as an equivalent of a contract law form requirement for a handwritten signature, was expanded to include various types of attribution mechanisms. Importantly, different policy approaches emerged, reflecting cultural and legal differences in the use of trusted third parties such as public notaries in signatures, and the related procedures. The policy approach determines the oversight regime, which may rely on an optional or mandatory accreditation system, as well as on the role of public entities, which may be regulators or service providers – at times, monopolistic. The importance of public entities is inversely proportional to the relevance given to party autonomy in the choice of technologies and methods for electronic signatures.

With time and experience, it became evident that different use cases of electronic signatures called for different levels of reliability. One common manner of describing levels of reliability is linked with authentication factors, which may be features of the signature creation device. Authentication factors can refer to: something possessed (for example, a token, or a mobile phone); something known (for example, a code, a drawing or a password); or an intrinsic (biometric) quality of a person. The more authentication factors are required, the more secure the electronic signature is considered.[15]

Rules on electronic signatures that allow identification and authentication of the parties may be found in: model laws; regional and national legislation, often based on those model laws; self-regulatory instruments such as codes of conducts; and contractual agreements. Because of their practical importance, free trade agreements also contain provisions on electronic signatures. The recent 'stabilised text' of the draft Agreement on Electronic Commerce,[16] prepared in the framework of the Joint Statement Initiative on Electronic Commerce, contains an updated restatement of such provisions. Article 5 of the draft Agreement, on 'Electronic Authentication and Electronic Signatures', defines 'electronic signature' akin to the definitions contained in the UNCITRAL Model Law on Electronic Commerce (MLEC) and the United Nations Convention on the Use of Electronic Communications in International Contracts (ECC). It also

[15] The use of different authentication factors was the rationale supporting the adoption of three levels of electronic signatures (simple, advanced, and qualified) in European Union law.

[16] World Trade Organization, 'Joint Statement Initiative on Electronic Commerce. Agreement on Electronic Commerce' (26 July 2024) WTO Doc INF/ECOM/87.

defines 'electronic authentication' as the act of identifying a party of an electronic communication or transaction, or the integrity of an electronic communication.

Article 5, para 2 of the stabilised text contains the principle of non-discrimination against the legal effect, legal validity, or admissibility as evidence in legal proceedings of an electronic signature solely on the basis that the signature is in electronic form. The provision is drafted in the UNCITRAL style, and its legal effects are similar to those of the MLIT, art 13, which, however, refers specifically to the result of the application of the trust service, including an electronic signature.

Article 5, para 3 of the stabilised text prohibits the adoption of measures that prevent parties from agreeing on the preferred electronic signature or electronic authentication method, and from proving in front of courts or administrative authorities that the method chosen complies with any applicable legal requirement. This paragraph may be derogated for special categories of transactions.

Article 5, para 5 of the stabilised text extends the application of art 5 to electronic seals, electronic time stamps, and electronic registered delivery services. This broader approach has also been adopted in the Protocol to the Agreement establishing the African Continental Free Trade Area on Digital Trade, art 8.[17]

Finally, art 5, paras 6 and 7 of the stabilised text encourages parties to use interoperable electronic authentication methods and to promote mutual legal recognition of electronic signatures.

Interestingly, art 9, para 3 of the stabilised text encourages parties to 'implement a reference number or other identity verification tool to uniquely identify data relating to an individual transaction' with regard to single window operations. A similar requirement to provide a unique electronic link identifying a shipment and the related data elements is contained in the eFTI Regulation. These provisions highlight the need to provide reliable identification of electronic transactions, documents and entities that may be addressed with the use of identity management and trust services.

7.3.2. Policy Approaches to Electronic Signatures

Similar to the reliability assessment,[18] legislation dealing with electronic signatures may be grouped under three main approaches: (a) the minimalist approach; (b) the technology specific or prescriptive approach; and (c) the two-tier or two-pronged approach.

Under the minimalist approach, all technologies, methods and products used for creating and managing electronic signatures are recognised on an equal basis, provided that they fulfil the functions of handwritten signatures. This approach is in strict compliance with the principle of technology neutrality.

[17] Protocol to the Agreement Establishing the African Continental Free Trade Area on Digital Trade (AfCFTA Digital Trade Protocol) (adopted 18 February 2024).

[18] See ch 6, section 6.5, commentary on the MLIT, art 10.

The MLEC, art 7, para 1, which applies the minimalist approach, requires as conditions for functional equivalence with the notion of handwritten signature to: identify the signatory; express the signatory's approval of the information contained in the message; and use a method that is as reliable as appropriate in light of the circumstances. As noted, the identification of the signatory may take place at a later stage, and on the basis of external elements (for example, signature using a pseudonym and eventual identification of the physical person who signed).

The minimalist approach calls for the ex post assessment of reliability, with which it shares the same advantages and disadvantages in terms of being future-proof, flexible to accommodate the needs of the parties, but also less predictable in legal effects.

On the other hand, legislators may require a particularly high level of predictability and security in electronic transactions due to the speed of electronic communications and the ability to replicate their content instantaneously, at low cost and in high volumes. As a result, more stringent conditions may be set forth for identification and authentication in electronic transactions than in paper-based ones. These considerations lead to prescribing the use of a specific technology and the underlying approach is therefore called technology-specific or prescriptive.

The prescriptive or technology-specific model typically demands the use of digital signatures, ie signatures based on cryptography and public key infrastructures (PKI). The role of governments in managing such systems may vary, as providers of certification services may be required to obtain prior authorisation or licensing from a public authority or may be encouraged to join voluntary schemes. Moreover, the establishment of a central certification authority may greatly influence the development and features of the electronic signatures market. Control may be further increased by establishing an exclusive electronic signatures service provider, which leads to mandating not only the use of a specific technology but also of a specific product.

The technology-specific approach is linked with the ex ante assessment of the reliability of the methods used. The disadvantages of this approach include the possible violation of the principle of technology neutrality, and the possible denial of legal validity of an electronic communication despite certainty of the signatory's intention and identity. At the cross-border level, technology-specific legislation may significantly hinder the recognition of foreign electronic signatures.

As noted, the two-tier or two-pronged approach strikes a balance between security and flexibility. Under this approach, all electronic signature methods have legal recognition and effect, subject to judicial confirmation in case of dispute ('first tier'). Moreover, methods offering higher levels of security are associated with certain presumptions such as reversing the burden of proof on the origin and integrity of the message, provided certain requirements are met ('second tier').[19] Those requirements may be described in technology neutral terms or may refer to

[19] The MLES, art 6 is based on this approach.

specific technologies; they may also demand specific certification models, so that only certain certification services would qualify to offer electronic signatures for specific applications. In practice, second tier technologies are often associated with the use of PKI technology to benefit from the legal presumptions on the origin and integrity of the signed electronic communication.

> ***Article 16. Electronic signatures***
>
> *Where the law requires a signature of a person, or provides consequences for the absence of a signature, that requirement is met in relation to a data message if a reliable method in accordance with article 22, paragraph 1, or article 22, paragraph 4, is used:*
>
> *(a) To identify the person; and*
>
> *(b) To indicate the person's intention in respect of the information contained in the data message.*

Similar to other trust services in the MLIT, the MLIT, art 16 is technology neutral, operates independently of the place of origin or use of the electronic signature, and relies on both ex ante and ex post assessments of reliability, thus following the two-tier approach. It also accommodates the joint use of electronic and non-electronic means.

The MLIT, art 16 is drafted as a functional equivalence rule for electronic signatures.[20] This means that, on its face, it should apply when there is a form requirement calling for a handwritten signature. However, as noted, trust services operate independently of a legal requirement. At the same time, electronic signatures that fall under the scope of the MLIT, art 16 may also be used to satisfy form requirements to use handwritten signatures established by law or parties' agreement. Consequently, there may be no practical difference between these two functions of electronic signatures as the same methods, processes and means could be used.

The MLIT, art 16 requires the use of a reliable method to identify the signatory of a data message and indicate its intention in respect of the information contained in the data message. The methods do not need to be used in a single procedure or process. For instance, identification could be achieved by logging into a system by using a secure login procedure, and indication of intent could be expressed by clicking the button 'I agree' in a virtual basket. These conditions for establishing functional equivalence were first set out in the ECC, art 9, para 3(a). As noted, since this definition focuses on the attributes of a method (as opposed to the notion of signature data used in certain legislative texts), it broadens the range of processes and technologies available. Identification may take place with respect to a pseudonym, unless forbidden by other law.

In line with the general principle of non-interference underpinning UNCITRAL texts on electronic commerce, the MLIT, art 16 does not affect any

[20] The same applies to the other trust services named in the MLIT except website authentication.

requirement contained in other law that limits the types of admissible electronic signatures.[21]

Certain paper-based signatures do not express approval of the signed document but satisfy other functions such as knowledge of content, or witnessing. Thus, the MLIT, art 16 refers to the neutral notion of the party's 'intention' which does not necessarily imply agreement with or endorsement of the content of the data message. The method should clearly indicate the intention of the party both in terms of content of the intention and of consent to embrace that intention.[22] This solution is in line with the MLETR, art 9 and with the ECC, art 9, para 3(a).

7.3.3. Relationship between Identity Management and Electronic Signatures

While the MLIT, art 16 may be mostly explained in light of pre-existing UNCITRAL texts, the qualification of electronic signature as a trust service raises novel questions. The relationship between the result of identity management, and the identity component of certain trust services, which is derived from identity management, is an issue that requires careful analysis.[23] On the one hand, identity management may be used to identify a signatory, among several uses. On the other hand, several methods, including identity management, may be used to identify persons in trust services.

There should be a difference between the outcome of the application of identity management and that of an electronic signature as a trust service, although both outcomes may lead to identification of a person. The outcome of identity management leads to verification of identity, and the outcome of electronic signatures and other trust services is to satisfy a legal requirement or provide assurance of data quality. Similar considerations apply to other trust services that contain an identity element such as electronic seals and electronic registered delivery services.

However, in practice the distinction between identity management and trust services may not be simple. Identity is asserted and verified by using trust services, namely electronic signatures. It may be argued that the obligations of the identity

[21] For instance, in the United States scanned handwritten signatures may not be used in medical prescriptions, as the method for their generation is similar to a rubber signature stamp, which is also forbidden: National Council for Prescription Drug Programs, 'White Paper: Electronic Signature Guidance' (2014) version 1.0, 13. In general, scanned signatures do not provide assurance of specific intention, and therefore fail the test of the MLIT, art 16.

[22] With regard to the ECC, art 9, para 3, see T Smedinghoff, 'Article 9: Form Requirements', in AH Boss and W Kilian (eds), *The United Nations Convention on the Use of Electronic Communications in International Contracts: An In-depth Guide and Sourcebook* (Frederick, Md, Kluwer Law International, 2008) 136, 153.

[23] Tullis, Constantine and Cooper, 'Electronic Signatures' (2024), 6.3.

management service provider and those of the trust service provider could separately and cumulatively apply but this solution may not be easy to implement.

It is necessary to add to the already complex picture the notion of digital identity wallets and the trust services of electronic attestation of attributes and of electronic ledger, which were introduced by the eIDAS 2 Regulation. The European Digital Identity Wallet is both an identity management tool (or, if preferred, an application), and a trust service to be used in conjunction with electronic signatures and electronic seals.[24] The electronic attestation of attributes is an online statement about qualities of a person such as age, education, professional qualification and ability to carry out certain actions (for example, driving; giving qualified professional advice).[25] As this statement is about a quality of an entity, and not of data, it is doubtful that it could qualify as a trust service under the MLIT. It may however be a component of an identity management scheme to confirm specific attributes. In practice, the concerned person could identify itself online with the provider of the electronic attestation of attributes, for instance by using an identity wallet, and then use the attestation with a third party, for instance to certify income or residence that qualify for certain services.

The trust service of electronic ledger is closely related with the use of blockchain.[26] An electronic ledger provides assurance of the chronology of information. While the definition of electronic ledger is technology neutral to include both distributed and non-distributed ledgers, this trust service is promoted in association with the use of blockchain technology. On the other hand, technical details of this trust service are still to be defined, and it is possible that the trust service will be limited to certain types of distributed ledgers, for example, permissioned ledgers, which are ledgers that may be accessed only upon prior approval.

7.4. Other Trust Services Named in the MLIT

Article 17. Electronic seals

Where the law requires a legal person to affix a seal, or provides consequences for the absence of a seal, that requirement is met in relation to a data message if a

[24] See the definition in art 3, point 42 of the revised eIDAS Regulation: '"European Digital Identity Wallet" means an electronic identification means which allows the user to securely store, manage and validate person identification data and electronic attestations of attributes for the purpose of providing them to relying parties and other users of European Digital Identity Wallets, and to sign by means of qualified electronic signatures or to seal by means of qualified electronic seals;'.

[25] See the somehow circular definition in art 3, point 46 of the revised eIDAS Regulation: '"electronic attestation of attributes" means an attestation in electronic form that allows attributes to be authenticated;'. Some attributes may be dynamic, such as a bank account statement.

[26] See the definition in art 3, point 52 of the revised eIDAS Regulation: '"electronic ledger" means a sequence of electronic data records, ensuring the integrity of those records and the accuracy of the chronological ordering of those records;'. For an introduction, see I Alamillo-Domingo and ors, 'Qualified Ledgers: Bridging the Gap between Blockchain Technology and Legal Compliance' *Medium* (medium.com) 29 January 2024.

reliable method in accordance with article 22, paragraph 1, or article 22, paragraph 4, is used:

(a) To provide reliable assurance of the origin of the data message; and
(b) To detect any alteration to the data message after the time and date of affixation, apart from the addition of any endorsement and any change that arises in the normal course of communication, storage and display.

Electronic seals are trust services of significant practical importance as they provide assurance of origin and integrity of a data message. Besides fulfilling the functions of electronic signatures, electronic seals may be used to satisfy the functional equivalence requirements for the notion of 'original' and other notions that require assurance of integrity. Because of these intrinsic features, they are evidence of the existence of a document issued by a legal person. Electronic seals may also be used for machine-to-machine interaction, including to confirm origin and integrity of data originating from machines such as oracles.[27]

Providing assurance of origin and integrity is associated with the use of digital signatures based on encryption, and this has already been acknowledged in the MLES, art 6, para 3(d), which indicates among the possible purposes of the legal signature requirement 'to provide assurance as to the integrity of the information to which it relates'. This function is missing in 'simple' electronic signatures. Jurisdictions that have enacted provisions on electronic signatures similar to the MLES, art 6, para 3(d) and that allow their use by legal persons may not need to enact a provision on electronic seals.[28]

Like the approach taken in the eIDAS Regulation, electronic seals in the MLIT are available only to legal persons. Jurisdictions enacting the MLIT may wish to consider whether they should be made available to physical persons, too, bearing in mind that electronic signatures are available to both physical and legal persons.

Electronic signatures and electronic seals may operationalise corporate digital identity, which is a tool that may bring significant clarity to corporate operations, reducing costs and increasing the compliance rate.[29] Business areas that may particularly benefit from a comprehensive, consistent and effective use of corporate digital identity include banking and finance, and taxation. For instance, with corporate digital identity any purported delegated authority to carry out a certain transaction may be verified instantaneously. To achieve these goals, legal persons need to maintain a real-time record of the credentials and authority given to each individual entitled to use electronic seals and electronic signatures.

[27] INNOPAY, 'Market Impact of the eIDAS Revision on Trust Services' (2024), 15.

[28] The issue may be different in EU law as the eIDAS Regulation does not define a unitary notion of signature, which is left to national laws. For that reason, it must be verified under national law whether an electronic seal also performs the functions of an electronic signature: see G Finocchiaro, 'Una prima lettura del reg UE n 910/2014 (cd eIDAS): identificazione on line, firme elettroniche e servizi fiduciari' (2015) XXXVIII *Le Nuove Leggi Civili Commentate* 419, 426.

[29] D Leung and ors, 'Corporate Digital Identity: No Silver Bullet, but a Silver Lining' (2022) Bank for International Settlements Papers No 126.

The MLIT, art 17(b) is based on the MLEC, art 8, para 3. It clarifies that purely technical modifications of the data message do not compromise its integrity. The term 'endorsement' has a broad meaning and is not limited to the notion of endorsement in documents of title (see the MLETR, art 15).

The trust service of electronic seal as defined in the MLIT should not be confused with the notion of seal in electronic form that may be found in national legislation, especially of certain common law jurisdictions, and that is aimed at satisfying the requirement of affixing a seal on a paper-based document: the constitutive elements of the MLIT, art 17 transpose the eIDAS notion of electronic seal, albeit drafted nominally in functional equivalence terms, while those national provisions may be based on different constitutive elements.[30]

Article 18. Electronic timestamps

Where the law requires a document, record, information or data to be associated with a time and date, or provides consequences for the absence of a time and date, that requirement is met in relation to a data message if a reliable method in accordance with article 22, paragraph 1, or article 22, paragraph 4, is used:

(a) To indicate the time and date, including by reference to the time zone; and
(b) To associate that time and date with the data message.

Associating a data message with an event occurring at a certain point in time is of great legal importance: in this manner, it is possible, for instance, to determine when an electronic communication has been received, a bill of lading has been transferred, or a security interest has been perfected. For this reason, electronic timestamps are gaining popularity not only in business practice but also among legislators.

The electronic timestamp does not provide evidence that the data message was created at a certain point in time, but that at that point in time it existed in a certain form and therefore had been created. The definition of electronic timestamp in the MLIT does not require assurance of integrity of the timestamped data message, but is not incompatible with it.

The result of the application of electronic timestamps may be used not only between the parties to an electronic transaction, but also for the opposability of that transaction to third parties. This function may apply also to other trust services, but is particularly evident in this case.

The MLIT, art 18 refers to the broad notion of 'data' to indicate that timestamps may be used in conjunction with data that is not structured in a document or otherwise.

[30] See, eg, British Virgin Islands, Electronic Transactions Act 2021, Act No 6 of 2021, s 13(2): 'Where a seal is required by law to be affixed to a document and such law does not prescribe the method or form by which such document may be sealed electronically, that requirement is satisfied if the document indicates that it is required to be under seal and it includes the secure electronic signature of the person by whom it is required to be sealed'.

Unlike the eIDAS 2 Regulation, the MLIT does not contain a trust service named 'electronic ledger' that ensures integrity and accuracy of chronological data ordering of data messages (eIDAS 2, recital 68); however, this does not exclude the application of timestamps to achieve the same result. Alternatively, the legislator may define electronic ledger as a discrete trust service when enacting the MLIT, or the parties may agree on its use.

Article 19. Electronic archiving

Where the law requires a document, record or information to be retained, or provides consequences for the absence of retention, that requirement is met in relation to a data message if a reliable method in accordance with article 22, paragraph 1, or article 22, paragraph 4, is used:

(a) *To make the information contained in the data message accessible so as to be usable for subsequent reference;*
(b) *To indicate the time and date of archiving and associate that time and date with the data message;*
(c) *To retain the data message in the format in which it was generated, sent or received, or in another format which can be demonstrated to detect any alteration to the data message after that time and date, apart from the addition of any endorsement and any change that arises in the normal course of communication, storage and display; and*
(d) *To retain such information, if any, as enables the identification of the origin and destination of a data message and the time and date when it was sent or received.*

Retention of data messages is a critical step to ensure their use as evidence, which is a complex matter.[31] For instance, reliable archiving is a requirement for change of medium in the MLETR, art 18. The trust service of electronic archiving should therefore be understood against the background of the rules on electronic evidence. Because of different legal traditions and policy choices, UNCITRAL has only provided general guidance in this area.

The MLEC, art 9 contains the principle of non-discrimination against electronic evidence, including a 'best evidence' rule. Moreover, it generally requires that information in the form of data messages be given evidential weight, having regard to the manner in which data has been stored, among other circumstances.

The MLEC, art 10 provides a functional equivalence rule on retention of data messages that contains some basic elements of the MLIT, art 19. In particular, the MLEC, art 10, para 1(a) contains the same requirements for functional equivalence with the notion of 'writing' as the MLIT, art 19(a) does. The MLEC, art 10, para 1(b) requires that the data message is retained in the format in which it was generated, sent or received, or in a format that accurately represents the original format. The MLIT, art 19(c) contains the same requirement, and clarifies that

[31] For an introduction (not focusing on UNCITRAL texts), see S Mason and D Seng (eds), *Electronic Evidence and Electronic Signatures*. See also M Demoulin and A Vernusset, 'La réversibilité des données et l'archivage électronique. Ou comment éviter la dépendance technologique' (2015) 11 *Les Cahiers du numérique* n 2, 115.

accurate representation means the ability to detect any modification to the original message. The data message does not need to be sent or received to be archived, and the rule enables not only archival from the application where the data message was generated, sent or received, but also migration of archives to prevent technological obsolescence. Finally, the MLEC, art 10, para 1(c) and the MLIT, art 19(d) require that information relating to origin, destination, and time and date of dispatch and receipt should also be retained, if available.

Despite being formulated in functional equivalence terms, the MLIT, art 19 differs from the MLEC, art 10 as the former refers to the trust service used to satisfy the functional equivalence rule, while the latter refers to the functional equivalence rule itself.[32] Moreover, the MLIT, art 19(b) requires timestamping the data message at the time of archiving, which is a requirement absent in the MLEC, art 10.

UNCITRAL texts do not deal with the complex issue of the duration of the archival period. On the one hand, legal information should be available at least until all foreseeable actions arising from the archived document are time-barred. On the other hand, data privacy law may require keeping data only for the time necessary to fulfil the purpose for which it was collected. UNCITRAL texts also do not deal with techniques such as anonymisation and encryption that may be mandated by regulation.

A trust service named 'electronic archiving' has been included in the eIDAS 2 Regulation.[33] In that Regulation, electronic archiving means a service ensuring the receipt, storage, retrieval and deletion of electronic data and electronic documents in order to ensure their durability and legibility as well as to preserve their integrity, confidentiality and proof of origin throughout the preservation period.[34] The description of qualified electronic archiving services refers, among others, to the capability of 'ensuring the durability and legibility of electronic data and electronic documents beyond the technological validity period and at least throughout the legal or contractual preservation period, while maintaining their integrity and the accuracy of their origin'.[35] As noted, such requirement may also apply to the MLIT, art 19, as the archived record should be available as long as legally relevant, ie until all possible related legal actions are time-barred.

Article 20. Electronic registered delivery services

Where the law requires a document, record or information to be delivered by registered mail or similar service, or provides consequences for the absence of delivery, that

[32] Guide to Enactment, para 212.

[33] The original eIDAS Regulation listed a trust service of 'preservation of electronic signatures and seals'; in addition, individual states could introduce the trust service of 'electronic archiving'. This was done in Belgium with the law of 21 July 2016, *Moniteur belge*, 28 September 2016, and in Luxembourg with the law of 25 July 2015 on electronic archiving: H Jacquemin, 'L'archivage électronique comme nouveau service de confiance : l'exemple belge' (2021) at researchportal.unamur.be.

[34] eIDAS 2 Regulation, art 1(j) and the revised eIDAS Regulation, point 48.

[35] eIDAS 2 Regulation, art 45(j), para 1(b).

requirement is met in relation to a data message if a reliable method in accordance with article 22, paragraph 1, or article 22, paragraph 4, is used:

(a) To indicate the time and date when the data message was received for delivery and the time and date when it was delivered;
(b) To detect any alteration to the data message after the time and date when the data message was received for delivery to the time and date when it was delivered, apart from the addition of any endorsement or information required by this article, and any change that arises in the normal course of communication, storage and display; and
(c) To identify the sender and the recipient.

The MLIT, art 20 deals with the electronic registered delivery service, a trust service which provides assurance of the delivery of a data message at a certain point in time, of the integrity of the message transmitted, and of the identity of sender and recipient. Hence, electronic registered delivery services have an identity component, and their function is not limited to confirming the delivery of the message.

This service has significant practical applications in private law, for instance in contract formation, and in e-government, for instance in administrative and tax law. A well-known application related to a specific technology is the use of registered electronic mail services.

The service may provide additional information, such as time and proof of despatch and time and proof of receipt (as opposed to delivery). This may help to fill any gap arising from the fact that the MLIT, art 20 does not refer to such notions, which are used in other UNCITRAL texts such as the ECC, art 10, because it was drafted with a focus on functional equivalence between registered mail services and electronic registered delivery services.[36] In other words, the MLIT, art 20 provides assurance of a certain event that may be useful to provide evidence needed in substantive rules such as the MLEC, art 15 and the ECC, art 10. However, the substantive rules may set additional requirements, such as designation of the electronic address, to achieve the intended result (for example, receipt of an electronic communication).

Article 21. Website authentication

Where the law requires website authentication, or provides consequences for the absence of website authentication, that requirement is met if a reliable method in accordance with article 22, paragraph 1, or article 22, paragraph 4, is used:

(a) To identify the person who holds the domain name for the website; and
(b) To associate that person to the website.

Internet users need to rely on the veracity of websites they visit to ensure that any information they provide, including payments, is exchanged with the intended party. This is reciprocal to the request of the website operator to reliably identify those users, for instance, by using electronic signatures and electronic seals.

[36] Guide to Enactment, para 218.

According to the MLIT, art 21, website authentication aims to provide assurance of the domain name holder of a website. This is part of the process that links the resource, identified by an internet protocol number, the domain name that identifies it in a human-friendly manner, and the uniform resource locator that completes the internet protocol number with additional information.[37]

The definition of 'website authentication' contained in the MLIT is different from that contained in the eIDAS 2 Regulation, which points at the person to whom a certificate was issued and therefore may presuppose the use of a specific technical solution based on certificates.[38]

Website authentication is listed as a trust service in the MLIT, which is in keeping with the eIDAS model. It is drafted as a functional equivalence rule although there is no offline equivalent of website authentication. Website authentication is a technology-specific trust service. Websites are one of the main data repositories of the internet but are not the only ones. It is possible to imagine a similar service for authenticating applications, which is carried out by applications stores.

Because website authentication takes place through certificates that are recognised by browsers, there is a certain level of technical uniformity that promotes cross-border use of those certificates. This means that website authentication service providers must ensure that their services are compatible with the browsers, although the MLIT does not impose an obligation on providers of browsers to 'ensure support and interoperability with qualified certificates for website authentication' as the eIDAS 2 Regulation, art 45, para 1(a) does. This peculiar situation does not apply to other trust services.

The domain name holder is not necessarily the website owner, the website content provider, or the website operator. Information on those other entities may also be provided.[39] Moreover, content hosted on a platform may not be considered a website, and the platform operator may be responsible for identifying the provider of that content.

Website authentication may also be considered as an example of identification of a digital object. Namely, it requires identifying both the website and the domain name holder, and establishing a link between the two. The same mechanism may be applied to other digital and physical objects.

[37] For technical details, see H Xue, 'Website Authentication: New International Legal Standards Safeguarding Digital Trade' (2025) 31 *Computer and Telecommunication Law Review* 10.

[38] eIDAS 2 Regulation, art 1, point 38: '"certificate for website authentication" means an electronic attestation that makes it possible to authenticate a website and links the website to the natural or legal person to whom the certificate is issued;'. This definition amends the previous definition contained in the original eIDAS Regulation by adding the word 'electronic'.

[39] Xue, 'Website Authentication' (2025), 14.

8

Cross-border Recognition and Cooperation in Identity Management and Trust Services

While the expertise and experience at the national level is increasing, legal and technical discussions on the cross-border use and recognition of identity management and trust services are still at an early stage.[1] Enabling cross-border use and recognition is critical for global digital trade and is a major goal of the UNCITRAL Model Law on the Use and Cross-border Recognition of Identity Management and Trust Services (MLIT), as reflected in its title itself, as well as a defining element of Regulation (EU) 910/2014 of the European Parliament and of the Council of 23 July 2014 on electronic identification and trust services for electronic transactions in the internal market and repealing Directive 1999/93/EC (eIDAS Regulation), albeit mostly at the regional level.

Ideally, legal and technical mechanisms should enable cross-border legal recognition and technical interoperability of all documents and data based on technology-neutral standards. Legislative frameworks based on the MLIT and eIDAS avoid creating data silos for each document by defining general requirements for data quality assurance. This is indispensable to ensure that digital trade ecosystems may interact seamlessly. However, this goal is not universally pursued, as cross-border recognition mechanisms may focus on specific documents, transactions and applications.

The absence of uniform legal and technical mechanisms for cross-border recognition before the MLIT was adopted often led to defining piecemeal requirements for individual documents. Such an approach may address the recognition of a specific document among participating entities in the short term, but it may create significant obstacles in the medium and long term to recognition of all documents and data. Moreover, ad hoc recognition mechanisms mimic paper-based

[1] With regard to the United Kingdom, the Industry Working Group on the Electronic Execution of Documents, 'Final Report' (2023) recommends the adoption of the UNCITRAL Model Law on Electronic Signatures (MLES), art 12; with regard to China, discussing the possible adoption of a solution similar to the eIDAS Regulation, see Y Zhou and N Zheng, 'Research on the Legal System of Cross-Border Mutual Recognition of Electronic Signatures in China' (2024) *Information Security and Communications Confidentiality* 3 www.secrss.com.

business practice without acknowledging that paper-based documents represent data structured for human convenience. In digital trade, data should be first and foremost optimised for machine processing, while human readability, albeit important, is a secondary goal and should not drive system design.[2]

From a legal perspective, at least three approaches to cross-border recognition are possible.

According to the first approach, the legal validity of identity management and trust services depends on the law of the jurisdiction of origin, whose cross-border effects are predetermined. The mechanisms used to achieve legal recognition under this approach operate ex ante, granting legal status based on a prior assessment. This is the assumption underlying automatic mutual recognition in the European Union, which applies to all documents and data.[3]

Under the second approach, the law of the jurisdiction where recognition is sought determines the requirements for the legal validity of identity management and trust services. This is the assumption underlying the MLIT.

A third approach recognises the parties' ability to choose the law applicable to the determination of validity of identity management and trust services, and upholds, within limits, such choice. In practice, this model based on party autonomy may play an important role but is complementary to one of the previous models.

The existence of an institutional framework has significant impact on cross-border recognition. The eIDAS Regulation relies on a strong institutional framework that allows for automatic recognition thanks to peer review and other tools for close cooperation. This framework does not exist – or does not exist yet – at the global level. The MLIT therefore relies on several legal, rather than institutional, tools to facilitate cross-border use and recognition as much as possible. These solutions apply to both identity management and trust services.

One tool is the use of geographic-neutral rules for the assessment of reliability of the method used and the designation of reliable systems and services. The MLIT, art 10, para 3 and art 11, para 4 apply that mechanism to identity management; MLIT, art 22, para 3 and art 23, para 4 do the same to trust services.

Moreover, the MLIT, arts 25, 26 and 27 further facilitate cross-border recognition by offering dedicated guidance. Their underlying assumption is that legal recognition will be assessed under the law of the recognising jurisdiction.

At the same time, the MLIT is compatible with the establishment of centrally-managed mutual recognition mechanisms similar to those used by eIDAS, which may be foreseen especially at the regional and sub-regional level. The establishment of such mechanisms is not only a technical and a legal challenge, but especially a policy matter, as it requires significant commitment of

[2] For the time being, data structure is highly relevant. In the future, artificial intelligence may assist in processing unstructured data.

[3] eIDAS Regulation, art 14; and the European Parliament and Council Directive 1999/93/EC on a Community framework for electronic signatures [2000] OJ L 13/12, art 7.

the participating entities. For this reason, the deployment of such mechanisms requires favourable conditions such as leveraging on a regional integration process. Centrally managed mutual recognition mechanisms may also promote or impose technical obligations of interoperability that are missing in the MLIT. A related possible use of the MLIT is as a template for implementing bilateral and plurilateral agreements.[4]

Legal recognition needs to be complemented by technical interoperability and related measures. An attempt to provide a comprehensive model has been made with the European Telecommunications Standards Institute (ETSI) four-pillar methodology for comparing cryptographic trust services frameworks.[5] The four pillars are: trust representation based on the use of mutually intelligible trusted lists; equivalent oversight regimes on audit and supervision; best practices and standards to achieve interoperability; and equivalent legal requirements. While this model is tailored to eIDAS and may refer to components such as oversight that may not be required by law in all jurisdictions (although they may be voluntarily complied with), it relies on the use of MLIT as legal recognition facilitator.

The statutory mechanisms foreseen in the MLIT do not exclude the possibility of contractual agreements on the cross-border effect of identity management and trust services. A dedicated legislative provision may give explicit recognition to such agreements, which may be specific to a transaction or between commercial partners, or may be concluded between service providers to establish equivalence of services.[6] Such provision is missing in the MLIT but may be found in national laws.[7]

Article 25. Cross-border recognition of the result of electronic identification

1. *The result of electronic identification provided outside [the enacting jurisdiction] shall have the same legal effect in [the enacting jurisdiction] as electronic identification provided in [the enacting jurisdiction] if the method used by the identity management system, identity management service, or identity credential, as appropriate, offers:*
   - *(a) At least an equivalent level of assurance, where the assurance levels recognized by such jurisdictions are identical; or*
   - *(b) Substantially equivalent or higher level of assurance, in all other cases.*

[4] See ch 9, section 9.10.

[5] ETSI, ETSI TR 103684 V1.1.1 (2020–01) Technical Report, 'Electronic Signatures and Infrastructures (ESI); Global Acceptance of EU Trust Services' (2020). The UNCITRAL Model Law on Electronic Commerce and the MLES are discussed in section 5.2.1 of the Report.

[6] UNCITRAL, *Promoting Confidence in Electronic Commerce: Legal Issues on International use of Electronic Authentication and Signature Methods* (Vienna, United Nations, 2009), paras 165–168 (on cross-recognition) and 169–172 (on cross-certification).

[7] See, eg, British Virgin Islands, Electronic Transactions Act, Act No 6 of 2021, s 24(3): 'Where the parties to a transaction agree to the use of particular types of electronic signatures and certificates, that agreement shall be recognised as sufficient for the purpose of cross-border recognition in respect of that transaction.'

2. *For the purposes of determining satisfaction of paragraph 1, regard shall be had to recognized international standards.*
3. *An identity management system, identity management service or identity credential shall be presumed to satisfy paragraph 1 if [the person, organ or authority specified by the enacting jurisdiction pursuant to article 11] has determined the equivalence, taking into account article 10, paragraph 2.*

The MLIT, art 25 contains geographic-neutral rules on the assessment of reliability of the methods used for electronic identification and on the designation of reliable systems and services.

Article 25, para 1 sets forth the principle that the effect of electronic identification does not vary depending on the geographical place of provision. To do so, it requires that the level of assurance of the identity management scheme to be recognised is 'at least equivalent' to that required in the recognising jurisdiction, if the definition of levels of assurance used in the originating and recognising jurisdictions are identical; alternatively, the identity management scheme to be recognised should be at least 'substantially equivalent' to that required in the recognising jurisdiction if the definitions of levels of assurance in the two jurisdictions are not identical.

Article 25, para 1(a) was inserted in the MLIT to address the concern of certain European delegations wishing to preserve the application of the eIDAS Regulation and of any required level of assurance. However, this solution has been criticised on three grounds: first, because the term of level of assurance is defined only technically, and therefore there is no legal certainty on its meaning; second, because in several jurisdictions compliance with a level of assurance is not a pre-requisite for legal recognition of identity management; third, because level of assurance is already relevant for assessing the reliability of the method, and it is unclear how the same notion can be relevant twice, but with different effects.[8]

In practice, the two cross-border recognition mechanisms reflect the ex ante and ex post approaches in the sense that closer adherence to a certain level of assurance means more predictability of legal effects but also less flexibility. While it is true that the adoption of globally accepted definitions of levels of assurance could address the matter, this goal may be difficult, if not impossible, to achieve; and insisting on an identical level of assurance would hinder cross-border recognition due to the challenges in mapping levels of assurance with different descriptions. However, this undesirable outcome may be avoided by applying art 25, para 1(a) only in those jurisdictions that have already adopted identical definitions of levels of assurance (for example, jurisdictions that have done so in the framework of the European Union approximation process).[9] The levels of assurance are usually

[8] T Smedinghoff, 'Is It Legal? Will It Be Trusted? What Are the Rules? – Enabling Electronic Identity Management Under the New UNCITRAL Model Law' (2024), 27–28.

[9] States that wish to join the European Union have a duty to align their laws to those of the European Union. The legal alignment process is called 'approximation of national law with the acquis communautaire'. For more information see, eg, R Petrov and P van Elsuwege (eds), *Legislative Approximation*

identical if there is a bilateral or plurilateral agreement, or a regional recognition mechanism.

If there is no agreement or recognition scheme, reference is made to the notion of 'substantial equivalence' contained in art 25, para 1(b) and first developed in the UNCITRAL Model Law on Electronic Signatures (MLES), art 12. That notion aims to facilitate cross-border recognition without requiring perfect adherence to the exact wording used in national technical standards, which runs against the purpose of cross-border recognition: it suffices that the core requirements of national law are satisfied. On the one hand, foreign providers do not need to fully comply with the national law of the jurisdiction where recognition is sought; on the other hand, they should not be better placed in satisfying legal requirements relating to levels of assurance than local providers.[10] The reference to 'at least' substantial equivalence was inserted to ensure that the requirement to use an at least equivalent identical level of assurance would not preclude the use of a higher level of assurance when the levels of assurance are not identical. In the latter case, the levels of assurance could be determined equivalent by analysis.

Moreover, the requirement for 'substantial equivalence' was inserted to impede that the use of an equivalent standard would be used to bypass minimum mandatory levels of assurance. In practice, the equivalent standard should fully and objectively meet the required level of assurance, and the 'substantially equivalent' level of assurance should be considered (before or after use, as the case may be) to be substantially the same or higher than the required level of assurance. Absent a formal agreement or mechanism, it is possible that two or more jurisdictions decide to use the same description of levels of assurance, in which case art 25, para 1(a) would also apply.

The mechanism contained in the MLIT, art 25, para 1(b) applies when the descriptions of levels of assurance in the relevant jurisdictions are different, but also when no description of level of assurance is recognised by the law.[11] Absence of recognition does not mean that it is not possible to map the identity management service against a description of level of assurance – technically, this process is normally possible. In short, the notion of substantial level of equivalence means that the level of assurance must be equivalent to or higher than the one required but need not be identical to the national one.[12]

and Application of EU Law in the Eastern Neighbourhood of the European Union. Towards a Common Regulatory Space? (Abingdon, Oxon, Routledge, 2016).

[10] Guide to Enactment of the MLES, para 153.

[11] Smedinghoff, 'Is It Legal?' (2024), 29.

[12] The United Kingdom (UK) Data (Use and Access) Bill contains provisions on trust services, namely to facilitate the application of existing legislation based on the eIDAS Regulation, and to give to the Secretary of State the authority to recognise overseas trust services as qualified (ie 'provided by a person established in a country or territory outside the United Kingdom'). The condition for recognition is that the reliability of the overseas trust service is at least equivalent to the reliability of a comparable qualified trust product (art 45B, para 4 of the to-be revised UK eIDAS Regulations).

To sum up, the MLIT, art 25, para 1 may be an imperfect solution, but it is a good one in light of different policy approaches and the lack of globally accepted definitions of level of assurance. Article 25, para 2 refers to the notion of 'recognized international standards' for fulfilling the requirements in para 1, especially with regard to the notion of 'substantial equivalence'. Those standards, which are also referred to in the MLES, art 12, may take a variety of forms, including intergovernmental standards, technical standards, and business standards.[13]

Article 25, para 3 clarifies that the authority in charge of designating reliable identity schemes under the MLIT, art 11 may do so also with respect to foreign schemes. If it does so, it is presumed that the service or credential satisfies the requirements of art 25, para 1. The object of the designation is normally an identity service, as each identity management service provider may offer services with varying levels of assurance, but art 25, para 3 adopts a broad formulation to encompass various options (system, service, or credential).

Article 26. Cross-border recognition of the result of the use of trust services

1. *The result deriving from the use of a trust service provided outside [the enacting jurisdiction] shall have the same legal effect in [the enacting jurisdiction] as the result deriving from the use of a trust service provided in [the enacting jurisdiction] if the method used by the trust service offers:*
   (a) *At least an equivalent level of reliability, where the reliability levels recognized by such jurisdictions are identical; or*
   (b) *Substantially equivalent or higher level of reliability, in all other cases.*
2. *For the purposes of determining satisfaction of paragraph 1, regard shall be had to recognized international standards.*
3. *The trust service shall be presumed to satisfy paragraph 1 if [the person, organ or authority specified by the enacting jurisdiction pursuant to article 23] has determined the equivalence, taking into account article 22, paragraph 2.*

The MLIT, art 26 replicates the MLIT, art 25 with regard to the outcome of the application of trust services. It therefore refers to the level of reliability offered by the trust service instead of the level of assurance of the identity management service.

In light also of the general principle of party autonomy underpinning the MLIT, art 26 of the MLIT is compatible with private agreements on the recognition of the cross-border effects of the application of trust services. As noted, those agreements may be between providers, for specific services, or also between individuals, for specific transactions, and the law may explicitly recognise the validity of such agreements. Article 5, para 7 of the stabilised text of the draft Agreement on Electronic Commerce complements the MLIT, art 26 by encouraging states to cooperate in the mutual recognition of electronic signatures.

[13] Guide to Enactment of the MLES, para 159.

Article 27. Cooperation

[The person, organ or authority specified by the enacting jurisdiction as competent] may cooperate with foreign entities by exchanging information, experience and good practice relating to identity management and trust services, in particular with respect to:

(a) Recognition of the legal effects of foreign identity management systems and trust services, whether granted unilaterally or by mutual agreement;
(b) Designation of identity management systems and trust services; and
(c) Definition of levels of assurance of identity management systems and of levels of reliability of trust services.

The MLIT, art 27 deals with institutional mechanisms supporting legal and technical cross-border recognition. Those mechanisms are important to implement the eIDAS Regulation with regard to identity management, where they complement procedures with a binding outcome and contribute to achieving interoperability of identity management schemes.[14] Cooperation mechanisms under the MLIT regard both identity management schemes and trust services, and are voluntary, unless the enacting jurisdictions decide otherwise, for example, to promote regional integration. Cooperation mechanisms may consist of exchanges of information, technical experience and best practices. Thus, cooperation activities may assist in defining equivalence across identity management schemes and trust services.

A provision similar to article 27 MLIT may be found in digital trade agreements.[15]

[14] See European Commission Implementing Decision (EU) 2015/296 establishing procedural arrangements for cooperation between Member States on electronic identification [2015] OJ L53/14.

[15] For instance, art 7.1(d) of the Digital Economy Partnership Agreement suggests 'the exchange of knowledge and expertise on best practices relating to digital identity policies and regulations, technical implementation and security standards, and user adoption'. See also AfCFTA Digital Trade Protocol, art 14, para 2(d).

9

Trends and Perspectives in the Adoption and Implementation of Uniform Digital Trade Laws

9.1. Promoting MLETR Understanding, Use and Adoption

The promotion of the adoption and use of the UNCITRAL Model Law on Electronic Transferable Records (MLETR) is a complex task that is being tackled by a collective effort of the Secretariat of the United Nations Commission on International Trade Law (UNCITRAL) and of private and public partners. The variety of the measures undertaken and the depth of the analysis carried out are particularly significant. Many of these initiatives may be usefully replicated for promoting other uniform commercial law texts.

The number of enactments by jurisdictions and the use in business, as evidenced by reported case law, are significant indicators of the success of commercial laws, including the MLETR. These indicators are meaningful but need to be qualified.

First, transferable documents and instruments usually contain a choice of law clause, but the choice is limited to a handful of national laws. This means that the adoption of the MLETR in a handful of jurisdictions may provide coverage of a significant percentage of commercial transactions. For instance, bills of lading often contain a choice of English law even when the port of loading or the port of discharge are not in England or Wales. Thus, the adoption of the United Kingdom (UK) Electronic Trade Documents Act 2023 has enabled the use of those bills worldwide as long as the other jurisdictions will uphold that choice.

On the other hand, domestic enactment of the MLETR in each relevant jurisdiction is needed when electronic transferable records need to be exchanged with public entities. Public entities may not wish to accept electronic transferable records without statutory authorisation. This is the case, for instance, when electronic bills of lading are submitted to single windows for customs operations.

Moreover, implementation of the MLETR calls for a robust technical infrastructure and sophisticate human expertise that may not always be readily available, especially in least developed countries. These limitations may be mitigated by the ability of service providers to operate across borders.

The UNCITRAL Secretariat maintains a list of jurisdictions that have enacted the MLETR.[1] The list features jurisdictions that have enacted the MLETR following closely the original text, and jurisdictions that have enacted legislation that, although differing from the MLETR in certain respects, is based on the same fundamental principles of the MLETR. Commonality of principles ensures that electronic transferable records issued in any listed jurisdiction may find legal recognition in other jurisdictions enacting the MLETR. The list does not provide any information on ongoing efforts to adopt the MLETR, as this may be seen as influencing sovereign decisions by states. It is also challenging to gather and maintain accurate information on ongoing adoption. For instance, when Bills are not approved before the end of the term, the legislative consideration process must start anew, and different priorities under a new administration may postpone the reintroduction of the Bill, sometimes indefinitely. Reporting that the Bill is nearing adoption when a term is about to expire could be misleading, although not necessarily inaccurate.

Despite these challenges, the International Chamber of Commerce (ICC) Digital Standards Initiative (DSI) and the United Nations Social and Economic Commission for Asia and the Pacific (UN/ESCAP) maintain a MLETR Tracker[2] that provides information on the progress of MLETR consideration in each jurisdiction, thus complementing the information available on the UNCITRAL website. The MLETR tracker also lists jurisdictions that have enacted legislation predating the MLETR, but which is compatible with it, to provide an accurate picture of the global legal status of electronic transferable records.[3]

9.2. The MLETR Consideration Process

Each jurisdiction that intends to adopt the MLETR does so in line with its constitutional requirements and legislative practice. Moreover, the features of the trade finance market and of the logistics ecosystem, the amount of resources available and other circumstances determine the details of the legislative process.

Ideally, three studies will be prepared for consideration by a government: (a) a policy paper on the impact of MLETR adoption on the digital trade ecosystem; (b) a legal gap analysis, including obstacles to MLETR adoption arising from existing laws; and (c) an economic benefit study. ICC DSI has prepared several

[1] Available on the UNCITRAL website. The list is based on the information available to the UNCITRAL Secretariat, which may be incomplete or may be received late.

[2] Available at www.digitalizetrade.org.

[3] This information is not provided on the UNCITRAL website. In particular, the status page of the MLEC on the UNCITRAL website does not indicate which jurisdictions have enacted the MLEC, arts 16 and 17. Moreover, some jurisdictions have adopted national laws based on the Rotterdam Rules, but the UNCITRAL website does not report that information. See L Castellani, 'The Legal Status of Electronic Bills of Lading: A Panorama' (2023) *Logistik & Recht* 141 for additional information.

documents on the MLETR[4] that provide guidance to policymakers, legal drafters and technical implementers.

The policy paper may build on existing digital trade strategies. In least developed countries, these strategies often relate to paperless trade facilitation and the implementation of a customs single window to reduce trading costs and simplify related procedures. This is understandable given that these countries have limited or no trade finance practice. Therefore, the main use of electronic transferable records relates to logistics, and one main goal of that use is the reduction of transport costs and the simplification and acceleration of customs procedures.

The legal gap analysis is influenced by two main variables: whether the jurisdiction has already adopted UNCITRAL texts, namely the UNCITRAL Model Law on Electronic Commerce (MLEC); and whether the jurisdiction belongs to the common law or the civil law family. Prior enactment of the MLEC ensures familiarity with the general principles underlying the MLETR, thus simplifying its consideration. The difference in legal tradition is reflected in the gap analysis, despite the uniformity of the substantive law of many transferable documents and instruments. Singapore and the United Kingdom have produced extensive discussion papers that may provide useful insight, especially in common law jurisdictions.[5] The French white paper provides an extensive legal analysis that may serve as a model, especially in civil law jurisdictions.[6] The recent Australian discussion paper raises a number of pertinent questions related not only to law reform to accommodate electronic transferable records but also to paperless trade and its technical implementation.[7]

The outcome of the legal gap analysis may formulate suggestions for MLETR enactment and contain a draft bill for discussion. How the MLETR may be enacted depends on the features of the existing legislation and on other considerations. Enactment may take the form of a new chapter of the existing electronic transactions law or of a standalone statute. Additional legislative options include its incorporation in the general law on transferable documents and instruments, such as bills of exchange and cheques, and interspersing its provisions in existing commercial laws, possibly complemented by implementing regulations containing other MLETR articles.

[4] Available at www.dsi.iccwbo.org.

[5] INFOCOMM Media Development Authority (IMDA) and Attorney General's Chambers (AGC), 'Joint IMDA – AGC Review of The Electronic Transactions Act (Cap 88) – Review of Draft UNCITRAL Model Law on Electronic Transferable Records (Public Consultation Paper)' (2017) and IMDA, 'Consultation Paper Issued by the INFOCOMM Media Development Authority on Review of the Electronic Transactions Act (ETA) (Cap 88)' (2019); Law Commission of England and Wales, *Electronic Trade Documents: Report and Bill* (Law Com No 405, 2022).

[6] B Collot, P Henry and S Teper, 'Accélérer la digitalisation des activités de financement du commerce international' (2023). ICC France has announced that it will prepare a guidance document on MLETR adoption in civil law jurisdictions.

[7] Attorney General's Department, 'Consultation to Inform Options for Implementing the Model Law on Electronic Transferable Records in Australia' (2024).

The economic impact study is particularly important because quantifying the expected economic benefits is a major incentive for legislators to act on the MLETR. There have been several attempts to quantify those benefits, which vary significantly in forecasts and outcomes. Typical benefits including faster and more reliable information exchanges, savings on the use of paper, including couriers' costs, reduced compliance costs, improved information management, and possibly a smaller environmental footprint. Efforts to define a standard econometric model are ongoing.[8]

The UK government's Department for Digital, Culture, Media and Sport prepared an economic benefits study that estimates the economic benefits arising from the adoption and implementation of the Electronic Trade Documents Act 2023 over a period of ten years, and under three different adoption scenarios.[9] The best-estimate scenario (medium adoption rate) ranges from 5 per cent in year 1 to 45 per cent in year 10, with total estimated benefits of £1,137.0m. Under a low adoption rate ranging from 1 per cent in year 1 to 10 per cent in year 10, the total estimated benefits still amount to £249.8m. The study also aimed at measuring the environmental impact of the law; however, this was not possible due to uncertainty on the prevailing use of blockchain technology and on its carbon footprint.

The French white paper estimates economic benefits using a methodology similar to that of the UK paper.[10] The French paper estimates savings of $823 million per year, and a total of $4.15 billion over the first 10 years considering the progressive implementation of the law.

The Hong Kong Monetary Authority has also carried out an estimate of the economic benefits expected from the adoption of the MLETR using a similar methodology.[11] The total net cost savings could amount from a low estimate of HK dollars 16.4 billion to a high estimate of HK dollars 34.9 billion over the next decade, equivalent to 0.05–0.11 per cent of GDP per year on average. Moreover, the net reduction in trade costs resulting from the MLETR could increase Hong Kong's shipping trade value progressively, reaching a 16.7 per cent increase in 2036.

[8] Asia-Pacific Economic Cooperation (APEC) Committee on Trade and Investment, 'A Path to Paperless Trade: Analysing the Legal Gaps and Economic Benefit of Adopting or Maintaining a Legal Framework That Takes into Account the UNCITRAL Model Law on Electronic Transferable Records (MLETR)' (2025), contains an extensive annex on MLETR economic modelling results and methodology.

[9] Department for Digital, Culture, Media & Sport, 'Impact Assessment of the Electronic Trade Documents Bill' (2022).

[10] B Collot, P Henry and S Teper, 'Accélérer la digitalisation', Annexe n°6 : Présentation de la méthodologie retenue pour le calcul des bénéfices de la dématérialisation des documents transférables.

[11] Hong Kong Monetary Authority, 'Half-Yearly Monetary and Financial Stability Report' (March 2025) 24–26 'Box 3. Assessing the potential economic impact of digitalising trade documents in Hong Kong'.

9.3. MLETR Endorsements

MLETR promotion greatly benefits from support of states, intergovernmental and non-governmental organisations. The turning point in MLETR awareness was the adoption during the British presidency of the Group of 7 (G7) Digital and Technology Ministerial Declaration of 28 April 2021.[12] The Declaration noted the inefficiency and environmental impact of paper-based transactions and suggested that the use of electronic transferable records could not only address those issues but also more generally strengthen the resilience of the global economic system during the post-COVID 19 pandemic recovery. The Declaration endorsed a Framework for G7 Collaboration on Electronic Transferable Records to initiate a dialogue between experts towards compatible domestic reforms, and to support other international initiatives promoting the adoption of electronic transferable records. The Framework expressly championed UNCITRAL work and promoted the adoption of legal frameworks compatible with the MLETR.

The Framework for G7 Collaboration on Electronic Transferable Records, which has been endorsed also by Australia and the Republic of Korea, contained a commitment to conduct domestic scoping exercises and report by October 2021. The following steps were envisaged:

- addressing domestic legal barriers by promoting 'the adoption of legal frameworks compatible with the principles' of the MLETR, mindful of diversity of national laws. Importantly, 'Laws enabling electronic transferable records should be technology neutral, future proof and applicable to all transferable records';
- promoting and supporting legal reform internationally, including in relevant legal forums such as UNCITRAL and through development agencies;
- bridging technical and interoperability issues, including by developing technical standards and supporting ongoing work on data modelling at the International Maritime Organization, World Customs Organization and the United Nations Centre for Trade Facilitation and Electronic Business (UN/CEFACT); and
- cooperating on cross-cutting regulatory issues relevant to the use of electronic transferable records, such as data protection regulations, capital requirements regulations, know-your-customer and anti-money laundering regulations, and regulations concerning trust services.

In short, the Declaration and the Framework provided a first comprehensive roadmap for global electronic transferable records adoption and implementation.

The 2021 G7 Ministerial Declaration was complemented by a Declaration adopted at the G7 Digital Ministers' meeting of 11 May 2022 during the German

[12] The Declaration is available at www.gov.uk.

Presidency.[13] Building on the Framework for G7 Collaboration on Electronic Transferable Records, the Declaration continued promoting 'appropriate legal frameworks consistent with' the MLETR, focusing on best practices and solutions for the exchange of freight transport information and documents using electronic platforms. The focus, upon which the Declaration further elaborates, reflects the need to coordinate the use of electronic transferable records with relevant European Union legislation, namely the eIDAS and eFTI Regulations. The Declaration is complemented by the 'Principles for domestic legal frameworks to promote the use of electronic transferable records' as contained in its Annex 2.[14] The Principles are:

- legal clarity, namely regarding MLETR legal notions that require technical implementation such as reliability, singularity, and (exclusive) control;
- technological neutrality;
- functional equivalence and non-discrimination;
- interoperability to prevent proprietary lock-in, foster competition among electronic transferable records service providers and improve confidence in their reliability;
- global acceptance, ie seamless cross-border recognition regardless of place of origin or use;
- transparency and stakeholder engagement in developing legislation on electronic transferable records.

The G7 endorsements paved the way to the inclusion of MLETR adoption as a target of regional initiatives. For instance, the Work Plan on the Implementation of the Association of Southeast Asian Nations (ASEAN) Agreement on Electronic Commerce[15] foresees the adoption of the MLETR, together with other UNCITRAL legislative texts, under objective B.1.1, requiring that all ASEAN member states 'adopt laws and regulations governing electronic transactions, taking into account applicable international conventions or model laws relating to e-commerce'. Similarly, the Pacific Regional E-commerce Strategy and Roadmap, which was adopted by the Pacific Islands Forum in the framework of the Pacific E-Commerce Initiative, foresees the adoption of the MLETR together with other UNCITRAL legislative texts under its strategic objective 4.1, requiring that laws on electronic commerce be drafted or amended based on UNCITRAL model laws and other best international practices.[16]

[13] The Declaration is available at bmdv.bund.de.

[14] Annex 2 to the Declaration is available at bmdv.bund.de.

[15] ASEAN, 'Work Plan on the Implementation of the ASEAN Agreement on Electronic Commerce 2021–2025' (2021).

[16] Measure 4.1.1 of the Pacific Regional E-commerce Strategy and Roadmap refers to adopting UNCITRAL model laws on electronic transactions.

9.4. Technical Cooperation Activities

The accelerating rate of adoption and use of the MLETR has increased the demand for cooperation and assistance in this area, especially by middle-income and developing countries. The offer of technical assistance services has increased accordingly, and efforts are being made to coordinate its delivery across stakeholders.

The UNCITRAL Secretariat is often the first stop for requests relating to the enactment of UNCITRAL texts. Legal expertise may be required in projects that cut across multiple digital trade matters and involve several international and national governmental and non-governmental organisations.

The UNCITRAL Secretariat may also recommend MLETR adoption when consulted during the preparation of general legislation on electronic transactions. Such a recommendation is based on a country's needs, namely the foreseeable use of electronic transferable records. In developing and least developed countries, especially landlocked countries and small island states, needs are often assessed in the context of paperless trade facilitation. Diagnostic tools that assess the readiness of existing legislation to enable electronic transactions[17] or to facilitate paperless trade[18] may highlight the desirability of MLETR adoption. In several cases, the suggestion to adopt the MLETR is based also on regional trends and recommendations. This explains why certain jurisdictions with limited exposure to digital trade, such as Kiribati, have become early enactors of the MLETR.

Multilateral development banks have been actively promoting MLETR adoption and implementation in the framework of their work on digitalising supply chain financing. The Asian Development Bank (ADB) Trade and Supply Chain Finance Program[19] has been a pioneer in the field, promoting awareness and adoption of the MLETR, as appropriate, in countries such as Cambodia, China and Georgia in the pursuit of its goal to 'make global trade and supply chains green, resilient, inclusive, transparent, and socially responsible'.[20] Similarly, the European Bank for Reconstruction and Development (EBRD) has promoted awareness and adoption of the MLETR in countries such as Egypt, Morocco and Türkiye.[21] Other multilateral development banks have expressed interest in these activities.

MLETR adoption is also being actively discussed at the Asia-Pacific Economic Cooperation (APEC). APEC is generally supportive of UNCITRAL texts on

[17] See the UNCTAD eTrade Readiness Assessments. UNCITRAL is a partner of the 'eTrade for all' initiative coordinated by UNCTAD.

[18] See the UN/ESCAP Readiness Assessments for Cross-Border Paperless Trade. UNCITRAL and UN/ESCAP are working closely together on paperless trade matters.

[19] See the Program's website at www.adb.org.

[20] For additional information on the work of the ADB in promoting the MLETR, CM Ramirez Ortiz and L Castellani, 'Driving Digitalization of Global Trade: UNCITRAL Model Law on Electronic Transferable Records' (2023) ADB Briefs No 280.

[21] See also the report commissioned by the EBRD: T Christou and J Taylor, 'Blueprint Paper on Digital Trade and the UNCITRAL Model Law on Electronic Transferable Records' (2023).

electronic commerce, and has recently started encouraging alignment of the APEC economies' legal frameworks with the MLETR.[22] Mindful of 'different levels of readiness and capacity' within APEC member economies, a project promoted by Australia offers support to APEC member economies interested in carrying out a legal gap analysis and an economic analysis of MLETR adoption or maintenance.[23]

Finally, a significant contribution to MLETR technical cooperation activities comes from the ICC DSI, which aims at promoting digital trade based on shared technical and legal standards, namely the MLETR, and at promoting policy decisions endorsing the MLETR. ICC DSI was set up to promote trade digitalisation to mitigate the challenges arising from the COVID-19 pandemic.

9.5. MLETR and Digital Trade Agreements

A feature of the evolution of trade law in the last years has been the inclusion of provisions on digital trade in free trade agreements.[24] Bilateral, plurilateral, and regional trade agreements increasingly refer to UNCITRAL texts for implementation to increase the chances of reaping the expected benefits.[25] While the development of electronic commerce provisions in free trade agreements has been progressive and on an ad hoc basis, the resulting corpus of provisions is useful in building a conducive, if not comprehensive, legal and regulatory environment for digital trade. The most relevant feature of this effort from the UNCITRAL perspective is the creation of a legal framework enabling end-to-end trade digitalisation. The MLETR and the UNCITRAL Model Law on the Use and Cross-border Recognition of Identity Management and Trust Services (MLIT) are key enablers of that goal as they respectively close the gap on digitalisation of transferable documents and instruments and provide ground rules on the legal recognition of data.

[22] APEC, 'Joint Ministerial Statement, 35th APEC Ministerial Meeting 2024, Lima, Peru' (14 November 2024), para 18; APEC, '2025 APEC Ministers Responsible for Trade Joint Statement, Jeju, Republic of Korea' (15–16 May 2025), para. 9.

[23] APEC Project Number CTI_02_2024S 'A Path to Paperless Trade: Analysing the Legal Gaps and Economic Benefit of Adopting or Maintaining a Legal Framework That Takes into Account the UNCITRAL Model Law on Electronic Transferable Records' (2024). For more information, see APEC Committee on Trade and Investment, 'A Path to Paperless Trade'.

[24] M Burri, M Vásquez Callo-Müller and K Kugler, 'The Evolution of Digital Trade Law: Insights from TAPED' (2024) 23 *World Trade Review* 190. The Trade Agreement Provisions on Electronic-commerce and Data (TAPED) dataset value 1.6.2 deals with the inclusion of a reference to the MLETR in trade agreements. By parsing the TAPED database it is therefore possible to retrieve trade agreements which contain a reference to the MLETR, and if that reference is legally binding or consists of best efforts. TAPED is available at unilu.ch/taped. On the relationship between trade agreements and standards, see S Klotz, *International Standardization and Trade Regulation* (Leiden, Brill | Nijhoff, 2024). The author lists UNCITRAL as a standard setter in the information and communication technology field at 187.

[25] See, eg, the Comprehensive and Progressive Agreement for Trans-Pacific Partnership, art 14.5.1; the Regional Comprehensive Economic Partnership, art 12.10.1.

Trade agreements may refer to UNCITRAL texts in three ways: (a) by making a direct reference; (b) by incorporating provisions originating from UNCITRAL texts; and (c) by making indirect reference. Direct reference means that the trade agreement contains an obligation to adopt or maintain legislation based on UNCITRAL texts or a 'best endeavour' clause to consider adoption of UNCITRAL texts. Incorporating provisions means that the trade agreement contains a binding provision that reproduces or is modelled after a pre-existing UNCITRAL provision. Indirect reference means that the trade agreement refers to goals and objectives that presuppose the adoption of UNCITRAL texts for their achievement.[26]

It is not unusual to have references to the MLEC in free trade agreements,[27] and references to the MLETR are increasingly common. They can be found, among others, in the draft agreement on electronic commerce, and in digital economy agreements. References to the MLETR may be found also in dedicated regional[28] and bilateral agreements.[29]

As noted,[30] a 'stabilised text' of the draft Agreement on Electronic Commerce has been made available to the public. The text is the outcome of five years of work in the framework of the Joint Statement Initiative on Electronic Commerce, an effort to create a modern and conducive legal framework for digital trade spearheaded by Australia, Japan and Singapore. Section B of the stabilised text, titled 'Enabling Electronic Commerce', draws significantly on UNCITRAL principles and provisions.[31]

Article 4 of the draft Agreement, on 'Electronic Transactions Framework', contains two 'best endeavour' clauses to adopt or maintain a legal framework governing electronic transactions that: (a) is consistent with the principles of the MLEC; and (b) takes into account the MLETR. The language of art 4 is non-committal, which maximises the ability to adapt the model laws to domestic law

[26] Eg, art 5, para 1 of the Framework Agreement on Facilitation of Cross-border Paperless Trade in Asia and the Pacific (CPTA) states that: 'The present Framework Agreement shall be guided by the following general principles: (a) Functional equivalence; (b) Non-discrimination of the use of electronic communications; (c) Technological neutrality; […]', which are the general principles underpinning UNCITRAL texts.

[27] For a recent example in a bilateral treaty, see art 96E of the Protocol Amending the Agreement between Japan and the Republic of Indonesia for an Economic Partnership, 2024, on the duty to maintain a legal framework governing electronic transactions that takes into account the MLEC, the United Nations Convention on the Use of Electronic Communications in International Contracts or 'other applicable international conventions and model laws related to electronic commerce'. Japan and Indonesia were not listed as having adopted UNCITRAL texts on electronic commerce in the UNCITRAL website at the time of the conclusion of the Protocol, but Japan announced its intention to adopt MLETR.

[28] AfCFTA Digital Trade Protocol, art 17 establishes an obligation to adopt or maintain mechanisms to facilitate the use of electronic transferable records taking into account, among other things, model laws adopted by international organisations.

[29] Digital Trade Agreement between the United Kingdom of Great Britain and Northern Ireland and Ukraine, 2023, art 132C, para 3.

[30] See ch 7, section 7.3.

[31] L Castellani, 'Le projet d'Accord de l'OMC sur le commerce électronique et les instruments de la CNUDCI : première analyse' (2024) 127 *Échanges internationaux* 14.

requirements and curbs possible claims of non-compliance. With regard to electronic transferable records, this approach may also preserve pre-existing laws and legacy systems, for instance those dealing with electronic promissory notes. However, the network effect of legal harmonisation may be achieved only if a certain level of commonality is maintained and fundamental principles are not violated, which is recognised in art 4 by acknowledging that 'The Parties recognize the importance of facilitating the use of electronic transferable records'.

Moreover, a new type of trade agreement, called digital economy agreements (DEAs) and championed by Singapore, has recently emerged.[32] DEAs are based on a flexible and modular approach that complements and implements regional trade agreements depending on the parties' capacity and needs. DEAs generally promote end-to-end trade digitalisation through paperless trade facilitation, including electronic invoicing, and ancillary matters such as electronic payments and the prohibition to apply customs duties on electronic transmissions.

Module 2 of the digital economy agreements, on 'Business and trade facilitation', introduces a best-efforts obligation to adopt the MLETR. Most states that are parties to a digital economy agreement have, however, yet to begin MLETR consideration.

9.6. The Implementing Ecosystem

The MLETR has enabled digitalisation of transferable documents and instruments, which were the last trade documents missing in the digital trade space. Filling that gap allowed consideration of the implementing ecosystem from a different perspective: instead of exchanging individual trade documents, it was possible to focus on exchanging trade data to improve the quality of the information contained in each trade document. The possibility of managing all commercial documents in a coordinated manner so as to fully benefit from data analysis and reuse was mentioned already at an early stage of the preparation of the MLETR.[33]

One recurring consideration regards the desirability of creating digital trade ecosystems (also referred to as digital trade platforms or digital exchange layers) that contain all trade-related data and documents and that are able to exchange information with other platforms and ecosystems.[34] One such solu-

[32] E Jones, B Kira and R Tavengerwei, 'Norm Entrepreneurship in Digital Trade: The Singapore-led Wave of Digital Trade Agreements' (2024) 23 *World Trade Review* 208.

[33] UNCITRAL, 'Present and Possible Future Work on Electronic Commerce' (22 March 2011) UN Doc A/CN.9/728/Add.1, para 29.

[34] Similarly, see the definition of 'digital trading systems' that includes digitalisation of both regulatory and commercial documents, and advanced single window systems and other platforms that facilitate exchange of digital trade documents in LSE Trade Policy Hub, 'Benefits of the digitalisation of trade processes and cross border barriers to their adoption, Final Report' (2023).

tion is Singapore's TradeTrust, described as an interoperable blockchain-based ecosystem open to all service providers that meet basic technical requirements.[35] TradeTrust has prepared a set of Model Terms, accompanied by a Guidance Note, to foster interoperability among service providers through contractual harmonisation. The Model Terms are primarily intended for use with electronic bills of lading but may be adjusted to other electronic trade documents.[36] Private companies offer to corporate clients and public entities similar solutions based on open digital trade ecosystems.[37]

Strong arguments lie behind promoting open digital trade ecosystems. Streamlining practices related to commercial documents is a key objective in modern trade. For instance, bank payment obligations were introduced to replace time-consuming procedures related to letters of credit, although they have not gained broad acceptance. The use of electronic transferable records may provide a major contribution to this objective. Dematerialising all commercial documents enables the integrated management of all data generated by the supply chain, which may truly transform the governance of trade processes.[38] Once regulatory documents are included, the concept of data pipeline, which combines data from all sources in the supply chain, may be implemented in the national trade platform.[39]

Information needed for all commercial and regulatory purposes may be contained in a single electronic record of high data quality whose attributes may be shared with business partners for both commercial exchanges and exchanges with public entities. That solution ensures consistency of information across the supply chain and avoids the need to input the same information multiple times, which may lead to input errors, omissions and other discrepancies. Moreover, using a single electronic record as the source of all documents relating to a commercial transaction may greatly facilitate documents' monitoring and management.

[35] For a business description of TradeTrust, see S Poddar, 'Bringing Trade into the Web 3.0' (Hinrich Foundation, 2024). The documents originating in TradeTrust may be exchanged in the Singapore Trade Data Exchange, which is a digital infrastructure that facilitates data sharing between supply chain partners. The Singapore Trade Data Exchange maintains a website at sgtradex.com.

[36] For further details see the TradeTrust website at tradetrust.io/about/legality-guide/.

[37] See, eg, Distichain, a private company offering a B2B platform for cross-border trade that allows automating import and export processes.

[38] On the MLETR in the context of supply chain management and trade facilitation, A Basu Bal, T Rajput and P Alizada, 'International Single Window Environment: Prospects and Challenges' (2017) ADBI Working Paper Series, vol 744.

[39] D Hesketh, 'Seamless Electronic Data and Logistics Pipelines Shift Focus from Import Declarations to Start of Commercial Transaction' (2009) 3 *World Customs Journal* 27; E van Stijn and ors, 'The Data Pipeline', discussion paper presented at the UN Economic Commission for Africa/Economic Commission for Europe/Economic and Social Commission for Asia and the Pacific/Economic Commission for Latina America and the Caribbean/Economic and Social Commission for West Asia Global Trade Facilitation Conference 2011 'Connecting International Trade: Single Windows and Supply Chains in the Next Decade' (2011); R Hu and ors, 'A New Approach to E-Commerce Customs Control in China: Integrated Supply Chain – A Practical Application Towards Large-Scale Data Pipeline Implementation' (2016) 10 *World Customs Journal* 65; G Bowering, 'Does E-Commerce and the Growing Availability of Trade Data Mean that the Customs Declaration May No Longer Be Required?' (2018) 12 *World Customs Journal* 3.

With respect to scalability, management systems able to manage electronic transferable and non-transferable records are more cost-effective than those managing a single type of electronic transferable record.[40]

The open and interoperable nature of digital trade ecosystems may address concerns of commercial operators on being locked into proprietary solutions and data silos as well as the 'membership requirement' problem. The core issue of that problem lies in the fact that the involvement of potential competitors of systems users, such as shipping lines and banks, in the management of the electronic transferable records system, which takes place in the context of vertical market integration,[41] may give rise to concerns about data confidentiality. Open digital trade ecosystems encourage competition among service providers, while the role of the ecosystem operator is limited to providing the infrastructure for the exchanges. Moreover, the role of rulebooks in this solution is minimised, as only a few basic rules are needed to set out the obligations of the service provider vis-à-vis the ecosystem operator. Contractual provisions between the subscriber and the service provider are stipulated elsewhere.

The creation of open digital trade ecosystems requires fulfilling several technical, legal, and operational conditions. Digital trade ecosystems are open to all service providers as long as their services are interoperable. Ecosystems may interact. To be effective, all relevant parties must be able to interact with each other in the ecosystem. This means harmonising regulatory requirements, for instance, with regard to data exchange with and among public entities, but also with regard to data privacy and data protection, and to commercial secrets and banking confidentiality.

To sum up, MLETR adoption plays a role in triggering changes in the management of electronic trade documents and data that may have far-reaching consequences. In the short term, the change of business model from proprietary registries to service providers competing in interoperable open ecosystems has promoted confidence by users and increased uptake.[42] In the longer term, this may translate into business process re-engineering with a complete shift from documents to data and may improve accordingly supply chain data management.

9.7. Paperless Trade Facilitation

Digital transformation is necessary for achieving paperless trade, which is, in turn, key for trade facilitation. Hence, a vigorous movement towards

[40] Non-transferability of certain types of documents depends on the agreement of the parties (eg, a straight bill of lading); however, the management of those documents in a separate system would increase costs and may create interoperability obstacles. Additional issues arise in case a negotiable document is made non-negotiable during its negotiation.

[41] For electronic bills of lading, see I Ioannou, 'Relational Trade Networks' (2023) 82 *CLJ* 450.

[42] ICC, 'Survey shows steady rise of global adoption of electronic bills of lading' (12 December 2024) at iccwbo.org.

digitalisation of trade documents has grown around the notion of trade facilitation as understood at the World Trade Organization and embodied in the Trade Facilitation Agreement,[43] mindful that the focus of paperless trade facilitation may be on business-to-government interaction rather than business-to-business exchanges.[44]

The adoption and implementation of UNCITRAL texts on electronic commerce in general, and of the MLETR and the MLIT in particular, are often advocated to advance paperless trade.[45]

When endorsing the MLETR, the United Nations General Assembly acknowledged the implications of the MLETR for paperless trade facilitation by asking intergovernmental organisations 'to coordinate their legal activities in the area of electronic commerce, including paperless trade facilitation, with those of the Commission, to avoid duplication of efforts and to promote efficiency, consistency and coherence in the modernization and harmonization of legislation on electronic commerce'.[46]

UNCITRAL tasked its Secretariat with conducting work on legal aspects of paperless trade with other organisations,[47] namely the United Nations Economic and Social Commission for Asia and the Pacific (UN/ESCAP).[48] Recently, that mandate was expanded to carry out a broad stocktaking exercise that aims at presenting the relevance of UNCITRAL texts for trade in a systematic manner.[49]

The bill of lading is a commercial document that contains high quality commercial data, and is therefore often placed at the centre of the paperless trade ecosystem.[50] The information contained in a bill of lading may be submitted to customs and other regulatory agencies via single windows for customs operations,[51] thus replacing customs declarations.

[43] Protocol amending the Marrakesh Agreement establishing the World Trade Organization (Agreement on Trade Facilitation) (adopted 27 November 2014, entered into force 22 February 2017) 3247 UNTS 1.

[44] See the illustration of digital trade systems in LSE Trade Policy Hub, 'Benefits of the Digitalisation', 11–13.

[45] In general, on the relationship between UNCITRAL texts and paperless trade, see J Gregory 'Legal Implementation Guide for Cross-border Paperless Trade' (2024) UNNExT Working Paper Series No 12 at unnext.unescap.org.

[46] UNGA Res 72/114 (7 December 2017), 5.

[47] UNGA, 'Report of the United Nations Commission on International Trade Law. Forty-fourth Session' (2011), UN Doc A/66/17, para 240.

[48] The UNCITRAL and UN/ESCAP secretariats cooperated in drafting and are cooperating in implementing the CPTA, which is the first international agreement in the field of paperless trade and aims at promoting legal recognition, interoperability, and technical cooperation among its state parties. On the CPTA generally, see H Xue, 'The Newest UN Treaty to Facilitate Cross-Border Paperless Trade in Asia and the Pacific: An Insight Preview' (2017) 51 *Journal of World Trade* 959.

[49] UNGA, 'Report of the United Nations Commission on International Trade Law. Fifty-seventh Session' (2024), UN Doc A/79/17, para 299.

[50] M Lind, W Lehmacher, A Simha and others, 'The Dynamics around the Digitisation of Documents. The eBL as Vehicle towards a More Data-Driven Approach' (2021) at maritimeinformatics.org. See also CM Ramirez Ortiz and L Castellani, 'Driving Digitalization', figures 1 and 2 for a description of the exchanges relevant for paperless trade facilitation.

[51] On the various solutions available for paperless trade, see A Wirjo, A Bayhaqi and ET Oh, 'Digitalising Trade: The Role of Paperless Platforms' (2024) APEC Policy Support Unit Policy Brief No 59.

However, information sharing with public entities may raise peculiar challenges because historically public entities have the authority to define the conditions and requirements for data exchange with them, and have often done so on a case-by-case basis. On the other hand, coordination across the public sector requires that the same data sharing policy, based on uniform technical standards, would apply to all public entities.

In short, customs authorities may not be ready to accept for compliance purposes the submission of electronic bills of lading, or the extraction of information contained therein, instead of the customs declaration. The legal and technical solution requires the adoption of client-friendly data sharing policies and the extension of cross-border recognition of documents and data to exchanges with public entities. Yet, significant obstacles of cultural and economic nature may linger, such as distrust for electronic submissions, data security concerns, fear of job losses and disfavour for what may be considered inappropriate transparency and accountability.

9.8. MLETR for Transport and Logistics

Legally enabling the digitalisation of bills of lading has been a goal of the work of UNCITRAL for decades and a prominent consideration during the preparation of the MLETR. The MLETR became a catalyst for the uptake of electronic bills of lading and MLETR-based electronic bills of lading are increasingly used in business operations.[52] Prominent reasons behind this trend are: the timing of the preparation of the MLETR, which shortly preceded the COVID-19 pandemic; the statutory basis for the use of electronic bills of lading provided by the MLETR, which enables reproducing all functions of a bill of lading; and the openness to technology neutrality and interoperability as opposed to the registry and rulebook based model. Importantly, the MLETR may interact with any substantive law regime, which allows preserving the delicate status quo on carrier liability without entering into the intricate debate on harmonising maritime law.[53]

The MLETR is a legislative framework that enables digital trade ecosystems by setting high standards for electronic records quality assurance. Moreover, by giving recognition to the use of dynamic information originating from an oracle, such as a sensor in a container or a global positioning system device, the MLETR

[52] See the figures in Future International Trade Alliance, 'eBL Report 2024' (2024) at www.fit-alliance.org.

[53] L Castellani, 'The UNCITRAL Model Law on Electronic Transferable Records as Enabler of the Use of Electronic Bills of Lading' in CJ Chae and ors (eds), *WMU Maritime Week 2024. Maritime Digitalization and Decarbonization: A Sustainable Future* (Malmö, World Maritime University, 2025) 128. On the limits of law harmonisation efforts in this field, see G Branellec and A Choquet, 'Transport maritime de marchandises : la construction d'un système juridique complexe dépassant le mythe de l'uniformité' (2022) 76–77 *Les Cahiers Scientifiques du Transport/Scientific Papers in Transportation* 67.

supports real-time cargo information sharing. This is critical to build more resilient supply chains and to improve their management.

The private sector is strongly supportive of broader use of electronic bills of lading not only to increase efficiency of transport but also to reduce its environmental footprint.[54] It is important that legal and technical standards for electronic transport documents will converge, so that transferable and non-transferable documents may be managed in the same systems and may be exchanged in open digital trade ecosystems. The alignment of the ongoing UNCITRAL work on negotiable electronic cargo documents with the provisions of the MLETR is a welcome step in that direction.

Another critical element is acceptance by smaller jurisdictions and by developing countries, especially for paperless trade facilitation purposes. The use of bills of lading for business-to-business exchanges is an important driver of their increased acceptance, but significant innovation opportunities may be missed if the data contained in the bill of lading cannot be reused for customs declaration purposes. However, as noted, significant technical and cultural obstacles may hinder opening up electronic single windows for customs operations to data structured according to business standards. Yet, the goal of reducing transport costs and increasing transparency and efficiency in customs operations is critical for global economic development and should be pursued relentlessly.

9.9. MLETR for Trade Finance

Trade finance plays a major role in cross-border trade by facilitating financing and payments and mitigating related risks. The increasing trade finance gap, ie the difference between trade finance demand and supply, is a major obstacle to global trade development. According to one study,[55] the global trade finance gap reached an estimated $2.5 trillion in 2022, or 10 per cent of global merchandise trade. The trade finance gap is particularly affecting small and medium-sized enterprises, which may not be able to provide adequate evidence of their assets and expected turnover.

The impact of trade finance on the uptake of electronic trade documents should not be underestimated.[56] While the digitalisation of electronic transferable records has been often seen through the lens of transport, effective private sector

[54] Baltic and International Maritime Council (BIMCO), 'BIMCO's "25 by 25" Campaign Reaches 25.1% eBL Adoption in First Year' (17 July 2024) at www.bimco.org. The 25 by 25 campaign requires shippers in the bulk sector to use electronic bills of lading for at least 25% of their annual seaborne trade volume for one commodity by 2025.

[55] S Beck and ors, '2023 Trade Finance Gaps, Growth, and Jobs Survey' (2023) ADB Briefs No 256.

[56] For an introduction, see MK Alshaleel, 'Digitalizing the End-to-End International Trade Finance Process and the Law: A Mission for the Entire Ecosystem' (2024), 35 *European Business Law Review* 49; M Alba Fernández, 'Financial Services in the Supply Chain and Digital Representation of Goods' (2025) 30 *The Journal of International Maritime Law* 90.

buy-in has started only with the involvement of banks. Banks and other financial institutions have seen digitalisation of trade financing as a way to reduce back-office costs and simplify procedures. Digitalisation may also help in increasing the appeal for investors of trade finance operations, which are seen as low-risk, low-yield, by offering portfolios and innovative fintech products.

From the borrower's perspective, digitalisation may reduce the cost of access to credit, especially for small and medium-sized enterprises, whose assets and cash-flow may be better assessed thanks to data aggregation and the use of persistent identifiers. Risk control may also be more effective thanks to the availability of larger datasets.

The possible contribution to addressing the massive trade financing gap has provided a strong motivation for getting involved in MLETR promotion to both commercial and multilateral development banks. Thus, the MLETR has become part of the digital lending ecosystem.

However, only selected banks have immediately taken advantage of the adoption of the MLETR. Traditional lenders may test fintech solutions cautiously despite the fact that many of the benefits relating to the digitalisation of trade finance come from improved access to data, such as persistent identification and better evaluation of the lender's assets, which can be applied to existing lending practices.[57] More often, non-banking entities have developed new business models taking advantage of the features of electronic transferable records.[58]

One critical issue for the future of digital trade financing is clarifying the status of electronic transferable records with respect to capital requirements. For instance, bills of lading are considered high-value collateral when issued on paper. Electronic bills of lading should have the same or higher value if they meet functional equivalence requirements. In that regard, monetary authorities should at a minimum review regulatory tools to ensure that they do not discriminate against the use of electronic transferable records. Ideally, they should assess improvements in digital trade finance monitoring over paper-based transactions, such as the easier availability of aggregate information based on the reliable identification of all concerned parties, to fully appreciate the value of electronic transferable records as collateral.

Another important element of digital trade ecosystems is the human component. In many countries, trade financing carried out according to traditional business practices seems not to attract the interest of younger workers. The possibility to rejuvenate the work environment, to take advantage of emerging

[57] For a discussion of the benefits arising from broader use of data in finance, see International Finance Corporation, 'The Emergence of New Data Ecosystems in Financial Services: Recent Developments in Southeast Asia' (2021) Discussion Paper; on legal aspects, see Asian Development Bank and Bankers Association for Finance and Trade, 'Deep-Tier Supply Chain Finance. Unlocking the Potential' (2024).

[58] For an introduction, see A Davidson, 'Implementation and Implications of the UNCITRAL Model Law on Electronic Transferable Records in Trade Finance' in C Hare and D Neo (eds), *Trade Finance: Technology, Innovation and Documentary Credits* (Oxford, Oxford University Press, 2021) 217.

technologies and to delegate to machines repetitive tasks may significantly help in regaining appeal and fill the workforce gap.

9.10. Promoting the Adoption and Use of the MLIT

The importance of MLIT for the digital economy, and for digital transactions more generally, is significant, particularly for cross-border exchanges. Reliable assurance of identity and of data quality is the cornerstone of trust in the information and in the documents being exchanged electronically. Moreover, persistent identification is the enabler of more effective governance at reduced cost: all other laws relating to digital trade, including the MLETR, must rely on the MLIT for addressing these needs. The relevance of such matters is likely to further increase in light of the increasing use of unilateral economic sanctions and the hefty penalties for their violation.

However, and despite recent high-level references,[59] there has been no MLIT enactment yet. Some states have indicated an interest in enacting the MLIT, but this has often happened either for the identity management part, or for the trust services part (or for selected trust services, especially electronic signatures and electronic timestamps).[60]

Significant work remains to be done to disseminate awareness of the MLIT and build capacity on its use and application. A significant contribution could come from the support of the European Union, including endorsement of the MLIT (possibly a slightly modified version to take into account the new elements contained in the eIDAS 2 Regulation) as a legal tool for approximation.

An important contribution to MLIT promotion may come from MLIT adoption as a regional or subregional framework. For instance, the MLIT could support the implementation of the ASEAN Digital Economy Framework Agreement.

Moreover, digital economy agreements contain an identity management module.[61] For instance, module 8 of the Digital Economy Partnership Agreement (DEPA),[62] recognising the possible different legal approaches to digital identities and their implementation, aims to promote interoperability between each state's digital identity regimes. To do so, it refers to the establishment or maintenance of appropriate frameworks to foster technical interoperability or common standards as well as the establishment or maintenance of broader international frameworks (DEPA, art 7.1(a) and (c)).

[59] Internet Governance Forum, 'Riyadh Declaration' (2024) Section 2 ('Global ID').

[60] An exception is the Thai Electronic Transactions Bill submitted for public consultation in July 2024, which contains provisions of both parts of the MLIT.

[61] On DEAs in general, see M Burri and M Vasquez Callo-Müller, 'Digital Economy Agreements: A Closer Look at the New Phenomenon in Digital Trade Rulemaking' (2024) WEF and AKCF Policy Brief No 1.

[62] Digital Economy Partnership Agreement (adopted 11 June 2020, entered in force 7 January 2021).

Article 7.1(b) of DEPA requires member states to grant 'comparable protection of digital identities afforded by each Party's respective legal frameworks, or the recognition of their legal and regulatory effects, whether accorded autonomously or by mutual agreement', which means that cross-border recognition of identity management may take place unilaterally, bilaterally or plurilaterally. Article 7.1(c) of DEPA calls for 'the establishment or maintenance of broader international frameworks', which is also an objective that may be achieved with the adoption of the MLIT.

DEPA is particularly significant because it is a plurilateral agreement binding Chile, New Zealand, and Singapore, and open to accession of more states, Canada and China having initiated the accession process. It may therefore work as an aggregator of digital-friendly countries, and as an implementing tool of any forthcoming agreement based on the stabilised text of the Joint Statement Initiative on E-Commerce. Singapore has concluded several similar, but separate agreements with other states and the European Union.[63]

The AfCFTA Digital Trade Protocol, art 14, para 2 foresees the preparation and adoption of an Annex to the Protocol on Digital Identities to 'foster interoperability between their respective digital identity systems' based on technical interoperability and the development of 'comparable protection of digital identities afforded by each state party's respective legal frameworks, or the recognition of their legal and regulatory effects, whether accorded unilaterally or by mutual agreement'. The two measures should lead to the mutual recognition of digital identity systems, which is listed as a separate goal. The MLIT may play an important role in implementing the Annex.

9.11. MLIT Policy Issues

There is no doubt that a robust and reliable legal and technical framework for identity management and trust services is necessary for advancing commercial and non-commercial electronic exchanges. The associated benefits are not only economic (for example, reduced onboarding costs), but extend to improving governance of electronic exchanges and, beyond that, to human rights preservation and implementation. This is why the MLIT is of critical importance. However, the MLIT deals with matters that are novel and evolving, and policymakers may wish to consider certain policy issues when deciding whether to adopt the MLIT, and how.

[63] These agreements are listed on the website of the Ministry of Trade and Industry of Singapore (see www.mti.gov.sg) and include, besides DEPA: the Singapore – Australia Digital Economy Agreement (adopted 6 August 2020, entered into force 8 December 2020); the United Kingdom – Singapore Digital Economy Agreement (adopted 25 February 2022, entered into force 14 June 2022); the Republic of Korea – Singapore Digital Partnership Agreement (adopted 21 November 2022, entered into force 14 January 2023); and the European Union – Singapore Digital Partnership (adopted 1 February 2023, not in force).

9.11.1. Identity Management vs Trust Services

As noted,[64] it is necessary to distinguish between identity management and trust services for practical and other reasons. For instance, different entities may oversee the two areas and may pursue conflicting interests, which makes coordination challenging.

This consideration raises a fundamental question about whether it is necessary to deal with identity management and trust services in the same piece of legislation. The MLIT has followed the blueprint of the eIDAS Regulation in offering a joint solution, and a discussion on separating the two parts has not officially taken place during its drafting. States may, however, enact the MLIT only for identity management or trust services, depending on their priorities. Early observations indicate that enactment of the two parts could be sought separately, and possibly more frequently for the part on trust services. While separation of the two parts is technically possible and may be desirable, coordination between identity management and trust services with an identity component should be pursued not to inadvertently create barriers to identity management implementation through trust services.

9.11.2. Promoting Public Services vs Facilitating Commercial Transactions

In principle, both the eIDAS Regulation and the MLIT apply to all types of transactions, regardless of whether they are with a public or with a private entity. However, there may be a perception that the eIDAS Regulation focuses on delivery of public services, especially in its original form and for identity management. For instance, certain identification services offered by private providers may not receive legal recognition in the eIDAS framework.[65]

The mandate of UNCITRAL pertains to facilitating cross-border trade and, for that reason, its work is focused on the private sector, excluding transactions with consumers. The MLIT reflects that mandate by clearly placing on the same level, with respect to legal effects, all types of identity management schemes and trust services.

It is however not easy to predict whether private providers will take advantage of the MLIT. On the one hand, especially in countries that follow the civil law tradition, the involvement of private identity service providers may conflict with an entrenched tradition of monopolistic governmental services. On the other

[64] See ch 7, section 7.3, commentary on the MLIT, art 16.

[65] European Commission, Directorate-General for Communications Networks, Content and Technology, *Study to Support the Impact Assessment for Revision of the eIDAS Regulation, Final Report* (2021) 8.

hand, major global private sector service providers have expressed interest in including digital wallets among their services.

9.11.3. Private Service Providers vs Public Service Providers

The MLIT places all service providers, regardless of their private or public nature, on an equal footing with regard to obligations and liabilities. This may not be possible in jurisdictions that generally provide a special liability regime for public entities.

This is particularly true for identity service providers: the issuer of a passport typically bears no liability for misuse or for failure to prevent forgery, regardless of the quality of its built-in security measures. Exemption from liability of identity service providers is well-rooted with regard to managing civil records and vital statistics, and may be carried over in the online environment. Similar considerations may apply to public trust service providers, which may be licensed or even monopolies under the national regulatory regime.

The disparity of liability treatment may introduce tensions in the MLIT that may affect, among other things, fair competition among providers. With respect to eIDAS implementation, the issue may arise regarding the ability of private providers to deliver identity wallets. The eIDAS experience will be precious for MLIT implementation.

9.11.4. Regulation vs Enabling Legislation

The eIDAS Regulation is designed to promote regional integration building on solid political commitment and in line with European Union fundamental values. The original eIDAS Regulation was found to be not fully effective in pursuing its goals, and it was reviewed and complemented accordingly.[66]

However, different models for identity management and trust services have emerged in the main economic powers. For the sake of illustration, it may be said that the United States (US) model is market-driven, while the European model is regulation-driven. A hybrid approach is emerging in China, fostering innovation in a regulated market. The various approaches have strong and weak points: for instance, while the market-driven model maximises the chances that economically viable and sustainable solutions will be offered to the public, it does not assure compliance with fundamental values such as data privacy. On the other hand, the

[66] European Commission, Proposal for a Regulation of the European Parliament and of the Council amending Regulation (EU) No 910/2014 as regards establishing a framework for a European Digital Identity, COM(2021) 281 final, 2021/0136 (COD) (2021), 1–3; see also European Commission, *Study to Support the Impact Assessment*, 7–11.

regulatory-driven model focuses on preserving those fundamental values, but may lead to the establishment of a costly oversight mechanism, and the proliferation of publicly-funded service providers in immature markets while preventing the establishment of global market leaders. The latter issue may be particularly problematic in developing countries.

9.12. Harnessing Technical Convergence to Complement Legal Harmonisation

The difference in policy approaches is reflected in the law but also in the adoption of technical standards. The US and the EU have started a dialogue to fill this gap at the EU-US Trade and Technology Council,[67] and the MLIT may be an important part of the envisaged solution, together with texts such as the Recommendation of the Council of the Organisation for Economic Co-operation and Development on the Governance of Digital Identity.[68]

Preliminary findings are available.[69] For instance, the EU approach is considered more prescriptive, while the US approach is seen as more based on technical guidelines.[70] This may reflect the fact that legislation in the EU is more detailed compared to the one in the US. In any case, it is important to bear in mind that the goal of the mapping exercise is not (or not yet) to come to a uniform definition of standards, but rather to understand which technical standards are equivalent or substantially equivalent so that they can be used for the same purposes. In the end, what counts is the reliability of the result of the application of identity management or trust services. If schemes and services deliver the same result under different approaches, the goal is achieved. This is in line with the MLIT, especially its arts 25 and 26.

Ideally, the dialogue on policy, technical and legal convergence of identity management and trust services should include other major players, such as China. It is also very important that smaller economies are informed about this ongoing process and of the benefits of adopting the MLIT. From their perspective, the MLIT may open the door to legal recognition of foreign service providers, which may suffice to address the limited demand of developing markets while not subtracting scarce human and financial resources. This would be a major contribution to addressing the digital divide.

[67] C Ford and P Rékasy, 'TTC WG1 Digital Identity Subgroup Roundtable Workshop Report' (2023), 20.

[68] See ch 6, section 6.4.

[69] US–EU Trade and Technology Council Working Group 1: Technology Standards, Subgroup on Digital Identity, 'Draft EU-US TTC Digital Identity Mapping Exercise Report' (2023).

[70] For an example of US technical guidelines, see National Institute of Standards and Technology, 'Special Publication 800-63-3, Digital Identity Guidelines' (2020).

The MLIT seems therefore a fully adequate legal tool for all involved parties. However, its implementation requires tripolar (ie China – EU – US) cooperation on the definition of interoperable standards, which may eventually address the lack of consensus on global technical standards.

The eIDAS Regulation requires the adoption of several implementing acts of an administrative and technical nature. It is therefore necessary to prepare the implementing acts, define the required technical standards, ensure that operators in EU member states comply with the acts, etc. This exercise requires significant human and financial resources and political commitment. These resources and the related commitment seem to be currently lacking at the global level, though additional regional initiatives are emerging. Possibly, a private entity could take upon itself the promotion of the adoption and implementation of the MLIT, akin to what ICC DSI does for the MLETR.

9.13. To Conclude

MLETR and MLIT are uniform laws that build on the solid foundation of UNCITRAL texts on electronic commerce. They were drafted in response to actual and urgent business demands to support digitalisation, reduce transaction costs and increase the governance and the resilience of supply chains. The MLETR and the MLIT complement provisions in digital trade agreements and are enablers of end-to-end trade digitalisation.

The use of increasingly complex electronic tools in the pursuit of greater efficiency, competitiveness and productivity seems unstoppable: the MLETR and the MLIT offer a solid, modern, comprehensive and predictable global legal template to do so. That framework can easily be tailored to national needs without affecting existing law.

Global trade law is shifting towards plurilateral initiatives whose agenda is aimed, among other things, at mitigating the effect of polycrisis: uniform digital trade law may offer an important contribution to accommodating those diverse, and at times conflicting, needs.

BIBLIOGRAPHY

Books and Chapters in Edited Books

Alamillo, I, Mouille, S, Röck, A and al, *Digital Identity Standards: Analysis of Standardisation Requirements in Support of Cybersecurity Policy* (Athens, European Union Agency for Cybersecurity (ENISA), 2023)

Bath, V, 'UNCITRAL and International Carriage of Goods by Sea' in Gulati R, John T and Köhler B (eds), *The Elgar Companion to UNCITRAL* (Cheltenham, Edward Elgar Publishing, 2023) 541–561

Blasco, AI, 'Digital Identity in a European User-Centric Ecosystem and Its Similarities with the Digital Euro Proposal' in Pastor Sempere C (ed), *Governance and Control of Data and Digital Economy in the European Single Market* (Cham, Springer, 2025) Law, Governance and Technology Series, vol 71, 453–471

Boss, AH and Kilian, W (eds), *The United Nations Convention on the Use of Electronic Communications in International Contracts: An In-depth Guide and Sourcebook* (Frederick, Md, Kluwer Law International, 2008)

Bruggeman, M, 'Etat civil et identité : quel(s) rapport(s) ?', in Eynard J (ed), *L'identité numérique : Quelle définition pour quelle protection?* (Bruxelles, Larcier, 2020) 59–73

Cachard, O, 'UNCITRAL Model Law on Electronic Transferable Records: The Missing Link Towards E-shipping?' in Soyer B and Tettenborn A (eds), *Disruptive Technologies, Climate Change and Shipping* (Abingdon, Oxon, Informa Law from Routledge, 2022), 32–39

Caprioli, É, Combarieu, C and Doise, D, 'La dématérialisation des titres transférables par la loi n°2024-537 du 13 juin 2024 : l'avènement du connaissement électronique en droit français' in Cremers T (ed), *40 ans de dématérialisation des titres en France* (Paris, IRJS Éditions, 2024) Bibliothèque de l'Institut de Recherche Juridique de la Sorbonne – André Tunc, Tome 133, 143–160

Caprioli, É, 'Les points d'ombre dans l'application du règlement eIDAS' in Eynard J (ed), *L'identité numérique : Quelle définition pour quelle protection ?* (Bruxelles, Larcier, 2020) 123–137

Caprioli, É, Fernandez Gonzalez, M and Gobert, D, 'Vers une internationalisation des principes du Règlement eIDAS' in Jacquemin H (dir), *L'identification electronique et les services de confiance depuis le règlement eIDAS* (Bruxelles, Larcier, 2016) 275–290

Castellani, L, 'Uniform Law and the Production and Circulation of Legal Models' in Low G (ed), *Convergence and Divergence of Private Law in Asia* (Cambridge, Cambridge University Press, 2022) 7–32

Castellani, L, 'UNCITRAL Texts on Electronic Commerce' in Gulati R, John T and Köhler B (eds), *The Elgar Companion to UNCITRAL* (Cheltenham, Edward Elgar Publishing, 2023) 512–524

Castellani, L, 'The UNCITRAL Model Law on Electronic Transferable Records as Enabler of the Use of Electronic Bills of Lading' in Chae, CJ and ors (eds), *WMU Maritime Week 2024. Maritime Digitalization and Decarbonization: A Sustainable Future* (Malmö, World Maritime University, 2025) 128–139

Castellano, GG, Selga, ĒK and Arner, DW, 'The Emergence of Financial Data Governance and the Challenge of Financial Data Sovereignty' in Chander A and Sun H (eds), *Data Sovereignty* (Oxford, Oxford University Press, 2023) 178–210

Commonwealth Telecommunications Organisation, *Digital Transformation: Critical Success Factors and Challenges in the Commonwealth* (London, Commonwealth Telecommunications Organisation, 2024)

Coopersmith, J, *Faxed: the Rise and Fall of the Fax Machine* (Baltimore, Md, Johns Hopkins University Press, 2015)
David, R, 'Le droit continental, la Common Law, et les perspectives d'un jus commune européen' in Cappelletti M (ed), *New Perspectives for a Common Law of Europe / Nouvelles perspectives d'un droit commun de l'Europe* (Leiden, Brill | Nijhoff, 1978–2024) 113–135
Davidson, A, 'Implementation and Implications of the UNCITRAL Model Law on Electronic Transferable Records in Trade Finance' in Hare C and Neo D (eds), *Trade Finance: Technology, Innovation and Documentary Credits* (Oxford, Oxford University Press, 2021) 217–229
Demoulin, M, *Droit du commerce électronique et équivalents fonctionnels. Théorie critique* (Bruxelles, Larcier, 2014)
Ellinger, P, 'Chapter 4. Negotiable Instruments' in Zweigert K and Drobnig U (gen eds), *International Encyclopedia of Comparative Law*, Ziegel J (ed), *Vol IX: Commercial Transactions and Institutions* (Leiden, Brill, 2000)
Favrod-Coune, P and Belet, K, 'Conflict of Laws and Tokens in Swiss Private International Law' in Bonomi A, Lehmann M and Lalani S (eds), *Blockchain and Private International Law* (Leiden, Brill | Nijhoff, 2023) 673–708
Fitzgerald, A and Moens, A, 'Regulating Electronic Commerce – Emerging Principles for the Regulation of Internet Transactions' in International Academy of Comparative Law, *Convergence of Legal Systems in the 21st Century. General Reports delivered at the XVIth International Congress of Comparative Law* (Bruxelles, Bruylant, 2006) 1565–1580
Fosgaard, L, *The Transfer of Rights in a Digitalised Age* (Aalborg, Aalborg Universitetsforlag, 2023)
Fujita, T, Sturley, M and van der Ziel, G, *The Rotterdam Rules: The UN Convention on Contracts for the International Carriage of Goods Wholly or Partly by Sea*, 2nd edn (London, Sweet & Maxwell, 2020)
Gama, L, *Recueil des cours de l'Académie de La Haye, Vol 406, Les principes d'UNIDROIT et la loi régissant les contrats de commerce* (Leiden, Brill, 2020)
Ganne, E, 'Blockchain's Practical and Legal Implications for Global Trade and Global Trade Law' in Burri M (ed), *Big Data and Global Trade Law* (Cambridge, Cambridge University Press, 2021) 128–159
Geva, B and Peari, S, *International Negotiable Instruments* (Oxford, Oxford University Press, 2020)
Gobert, D and Montero, E, 'La signature dans les contrats et les paiements électroniques : l'approche fonctionnelle' in Cavanillas Mugica S and ors (eds), *Commerce électronique : le temps des certitudes* (Bruxelles, Bruylant, 2000) 53–97
Goldby, M, *Electronic Documents in Maritime Trade. Law and Practice*, 2nd edn (Oxford, Oxford University Press, 2019)
Goldby, M, 'Can the Rotterdam Rules Co-exist with Laws Based on the MLETR?' in Comité Maritime International, *The Rotterdam Rules Convention* (Antwerp, Comité Maritime International, 2024), 91–99
Guo, Y, *Legislation on Electronic Transferable Records: the 'Singularity' Problem and Solution* (Beijing, Beijing University Press, 2019)
Hare, C and Neo, D (eds), *Trade Finance: Technology, Innovation and Documentary Credits* (Oxford, Oxford University Press, 2021)
Heiss, H and Drobnjak, S, 'Formal Requirements and Validity' in Basedow J and ors (eds), *Elgar Encyclopedia of Private International Law* (Cheltenham, Edward Elgar Publishing, 2017) 783–789
Herrenschmidt, C, *Les trois écritures : langue, nombre, code* (Paris, Gallimard, 2007)
International Chamber of Commerce (ICC), *Users Guide to the eUCP* (Paris, ICC, 2021)
International Monetary Fund, Organisation for Economic Co-operation and Development, United Nations Conference on Trade and Development, World Bank and World Trade Organization, *Digital Trade for Development* (Geneva, WTO, 2023)
Jacquemin, H (dir), *L'identification electronique et les services de confiance depuis le règlement eIDAS* (Bruxelles, Larcier, 2016)
Klotz, S, *International Standardization and Trade Regulation* (Leiden, Brill | Nijhoff, 2024)

Lampič, J and Ng, I, 'An Analysis on the Application of the UNCITRAL Model Law on Electronic Transferable Records on Contract Automation and Metadata' in Lopez Rodriguez AM, Green MD and Kubica ML (eds), *Legal Challenges in the New Digital Age* (Leiden, Brill, 2021) 45–65

Law Commission of England and Wales, *Electronic Trade Documents: Report and Bill* (Law Com No 405, 2022)

Law Commission of England and Wales, *Digital Assets: Final Report* (Law Com No 412, 2023)

Lloyd, M, *The Passport: The History of Man's Most Travelled Document* (Stroud, Sutton Publishing, 2003)

Madrid Parra, A, 'Identidad y autenticación electrónicas : la atalaya de UNCITRAL' in R Perea Ortega (ed), *Estudios sobre derecho digital* (Cizur Menor, Editorial Aranzadi, 2021), pt 2, 199–250

Magklasi, I, *The Rotterdam Rules and International Trade Law* (Abingdon, Oxon, Routledge, 2018)

Mason, S, *Electronic Signatures in Law* (London, University of London Press, 2016)

Mason, S and Seng, D (eds), *Electronic Evidence and Electronic Signatures*, 5th edn, OBserving Law (London, University of London Press, 2021)

Mason, S, *The Signature in Law. From the Thirteenth Century to the Facsimile*, OBserving Law (London, University of London Press, 2022)

Meynell, D, (ed), *Implementing URDTT Version 1.0* (Paris, ICC, 2022)

Meynell, D, *From a Bill to an Act. The Electronic Trade Documents Act* (London, ICC UK, 2023)

Millard, É, 'Le rôle de l'état civil dans la construction de l'Etat' in *Mélanges en l'honneur du Doyen F-P Blanc* (Perpignan – Toulouse, Presses Universitaires de Perpignan et Presses Universitaires de Toulouse 1 Capitole, 2011) 721–727

Møllmann, A, *Delivery of Goods under Bills of Lading* (Abingdon, Oxon, Routledge, 2017)

Neo, D, 'Drafting a Model Law on Warehouse Receipts', in Köhler B, Gulati R and John T (eds), *The Elgar Companion to UNIDROIT* (Cheltenham, Edward Elgar Publishing, 2023) 442–456

Organisation for Economic Co-operation and Development (OECD), *G7 Mapping Exercise of Digital Identity Approaches* (Paris, OECD Publishing, 2024)

Petrov, R and van Elsuwege, P (eds), *Legislative Approximation and Application of EU Law in the Eastern Neighbourhood of the European Union. Towards a Common Regulatory Space?* (Abingdon, Oxon, Routledge, 2016)

Robertson, C, *The Passport in America: The History of a Document* (New York, Oxford Academic, 2012)

Rodríguez De Las Heras Ballell, T, 'Tracing the Path of the Role of Technology in Unidroit Instruments', in Köhler B, Gulati R and John T (eds), *The Elgar Companion to UNIDROIT* (Cheltenham, Edward Elgar Publishing, 2024) 80–95

Rodríguez Delgado, JP and Albors Cano, J, 'El "control (exclusivo)" como concepto equivalente a la función posesoria en el conocimiento de embarque electrónico' in Pulido Begines JL, Alba Fernández M and Rodríguez Delgado JP (coords), *Liber Amicorum : Estudios de Derecho de la Navegación Marítima en Homenaje al Prof. José Luis Gabaldón* (Madrid, Dykinson, 2024) 603–643

Sacco, R, *Antropologia giuridica* (Bologna, Il Mulino, 2007)

Smedinghoff, T, 'The Legal Requirements for Creating Secure and Enforceable Electronic Transactions', in International Monetary Fund, *Monetary and Financial Law*, vol 3 (Washington, DC, International Monetary Fund, 2005) 757–797

Smedinghoff, T, 'Article 9: Form Requirements', in Boss, AH and Kilian, W (eds), *The United Nations Convention on the Use of Electronic Communications in International Contracts: An In-depth Guide and Sourcebook* (Frederick, Md, Kluwer Law International, 2008) 136–161

Smedinghoff, T, 'The Legal Framework for Digital Identity' in Finocchiaro G, Balestra L and Timoteo M (eds), *Major Legal Trends in the Digital Economy: The Approach of the EU, the US and China* (Bologna, Il Mulino, 2022) 245–262

Takahashi, K, 'Blockchain-based Negotiable Instruments: with Particular Reference to Bills of Lading and Investment Securities', in Bonomi A, Lehmann M and Lalani S (eds), *Blockchain and Private International Law* (Leiden, Brill | Nijhoff, 2023) 494–528

Torpey, J, *The Invention of the Passport: Surveillance, Citizenship and the State* (Cambridge, Cambridge University Press, 1999)

United Nations Centre for Trade Facilitation and Electronic Business (UN/CEFACT), *Buy Ship Pay Data Exchange Structures for Trade Finance Facilitation* (Geneva, United Nations, 2024)

UN/CEFACT, *Transfer of MLETR-Compliant Titles* (Geneva, United Nations, 2023)

United Nations Conference on Trade and Development (UNCTAD), *E-commerce and Digital Economy Programme Year in Review 2022 – Looking Beyond Current Crises: Boosting Digital Readiness in Developing Countries* (Geneva, UNCTAD, 2023)

United Nations Commission on International Trade Law (UNCITRAL), *Legal Guide on Electronic Funds Transfer* (New York, United Nations, 1987)

UNCITRAL, *Model Law on International Credit Transfers* (Vienna, United Nations, 1994)

UNCITRAL, *Model Law on Electronic Commerce with Guide to Enactment, 1996, With Additional Article 5 bis as Adopted in 1998* (New York, United Nations, 1999)

UNCITRAL, *Model Law on Electronic Signatures with Guide to Enactment* (New York, United Nations, 2002)

UNCITRAL, *Promoting Confidence in Electronic Commerce: Legal Issues on International Use of Electronic Authentication and Signature Methods* (Vienna, United Nations, 2009)

UNCITRAL, *Digest of Case Law on the United Nations Convention on Contracts for the International Sale of Goods* (United Nations, Vienna, 2016)

UNCITRAL, *Model Law on Electronic Transferable Records* (New York, United Nations, 2018)

UNCITRAL, *Model Law on the Use and Cross-border Recognition of Identity Management and Trust Services* (Vienna, United Nations, 2023)

United Nations, *Conference on the Carriage of Goods by Sea (Hamburg, 6–31 March 1978) Official Records* (New York, United Nations, 1981)

von Ziegler, A, Schelin, J and Zunarelli S (eds), *The Rotterdam Rules 2008: Commentary to the United Nations Convention on Contracts for the International Carriage of Goods Wholly or Partly by Sea* (Alphen aan den Rijn, Wolters Kluwer, 2010)

Winn, J, 'Will Blockchain Transform Trade Finance?' in Hare C and Neo D (eds), *Trade Finance: Technology, Innovation and Documentary Credits* (Oxford, Oxford University Press, 2021) 230–252

World Bank, *Federated Ecosystems for Digital ID: Current Approaches and Lessons* (Washington, DC, World Bank, 2022)

World Trade Organization (WTO), United Nations Economic and Social Commission for Asia and the Pacific and UNCITRAL, *Cross-border Paperless Trade Toolkit* (Geneva, WTO, 2022)

WTO and World Economic Forum, *The Promise of TradeTech: Policy Approaches to Harness Trade Digitalization* (Geneva, WTO, 2022)

WTO and ICC Digital Standards Initiative, *Standards Toolkit for Cross-border Paperless Trade* (Paris, ICC, 2022)

Wunderlich, S and Saive, D, 'The Electronic Bill of Lading' in Prieto, J and ors (eds), *Blockchain and Applications* (Cham, Springer, 2020) Advances in Intelligent Systems and Computing vol 1010, 93–100

Articles

Alavi, H, 'Mitigating the Risk of Fraud in Documentary Letters of Credit' (2016) 6 *Baltic Journal of European Studies* 1, 139

Alba Fernández, M, 'Electronic Commerce Provisions in the UNCITRAL Convention on Contracts for the International Carriage of Goods Wholly or Partly by Sea' (2009) 44 *Texas International Law Journal* 387

Alba Fernández, M, 'Financial Services in the Supply Chain and Digital Representation of Goods' (2025) 30 *The Journal of International Maritime Law* 90

Alshaleel, MK, 'Digitalizing the End-to-End International Trade Finance Process and the Law: A Mission for the Entire Ecosystem' (2024), 35 *European Business Law Review* 49

Argüello Rojas, LM, 'Los principios de los títulos valores electrónicos en Costa Rica: a propósito de la entrada en vigor de la Ley n° 10069, "Ley sobre letra de cambio y pagaré electrónico"' (2023) 16 *Revista IUS Doctrina* 1

Bloch, DS, 'Non-Fungible Tokens: A Solution to the Challenges of Using Blockchain Bills of Lading in the International Sales of Goods' (2022) 1 *Journal of Law, Market & Innovation* n 1, 49

Bowering, G, 'Does E-Commerce and the Growing Availability of Trade Data Mean that the Customs Declaration May No Longer Be Required?' (2018) 12 *World Customs Journal* 3

Branellec, G and Choquet, A, 'Transport maritime de marchandises : la construction d'un système juridique complexe dépassant le mythe de l'uniformité' (2022) 76–77 *Les Cahiers Scientifiques du Transport/Scientific Papers in Transportation* 67

Burman, H, 'United Nations: UNCITRAL Model Law on Electronic Commerce' (1997) 36 *International Legal Materials* 197

Burri, M, Vásquez Callo-Müller M and Kugler, K, 'The Evolution of Digital Trade Law: Insights from TAPED' (2024) 23 *World Trade Review* 190

Caprioli, É, 'La Loi-type de la CNUDCI sur les documents transférables électroniques : analyse et perspectives' (2023) *Journal du droit international 'Clunet'* 465

Castelán Luna, MDP and Aceves Mejía, M, 'El principio de equivalencia funcional en los títulos de crédito electrónicos' (2024) 2-2024 *Saberes Administrativos* v 5, 8

Castellani, L, 'The United Nations Convention on the Use of Electronic Communications in International Contracts at Ten: Practical Relevance and Lessons Learned' (2016) 3 *Journal of Law, Society and Development* 132

Castellani, L, 'The Legal Status of Electronic Bills of Lading: A Panorama' (2023) *Logistik & Recht* 141

Castellani, L and Finocchiaro, G, 'The UNCITRAL Model Law on Electronic Transferable Records: Introduction and Overview' (2023) *European Review of Private Law* 955

Castellani, L, 'Le projet d'Accord de l'OMC sur le commerce électronique et les instruments de la CNUDCI : première analyse' (2024) 127 *Échanges internationaux* 14

Choi, SB, 'Compliance of Electronic Bill of Lading Regulation in Korea with Model Law on Electronic Transferable Records' (2019) 23 *Journal of Korea Trade* 68

Chong, KW and Chao, JS, 'United Nations Convention on the Use of Electronic Communications in International Contracts: A New Global Standard' (2006) 18 *Singapore Academy of Law Journal* 116

Davidson, A, 'The Digitalisation of Transferable Documents and Instruments in International Trade' (2018) 22 *Documentary Credit World* 27

Demoulin, M and Vernusset, A, 'La réversibilité des données et l'archivage électronique. Ou comment éviter la dépendance technologique' (2015) 11 *Les Cahiers du numérique* n 2, 115

Dickinson, A, 'Electronic Trade Documents and the Conflict of Laws in the United Kingdom' (2024) *Lloyd's Maritime and Commercial Law Quarterly* 56

Douville, T, 'La présomption de fiabilité des signatures électroniques : un modèle pour le droit de l'Union ?', *Recueil Dalloz*, 20 avril 2023, n 15, 740

Dubovec, M, 'The Problems and Possibilities for Using Electronic Bills of Lading as Collateral' (2006) 23 *Arizona Journal of International and Comparative Law* 437

Dubovec, M and Elias, A, 'A Proposal for UNCITRAL to Develop a Model Law on Warehouse Receipts' (2017) 22 *Uniform Law Review* 716

Ferrari, F, 'Autonomous Interpretation Versus Homeward Trend Versus Outward Trend in CISG Case Law' (2017) 22 *Uniform Law Review* 244

Finocchiaro, G, 'Una prima lettura del reg UE n 910/2014 (cd eIDAS): identificazione on line, firme elettroniche e servizi fiduciari' (2015) XXXVIII *Le Nuove Leggi Civili Commentate* 419

Gabriel, H, 'The New United States Uniform Electronic Transactions Act: Substantive Provisions, Drafting History, and Comparison to the UNCITRAL Model Law on Electronic Commerce' (2000) 5 *Uniform Law Review* 651

Gabriel, H, 'The UNCITRAL Model Law on Electronic Transferable Records' (2019) 24 *Uniform Law Review* 261

Gabriel, H, 'The Concept and Necessity of "Control" in the Use of Emerging Technologies in Commercial Transactions' (2023) 28 *Uniform Law Review* 257–268

Gabriel, H, 'The Future of the Transnational Law of Security Rights: The Emergence of Security Rights in Electronic Data' (2024) 29 *Uniform Law Review* 244

Gabriel, H, 'The 2022 Amendments to Article 9 of the American Uniform Commercial Code' (2025) 18 *Law and Financial Markets Review* 6

Gaskell, N, 'Book Review' (2013) 27 *Australia & New Zealand Maritime Law Journal* 42

Geva, B, 'From Paper to Electronic Order: The Digitalization of the Check in the USA' (2015) 4 *Penn State Journal of Law & International Affairs* 96

Girvin, S, 'Evidentiary Aspects of Transport Documents and Electronic Transport Records Under the Rotterdam Rules' (2010) 2 *European Journal of Commercial Contract Law* 109

Goldby, M, 'What is Needed to Get Rid of Paper? A New Look at Delivery Orders' (2015) 21 *The Journal of International Maritime Law* 5

Granville Edge, P, 'Vital Registration in Europe. The Development of Official Statistics and Some Differences in Practice' (1928) 91 *Journal of the Royal Statistical Society* 346

Green, S, 'Happy Birthday to the Electronic Trade Documents Act!' (2024) 23 *Trade Finance Talks* 50

Hesketh, D, 'Seamless Electronic Data and Logistics Pipelines Shift Focus from Import Declarations to Start of Commercial Transaction' (2009) 3 *World Customs Journal* 27

Hjort, MA, Kalamees, P and Kask, L, 'Misuse of Electronic Signatures and eID Owner Liability: A Comparative Analysis of Estonian and Norwegian Legislative Frameworks and Practice' (2025) 36 *European Business Law Review* 287

Hu, R, Tan, Y-H and Heijmann, F, 'A New Approach to E-Commerce Customs Control in China: Integrated Supply Chain – A Practical Application Towards Large-Scale Data Pipeline Implementation' (2016) 10 *World Customs Journal* 65

Ioannou, I, 'Relational Trade Networks' (2023) 82 *CLJ* 450

Jones, E, Kira, B, and Tavengerwei, R, 'Norm Entrepreneurship in Digital Trade: The Singapore-led Wave of Digital Trade Agreements' (2024) 23 *World Trade Review* 208

Krebs, J, 'The Technological Practicality of Electronic Bills of Lading and Non-Fungible Tokens' (2023) 20 *Manchester Journal of International Economic Law* 34

Krebs, T, 'Electronic Bills of Lading, Transnational and English law: Blocking the Blockchain?' (2023) 28 *Uniform Law Review* 323

Lai, J, 'Tokenisation of Documentary Intangibles' (2023) *Lloyd's Maritime and Commercial Law Quarterly* 92

Lai, J, 'Conversion of cryptoassets' (2024) 55 *Computer Law & Security Review*, art 106060

Lehmann, M, 'Liberating the Individual from Battles between States: Justifying Party Autonomy in Conflict of Laws' (2008) 41 *Vanderbilt Journal of Transnational Law* 381

Livermore, J and Euarjai, K, 'Electronic Bills of Lading and Functional Equivalence' (1998) 2 *Journal of Information, Law and Technology*

Lu, Z, 'Optimization of Security Algorithms for Digital Authentication and Electronic Signatures in International Electronic Commerce Regulations' (2024) 12 *International Journal of Intelligent Systems and Applications in Engineering* 21s, 152

Mabrouk, H, 'Beyond Speculation: The Transformative Power of Blockchain Technology in Various Industries' (2023) *European Journal of Law Reform* 3

Madrid Parra, A, 'Contenido Esencial de la Ley Modelo de la CNUDMI/UNCITRAL sobre Documentos Transmisibles Electrónicos' (2018) 48 *Revista Aranzadi de derecho y nuevas tecnologías* 19

Mills, S, Lee, JK and Rassekh, BM, 'Benefits of Linking Civil Registration and Vital Statistics with Identity Management Systems for Measuring and Achieving Sustainable Development Goal 3 Indicators' (2019) 38 *Journal of Health, Population and Nutrition* (supp 1) art 18

Mugasha, A, 'Technological Innovation in Trade Finance and the Law: From the Bank Payment Obligation and Blockchain to the Uniform Rules on Digital Trade Transactions' (2022) 38 *Banking & Finance Law Review* 217

Nezhad, M, Rashidian, S and Botta, C, 'Revolutionizing Trade Finance: Leveraging the Power of Blockchain and AI in Electronic Letters of Credit' (2024) 29 *Uniform Law Review* 87

Niv, LS, 'Electronic Express Sea Waybill as Perceived in Sea-Land Service, Inc v Lozen International, LLC and Later Case Law' (2013) 30 *Arizona Journal of International and Comparative Law* 507

Noiriel, G, 'L'identification des citoyens : Naissance de l'état civil républicain' (1993) 13 *Genèses. Sciences sociales et histoire* 3

Oluwabunmi, MB and Henning, J, 'Beyond the Centennial of the Hague Rules: Assessing the UNCITRAL Model Law on Electronic Transferable Records (MLETR)' (2025) 30 *The Journal of International Maritime Law* 163

Ortalda, A and Leucci, S, 'Identità digitale e protezione dei dati personali: punti di incontro e rischi nelle discipline eIDAS e RGPD' (2022) 4 *Rivista italiana di informatica e diritto* 145

Pejovic, C and Lee, U, 'Towards Global Legal Recognition of Electronic Trade Documents: Control or Possession?' (2024) 59 *Texas International Law Journal* 101

Plank, TE, 'A New System of Electronic Chattel Paper: Notification of Assignment' (2019) 71 *South Carolina Law Review* iss 1, art 6

Purba, J, 'Ratio Decidendi, Agreement, Against the Decision of MA No 601K/PDT/2015 in the Case of Agreements that do not use Indonesian' (2021) 21 *Jurnal Penelitian Hukum De Jure* 517

Putzeys, J, 'Adapting the CMR to the Electronic Age' (2006) 11 *Uniform Law Review* 530

Robles-Carrillo, M, 'Digital Identity: An Approach to its Nature, Concept, and Functionalities' (2024) 32 *International Journal of Law and Information Technology* 1, eaae019

Sacco, R, 'Legal Formants: A Dynamic Approach to Comparative Law' (1991) 39 *American Journal of Comparative Law* 1 (Instalment I), 343 (Instalment II)

Šafranko, Z, 'The Notion of Electronic Transferable Records' (2016) III *Intereulaweast* 1

Sanitt, A, 'Digital Assets and Applicable Law: in Defence of the Lex Situs' (2025) *Lloyd's Maritime and Commercial Law Quarterly* 82

Schwartze, A, 'New Trends in Parties' Options to Select the Applicable Law? The Hague Principles on Choice of Law in International Contracts in a Comparative Perspective' (2015) 12 *University of St Thomas Law Journal* 87

Shah, H and Srivastava, A, 'Authentication and Recognition Issues in Cross-Border Single Window' (2013) 47 *Journal of World Trade* 1225

Suyudi, A and Budi, HS, 'Reconsidering the Mandatory Use of Indonesian Language in Private Commercial Contract' (2022) 2 *Global Legal Review* 2, 185

Takahashi, K, 'Blockchain Technology for Letters of Credit and Escrow Arrangements' (2018) 135 *Banking Law Journal* 89

Tescaro, M, 'Le regole di responsabilità del regolamento «eIDAS»' (2017) XL *Le Nuove Leggi Civili Commentate* 542

Wehling, P, 'A Roadmap for Legal Reform: The Future UNCITRAL/Unidroit Model Law on Warehouse Receipts' (2023) 38 *Butterworths Journal of International Banking & Financial Law* 553

Xue, H, 'The Newest UN Treaty to Facilitate Cross-Border Paperless Trade in Asia and the Pacific: An Insight Preview' (2017) 51 *Journal of World Trade* 959

Xue, H, 'Website Authentication: New International Legal Standards Safeguarding Digital Trade' (2025) 31 *Computer and Telecommunication Law Review* 10

Yntema, HE, '"Autonomy" in Choice of Law' (1952) 1 *American Journal of Comparative Law* 341

Zhou, Y and Zheng, N, 'Research on the Legal System of Cross-Border Mutual Recognition of Electronic Signatures in China' (2024) *Information Security and Communications Confidentiality* 3

Zhu, L and Pan, X, 'A Conceptual Analysis of the Electronic Bill of Lading' (2021) 4 *Journal of Business Law* 336

United Nations Documents

United Nations Commission on International Trade Law (UNCITRAL), 'Draft Uniform Rules on the Legal Aspects of Electronic Data Interchange (EDI) and Related Means of Trade Data Communication' (1992) UN Doc A/CN.9/WG.IV/WP.57
UNCITRAL, 'Electronic Data Interchange' (31 January 1996) UN Doc A/CN.9/WG.IV/WP.69
UNCITRAL, 'Transport Law: Possible Future Eork' (31 March 2000) UN Doc A/CN.9/476
UNCITRAL, 'Possible Future Work on Electronic Commerce. Transfer of Rights in Tangible Goods and Other Rights' (20 December 2000) UN Doc A/CN.9/WG.IV/WP.90
UNCITRAL, 'Transport Law: Preparation of a Draft Instrument on the Carriage of Goods [Wholly or Partly] [By Sea]. Proposed Revised Provisions on Electronic Commerce' (24 March 2005) UN Doc A/CN.9/WG.III/WP.47
UNCITRAL, 'Present and Possible Future Work on Electronic Commerce' (15 April 2010) UN Doc A/CN.9/692
UNCITRAL, 'Present and Possible Future Work on Electronic Commerce' (21 March 2011 and 22 March 2011) UN Doc A/CN.9/728 and Add.1
UNCITRAL, 'Legal Issues Relating to the Use of Electronic Transferable Records' (8 September 2011) UN Doc A/CN.9/WG.IV/WP.115
UNCITRAL, 'Legal Issues Relating to the Use of Electronic Transferable Records – Proposal by the Governments of Colombia, Spain and the United States' (3 August 2012) UN Doc A/CN.9/WG.IV/WP.119
UNCITRAL, 'Legal Issues Relating to the Use of Electronic Transferable Records' (17 August 2012) UN Doc A/CN.9/WG.IV/WP.118 and Add.1
UNCITRAL, 'Draft Provisions on Electronic Transferable Records' (4 March 2013) UN Doc A/CN.9/WG.IV/WP.122
UNCITRAL, 'Legal Issues Relating to the Use of Electronic Transferable Records' (27 September 2013) UN Doc A/CN.9/WG.IV/WP.125
UNCITRAL, 'Possible Future Work in the Area of Electronic Commerce – Legal Issues Related to Identity Management and Trust Services. Proposal by Austria, Belgium, France, Italy and Poland' (5 May 2015) UN Doc A/CN.9/854
UNCITRAL, 'Report of Working Group IV (Electronic Commerce) on the Work of its Fifty-third Session' (20 May 2016) UN Doc A/CN.9/869
UNCITRAL, 'Legal Issues Related to Identity Management and Trust Services' (3 May 2016) UN Doc A/CN.9/891
UNCITRAL, 'Draft Model Law on Electronic Transferable Records – Compilation of Comments by Governments and International Organizations' (25 April 2017) UN Doc A/CN.9/921/Add.1
UNCITRAL, 'Legal Issues Related to Identity management and Trust Services. Terms and Concepts Relevant to Identity Management and Trust Services' (6 February 2018) UN Doc A/CN.9/WG.IV/WP.150
UNCITRAL, 'Work Programme – Possible Future Work Regarding Railway Consignment Notes – Proposal by the Government of the People's Republic of China' (14 June 2019) UN Doc A/CN.9/998
UNCITRAL, 'Reconsideration of Approach to Identity Management and Trust Services – Submission by the United States of America' (30 September 2020) UN Doc A/CN.9/WG.IV/WP.165
UNCITRAL, 'Report of Working Group IV (Electronic Commerce) on the Work of its Sixty-fifth session' (25 April 2023) UN Doc A/CN.9/1132
UNCITRAL, 'Draft Model Law on Warehouse Receipts' (20 November 2023) UN Doc A/CN.9/WG.I/WP.133
UNCITRAL, 'Report of Working Group I (Warehouse Receipts) on the Work of its Forty-first Session' (16 February 2024) UN Doc A/CN.9/1165
UNCITRAL, 'Preliminary Draft Provisions for a New Instrument on Negotiable Cargo Documents. Submission from the Government of Singapore' (25 January 2024) UN Doc A/CN.9/WG.VI/WP.104
UNCITRAL, 'Negotiable Cargo Documents' (8 February 2024) UN Doc A/CN.9/WG.VI/WP.103
UNCITRAL, 'Report of Working Group VI (Negotiable Cargo Documents) on the Work of its Forty-fifth Session' (20 December 2024) UN Doc A/CN.9/1199

UN Economic Commission for Europe, 'Analysis of the Provisions of Article 5 to the eCMR Protocol' (26 July 2022) UN Doc ECE/TRANS/SC.1/GE.22/2022/2
United Nations General Assembly (UNGA), Resolution 2205 (XXI) (17 December 1966)
UNGA, 'Report of the United Nations Commission on International Trade Law. Eighteenth Session' (1985) UN Doc A/40/17
UNGA, 'Report of the United Nations Commission on International Trade Law. Twenty-seventh Session' (1994) UN Doc A/49/17
UNGA, 'Report of the United Nations Commission on International Trade Law Forty-second Session' (2009) UN Doc A/64/17
UNGA, 'Report of the United Nations Commission on International Trade Law. Forty-fourth session' (2011) UN Doc A/66/17
UNGA, 'Report of the United Nations Commission on International Trade Law. Forty-ninth Session' (2016) UN Doc A/71/17
UNGA, 'Report of the United Nations Commission on International Trade Law Fiftieth Session' (2017) UN Doc A/72/17
UNGA, 'Report of the United Nations Commission on International Trade Law. Fifty-seventh Session' (2024) UN Doc A/79/17
UNGA Resolution 72/114 (7 December 2017)
United Nations, 'Analysis of Comments and Proposals by Governments and International Organizations on the Draft Convention on the Carriage of Goods by Sea, and on the Draft Provisions Concerning Implementation, Reservations and Other Final Clauses Prepared by the Secretary-General' (10 November 1977) UN Doc A/CONF.89/8
United Nations Conference on Trade and Development, 'Maritime Transport in Times of Polycrisis' (14 August 2024) UN Doc TD/B/C.I/MEM.7/32
World Summit on the Information Society, 'Plan of Action' (12 December 2003) UN Doc WSIS-03/GENEVA/DOC/5-E

Other Documents

Alamillo-Domingo, I and ors, 'Qualified Ledgers: Bridging the Gap between Blockchain Technology and Legal Compliance' *Medium* (medium.com) 29 January 2024
APEC Committee on Trade and Investment, 'A Path to Paperless Trade: Analysing the Legal Gaps and Economic Benefit of Adopting or Maintaining a Legal Framework that Takes into Account the UNCITRAL Model Law on Electronic Transferable Records (MLETR)' (2025)
Asia-Pacific Economic Cooperation (APEC), 'Joint Ministerial Statement, 35th APEC Ministerial Meeting 2024, Lima, Peru' (14 November 2024)
APEC, '2025 APEC Ministers Responsible for Trade Joint Statement, Jeju, Republic of Korea' (15–16 May 2025)
Asian Development Bank and Bankers Association for Finance and Trade, 'Deep-Tier Supply Chain Finance. Unlocking the Potential' (2024)
Association of Southeast Asian Nations (ASEAN), 'Work Plan on the Implementation of the ASEAN Agreement on Electronic Commerce 2021–2025' (2021)
Attorney General's Department, 'Consultation to Inform Options for Implementing the Model Law on Electronic Transferable Records in Australia' (2024)
Australian APEC Study Centre and ors, 'A Path to Paperless Trade: Analysing the Legal Gaps and Economic Benefit of Adopting or Maintaining a Legal Framework That Takes into Account the UNCITRAL Model Law on Electronic Transferable Records (MLETR)' (2025)
Baltic and International Maritime Council (BIMCO), 'BIMCO's "25 by 25" Campaign Reaches 25.1% eBL Adoption in First Year' (17 July 2024)
Bank for International Settlements Innovation Hub, 'Project Dynamo: Catalysing Innovation for SME Growth' (2023)

Basu Bal, A, Rajput, T and Alizada, P, 'International Single Window Environment: Prospects and Challenges' (2017) ADBI Working Paper Series vol 744
Beck, S and ors, '2023 Trade Finance Gaps, Growth, and Jobs Survey' (2023) ADB Briefs No 256
Burri, M and Vasquez Callo-Müller, M, 'Digital Economy Agreements: A Closer Look at the New Phenomenon in Digital Trade Rulemaking' (2024) WEF and AKCF Policy Brief No 1
Chen, B, 'Tokenization in Shipping and the Securitization of Trade Flows' *Forbes* (Jersey City, NJ, 17 January 2024)
Christou, T and Taylor, J, 'Blueprint Paper on Digital Trade and the UNCITRAL Model Law on Electronic Transferable Records' (2023)
Collot, B, Henry, P and Teper, S, 'Accélérer la digitalisation des activités de financement du commerce international' (2023)
Department for Digital, Culture, Media & Sport, 'Impact assessment of the Electronic Trade Documents Bill' (2022)
Deutsche Bank, 'Fighting Trade-related Fraud' *Flow* (19 April 2023)
European Commission, Directorate-General for Communications Networks, Content and Technology, *Study to Support the Impact Assessment for Revision of the eIDAS Regulation, Final Report* (2021)
European Commission, Proposal for a Regulation of the European Parliament and of the Council amending Regulation (EU) No 910/2014 as regards establishing a framework for a European Digital Identity, COM(2021) 281 final, 2021/0136 (COD) (2021)
European Telecommunications Standards Institute (ETSI), ETSI TR 103684 V1.1.1 (2020-01) Technical Report, 'Electronic Signatures and Infrastructures (ESI); Global Acceptance of EU Trust Services' (2020)
Ford, C and Rékasy, P, 'TTC WG1 Digital Identity Subgroup Roundtable Workshop Report' (2023)
Future International Trade Alliance, 'eBL Report 2024' (2024)
Garrido, JM, 'Digital Tokens: A Legal Perspective' (2023) IMF Doc WP/23/151
Geva, B and Peari, S, 'Which Law Applies to Negotiable Instruments?' *OUPblog* (4 July 2021)
Gierten, D and Lesher, M, 'Assessing National Digital Strategies and their Governance' (2022) OECD Digital Economy Papers No 324
Global Shipping Business Network – SIA Partners, 'Impact of Digitalization in Driving Decarbonization in the Shipping Industry' (2024)
Global Trade Review, 'Industry Perspectives: Reliable Systems – Are They Really Something New?' (10 January 2024)
Goldby, M, 'The Electronic Trade Documents Act 2023 and the 2003 Amendments to Article 7 of the Uniform Commercial Code: Do They Do the Same Thing?' (2024)
Gregory, J, 'Legal Implementation Guide for Cross-border Paperless Trade' (2024) UNNExT Working Paper Series No 12
Hong Kong Monetary Authority, 'Half-Yearly Monetary and Financial Stability Report' (March 2025)
International Chamber of Commerce (ICC), 'Survey Shows Steady Rise of Global Adoption of Electronic Bills of Lading' (12 December 2024)
ICC Deutschland, 'Elektronische Transport- und Warenwertpapiere in Deutschland: Reformen und Verordnung als Katalysator des Papierlosen Handels' (2022)
ICC Digital Standards Initiative (DSI), 'Key Trade Documents and Data Elements: Digital Standards Analysis and Recommendations' (2024)
ICC DSI, 'Key Trade Documents and Data Elements: Digital Standards Analysis and Recommendations – An Integrated Framework for Digitalising the Entire Supply Chain' (2024)
ICC Sweden, 'Digitalisation of International Trade: The Legal Status of Electronic Transferable Records in Sweden' (2024)
INFOCOMM Media Development Authority (IMDA) and Attorney General's Chambers (AGC), 'Joint IMDA – AGC Review of The Electronic Transactions Act (Cap 88) – Review of Draft UNCITRAL Model Law on Electronic Transferable Records (Public Consultation Paper)' (2017)
Institut luxembourgeois de la normalisation, de l'accréditation, de la sécurité et qualité des produits et services (ILNAS), 'Trust Services under the eIDAS Regulation' V1.0 (2018)

IMDA, 'Consultation Paper Issued by the INFOCOMM Media Development Authority on Review of the Electronic Transactions Act (ETA) (Cap 88)' (2019)

Industry Working Group on the Electronic Execution of Documents, 'Final Report' (2023)

INNOPAY, 'Market Impact of the eIDAS Revision on Trust Services' (2024)

International Finance Corporation, 'The Emergence of New Data Ecosystems in Financial Services: Recent Developments in Southeast Asia' (2021) Discussion Paper

Internet Governance Forum, 'Riyadh Declaration' (2024)

Ioannou, I, 'Is Enabling Legislation Sufficient to Promote the Uptake of Electronic Paperless Trading Systems?' (2023) NUS Centre for Maritime Law Working Paper No 23/04

Jacquemin, H, 'L'archivage électronique comme nouveau service de confiance : l'exemple belge' (2021)

Japan International Cooperation Agency, 'Collaboration Program with the Private Sector for Disseminating Japanese Technology for Electronically Recorded Monetary Claims Service Project Completion Report' (2019)

Katayama, K, 'Electronic Claims: A Japanese Financial Innovation' (2008) Nomura Research Institute Lakyara vol 33

Leung, D and ors, 'Corporate Digital Identity: No Silver Bullet, but a Silver Lining' (2022) Bank for International Settlements Papers No 126

Lind, M and ors, 'The Dynamics Around the Digitisation of Documents. The eBL as Vehicle Towards a More Data-Driven Approach' (2021)

LSE Trade Policy Hub, 'Benefits of the Digitalisation of Trade Processes and Cross Border Barriers to their Adoption, Final Report' (2023)

National Council for Prescription Drug Programs, 'White Paper: Electronic Signature Guidance' (2014) version 1.0

National Institute of Standards and Technology, 'Special Publication 800-63-3, Digital Identity Guidelines' (2020)

Office for Digital Identities & Attributes, Department for Science, Innovation & Technology, 'Digital Identity Sectoral Analysis 2024: Interim Findings' (2024)

Organisation for Economic Co-operation and Development (OECD), 'Recommendation of the Council on the Governance of Digital Identity' (8 June 2023) OECD Doc OECD/LEGAL/0491

Poddar, S, 'Bringing Trade into the Web 3.0' (Hinrich Foundation, 2024)

Ramirez Ortiz, CM and Castellani, L, 'Driving Digitalization of Global Trade: UNCITRAL Model Law on Electronic Transferable Records' (2023) ADB Briefs No 280

Smedinghoff, T, 'Is It Legal? Will It Be Trusted? What Are the Rules? – Enabling Electronic Identity Management Under the New UNCITRAL Model Law' (2024)

Stella Richter, M, 'I titoli di credito nel nuovo sistema di diritto internazionale privato' (1996) Consiglio Nazionale del Notariato Studio n 1185/2

Stephenson Harwood LLP in collaboration with IMDA, 'TradeTrust-enabled Electronic Bills of Lading: A Legal and Practical Analysis of their Use in Global Trade' (2023)

Tullis, C, Constantine, N and Cooper, A, 'Electronic Signatures: Enabling Trusted Digital Transformation' (2024) World Bank Digital Transformation Policy Note Series

Tullis, C and Black, D, 'Public Key Infrastructure: Implementing High-Trust Electronic Signatures' (2025) World Bank Digital Public Infrastructure Policy Note Series

UK Protection and Indemnity Club, Circular 15/23: Electronic (Paperless) Trading – ICE Digital Trade Management Limited (8 November 2023)

US-EU Trade and Technology Council Working Group 1: Technology Standards, Subgroup on Digital Identity, 'Draft EU-US TTC Digital Identity Mapping Exercise Report' (2023)

van Stijn, E and ors, 'The Data Pipeline', discussion paper presented at the UN ECA/ECE/ESCAP/ECLAC/ESCWA Global Trade Facilitation Conference 2011 'Connecting International Trade: Single Windows and Supply Chains in the Next Decade' (2011)

Wirjo, A Bayhaqi, A and Oh ET, 'Digitalising Trade: The Role of Paperless Platforms' (2024) APEC Policy Support Unit Policy Brief No 59

World Trade Organization, 'Joint Statement Initiative on Electronic Commerce. Agreement on Electronic Commerce' (26 July 2024) WTO Doc INF/ECOM/87

INDEX

[all references are to page number]

www.ingramcontent.com/pod-product-compliance
Ingram Content Group UK Ltd.
Pitfield, Milton Keynes, MK11 3LW, UK
UKHW020803290926
15470UKWH00003B/935

9 781509 937417